Studying Shakespeare in

Also by John Russell Brown

King Lear (Shakespeare Handbooks)
Hamlet (Shakespeare Handbooks)
Macbeth (Shakespeare Handbooks)
A.C. Bradley on Shakespeare's Tragedies
Shakespeare Dancing
Shakespeare and the Theatrical Event
Shakespeare: The Tragedies
William Shakespeare: Writing for Performance

Studying Shakespeare in Performance

John Russell Brown

palgrave
macmillan

First published 2011 by
PALGRAVE MACMILLAN

Palgrave Macmillan in the UK is an imprint of Macmillan Publishers Limited, registered in England, company number 785998, of Houndmills, Basingstoke, Hampshire RG21 6XS.

Palgrave Macmillan in the US is a division of St Martin's Press LLC, 175 Fifth Avenue, New York, NY 10010.

Palgrave Macmillan is the global academic imprint of the above companies and has companies and representatives throughout the world.

Palgrave® and Macmillan® are registered trademarks in the United States, the United Kingdom, Europe and other countries.

ISBN 978–0–230–27373–3   hardback
ISBN 978–0–230–27374–0   paperback

This book is printed on paper suitable for recycling and made from fully managed and sustained forest sources. Logging, pulping and manufacturing processes are expected to conform to the environmental regulations of the country of origin.

A catalogue record for this book is available from the British Library.

Library of Congress Cataloging-in-Publication Data
Brown, John Russell.
Studying Shakespeare in performance / John Russell Brown.
p. cm.
Includes index.
Summary: "John Russell Brown is arguably the most influential scholar in the field of Shakespeare in performance. This collection brings together, and makes accessible, his most important writing across the last 40 years. Together these essays provide an authoritative and engaging account of how to study Shakespeare's plays as texts for performance"— Provided by publisher.
ISBN 978–0–230–27374–0 (pbk.)
1. Shakespeare, William, 1564–1616—Dramatic production.
2. Shakespeare, William, 1564–1616—Stage history. I. Title.
PR3091.B736 2011
822.3'3—dc22   2011016882

10   9   8   7   6   5   4   3   2   1
20 19 18 17 16 15 14 13 12 11

Printed and bound in Great Britain by
the MPG Books Group, Bodmin and King's Lynn

Contents

Acknowledgements

The studies brought together here had their origin while I was teaching at the Universities of Sussex, Michigan and Essex so that, in ways that are now inextricable, they owe much to my colleagues and students of those years. They are also indebted to everyone taking part in the productions I directed at that time in England and North America. I cannot begin to name everyone who inspired and guided me but, whenever I think back to those years, Kate Duchene, Reg Foakes, Peter Hall, Peter James, Athina Kasiou, G.W. [Skip] Mercier, Richard Nelson and Leon Rubin are sure to come to mind; this book is indebted to these and many others in ways that overflow particular memories.

Margaret Bartley, Anna Sandeman, Kate Haines and Sonya Barker have successively and most helpfully overseen the preparation of my books published by Palgrave Macmillan and in doing so have taught me much and saved me from many an error. Kate Haines has guided me when drawing together this collection of my writings originally published elsewhere. While the proofs of this book were being corrected Daniel Starza Smith gave me valuable assistance for which I am most grateful. To numerous journals, as detailed in the course of the book, I am grateful for permission to reprint articles (see below). Any excisions are marked by '...' and the very few substantive emendations enclosed within square brackets. Unless otherwise noted all quotations and references are from the edition of Peter Alexander (Collins, 1951 and many times reprinted).

The author and publishers wish to thank the following for permission to use copyright material:

Associated University Presses, for 'The Nature of Speech in Shakespeare's Plays', from Marvin and Ruth Thompson (eds): *Shakespeare and the Sense of Performance*, University of Delaware Press, 1989, pp. 48–59;

Cambridge University Press, for 'Writing about Shakespeare's Plays in Performance', from *Shakespeare Quarterly,* xiii (1962); 'Research in the Service of Theatre: the Example of Shakespeare Studies', from *Theatre Research International,* 18, 1 (2000), pp. 25–35; 'Learning Shakespeare's Secret Language: the Limits of "Performance Studies"', from *New Theatre Quarterly 95,* XXIV (2008), pp. 211–21; 'Free Shakespeare', from *Shakespeare Survey, 24* (1971), pp. 127–35; 'Representing Sexuality in Shakespeare's Plays', from *New Theatre Quarterly,* 51, XII (1997), pp. 205–13; 'Violence and Sensationalism in the Plays of Shakespeare and other Dramatists', from *Proceedings of the British Academy, 87* (1995), pp. 101–18; 'S. Franco Zeffirelli's *Romeo and Juliet'*, from *Shakespeare Survey,* 15 (1962), pp. 147–55; 'Three Kinds of Shakespeare', from *Shakespeare Survey,* 18 (1965), pp. 147–55;

Palgrave Macmillan, for 'Motivation and Subtext', from John Russell Brown: *Discovering Shakespeare* (Macmillan, 1981), pp. 108–12; 'Accounting for Space: Choreography', from John Russell Brown: *Shakespeare Dancing* (Palgrave Macmillan, 2005), pp. 87–113; and 'Playgoing and Participation', from *Shakespeare and the Theatrical Event* (Palgrave Macmillan, 2002), pp. 7–29;

The Johns Hopkins University Press, for 'Theatre Research and the Criticism of Shakespeare and His Contemporaries', from *Shakespeare Quarterly,* Vol. 13, No. 4 (Autumn 1962), pp. 451–61, © Folger Shakespeare Library;

Verlag und Druckkontor Kamp GmbH, for 'Asian Theatres and European Shakespeares', from *Shakespeare Jahrbuch 138* (2002), pp. 11–22.

Every effort has been made to trace all the copyright-holders, but if any have been inadvertently overlooked the author and publishers will be pleased to make the necessary arrangement at the first opportunity.

Introduction

Shakespeare wrote his plays for an acting company and, in contrast to an increasing number of his contemporaries, seems to have done nothing to ensure they were available in print. Perhaps he saw little reason for that because to read a text and imagine it in performance before an audience will not come naturally to any one and any play can be acted and produced in many different ways. To study Shakespeare's plays in performance is an endless task because it varies with each change of cast and production. The entire theatrical event should come into the reckoning: the occasion, location and context for performance, the composition and expectation of the audience, the form and equipment of the theatre building, the skill, training and experience of the actors. Daunting as all this is, a student of the plays must also remember that every reader and critic will bring a unique experience and imagination with them as they discover for themselves what the plays can offer. All of which brings uncertainties to the study of Shakespeare's plays in performance but also the discovery of their contemporary relevance, centuries after they were written and received their first performances.

The studies collected in this book represent a critical and scholarly journey taken during the last forty or so years. My first thought was to arrange them in chronological order to show how progress had been made but that would not have given the reader a clear path to follow because I had moved repeatedly from one critical or scholarly method to another. I have therefore grouped the chapters according to the kind of study each of them uses but starting, in Part I, with three articles that consider critical methods and chart my progress in response to plays and performances. They are, in effect, an introduction that distinguishes the study of plays from the study of other forms of writing. Together they stress the importance of theatre history as well as present-day productions and the significance of sensation alongside thought and verbalised meanings. The third chapter in this section shows how the study of theatre and performance can illuminate the study of Shakespeare's plays.

The group of chapters in Part II pays closer attention to play-texts, the first two considering speech and physical performance in relation to the printed words. By this means a student who reads a text, rather than seeing a performance, can begin to envision what might happen on stage, a step forward that every student of Shakespeare needs to take in order to realise the potential theatrical effect of the dialogue. The third and fourth chapters are more specialised, noting how a text can give the impression of thoughts of feelings that exist underneath the primary meaning of words and how speech in these plays calls for movements on stage that counteract, modify or reinforce the effect of words.

Part III looks at the entire process of production with attention at first focused on some recent staging of individual plays. Its second and third chapters consider the effect of changes in social custom and consciousness. When the plays were first performed, their female roles were played by boys or young men and in daily life sexual consciousness and behaviour were not as open as they are now. Television and film did not exist then and have changed how violence is experienced by bringing images of actual occurrences into every home and enabling instant and vivid reportage in newspapers and journals. Shakespeare's handling of these aspects of lived experience was very different and calls for an understanding of his use of the stage and dialogue as these two chapters show. Part IV concentrates on the work of three directors and only a few productions and by this means can deal in sufficient detail to investigate how meanings are modified and effects widened or sharpened in performance.

The effectiveness of what is seen on stage will depend on the audience that is watching and this varies greatly now that Shakespeare productions are more widely available. The two final chapters in Part V provide an introduction to this huge field of study that involves many languages and a great variety of spectators. One purpose of these chapters and much else in the book is to develop a reader's response to any performance that he or she may be able to see.

Part I
Study

1

Theatrical Study and Editions of the Plays*

With this first attempt to understand the consequences of trying to study Shakespeare in performance, I considered a number of approaches and came to a positive conclusion. I identified describing and analysing a production's use of time and space as basic and necessary tasks and introduced two phrases that were to recur frequently in my writing: the 'progressive experience' of an audience and the 'journey' undertaken by actors. I had also begun to consider a 'theatrical event' as the complex outcome of everyone's contribution to a performance, on stage, back stage and in the audience, both before and during a performance. These personal and shared experiences are influenced by the location and timing as well as the nature of a production. I was learning new ways of grappling with Shakespeare's plays in performance but not finding the task any easier.

Believing that Shakespeare set down words so that a company of actors would perform his plays before very varied audiences, readers have sought to respond to the texts as if in performance and have taken whatever opportunity arises to see them in the theatre. In both efforts they are often frustrated but critics and scholars provide further assistance by reporting on reviews and records of earlier productions and writing detailed accounts of performances they have witnessed. They also listen to actors, directors, and designers talking about their work and then try to distinguish between intention and achievement. Writing about performances of Shakespeare's plays has become such an accepted and often industrious academic pursuit that

---

★ Based on a paper read to the Society for Theatre Research, 15 March 1960 and published in *Shakespeare Quarterly*, xiii (1962).

it may be profitable to stop to consider exactly what the "theatrical dimension" in Shakespeare studies entails.

The basic questions are: "To what are we giving our attention, and what do we bring to this experience?" Neither "hearing" nor "seeing" a play are satisfactory words for this activity, because attending a performance involves far more than sight and hearing, and more than simple cognition of fixed signs. All our senses, instincts, and memories may be involved and will interact with each other. Both words and everyday actions can be given unexpected and exceptional powers in the theatre and so any full account of performance must go beyond mere quotation or factual description and call upon impressionistic and personal memories. Two other questions arise immediately: "How can we best describe or report on a theatre experience, and what do we gain by this exercise?"

In recent years, the study of what constitutes performance has occupied many scholars in university Departments of Theatre, Anthropology, Linguistics, and Sociology. In 1980 Keir Elam's *The Semiotics of Theatre and Drama* was the first book to provide analyses of speech-acts and so demonstrated the interweaving of many modes of perception and reception called upon by the performance of a dramatic text.[1] Later critics have built on this, giving more emphasis to the physical and corporeal elements of performance, to the actors' modes of preparation, to social and political contexts for performance, and to all the reactions and interactions that occur among individual members of an audience as they share the occasion and, in some measure, help to create it. It must seem strange to scholars in this new discipline of Performance Studies that so little writing about Shakespeare has made use of the distinctions and terminology that are now available. Perhaps one reason is that so much cannot be assimilated rapidly, especially at this time when new forms of literary, as well as theatrical, criticism are already busying more adventurous minds. Another reason for neglecting this new form of study may be that "Performance," as Marvin Carlson has put it, "by its nature resists conclusions, just as it resists the sort of definitions, boundaries, and limits so useful to traditional academic writing and academic structures."[2] To consider Shakespeare's plays in the light of recent Performance Studies is to enter forbidding territory in which perception must always be open to question.

The critical challenge, nevertheless, remains: we should respond to the plays as works for performance and therefore need to know how best to do this. Shakespeare's imagination was not simply full of words or speeches, but of men and women in action; his art was to write down what actors should speak while representing those imaginary individuals as if they were fully alive in continuous action on a stage before an audience. Necessarily such a performance is more difficult to comprehend than any number of written words. Much of it will contain a great deal which Shakespeare could not have foreseen and, even when he was alive, could not control. Moreover every single performance will be different from all others, even if the same actors are involved and use the same theatre building. Faced with describing such complex and ever-changing phenomena, a critic must decide, consciously or unconsciously, which incidents on stage and which impressions made upon him- or herself—and on other critics—should be given most attention. To notice everything is impossible but, even if it were not, the task of describing and assessing everything would remain. The critic's own mind and personal history are of crucial importance because they will control both the selection of material for study and the perception of it. The best person to describe performances would be someone of strong sensibilities but without conscious predilections or foreknowledge of the play's stage history; such a person might give attention to the show, entirely and openly, as it evolves moment by moment, seeing clearly and responding wholeheartedly and imaginatively. Yet, on the other hand, another person who is experienced enough to be on the lookout for what is new and what has been achieved with special power or in closest accord with Shakespeare's words might be the more useful, if more biased, critic.

★ ★ ★

Among the wide range of methods used in writing about Shakespearian performances some may be considered provocative rather than essential, because they fasten on modern stage techniques that would have been impossible in Shakespeare's day or are interpretative in ways alien to thought and perception at that time. So, for example, Jay L. Halio's volume on *A Midsummer Night's Dream* for the *Shakespeare in Performance* series has a concluding chapter which details the innovations of Robert Lepage and his designer, Michael Levine, in a production for the National Theatre in London in 1992:

> A large circular pool of water, about 25mm deep over an area of 120 square metres, surrounded by a bank of mud (made of Bentonite mixed with lignite and water), dominated the set from the first scene to the

last ... [T]his *Dream* was meant to take us back to the beginnings of life
and to suggest connections between the primitive world and the civilised
one; hence, the primordial mud, a violent coupling between an androgy-
nous Puck and a blue-faced fairy ..., the "group sex" in muddy water,
and the "noisy rutting" of Titania and Bottom.[3]

The critic is objective for the most part, noting, almost in passing, that
Titania "does not lie asleep in her bower but hangs above it, upside
down suspended by a rope" (121). However, he also allows himself a
few marks of approval, so he describes "some very nice touches ...
that somewhat softened the effect of the 'mud-wrestling'" (122–3).
These are comparatively simple actions that might have been found
in almost any twentieth-century production.

This review gives reasons for recounting much that has little direct
connection to the dialogue which Shakespeare wrote:

> the theatre often resorts to new, hitherto unimagined—even unimagi-
> nable—ways of presentation ...: "what works" [on stage] translates into
> what illuminates for us things we did not see or hear or feel, and there-
> fore did not comprehend as fully in previous productions. (26)

The critic recounts and marvels at new devices of theatre production and the results of long, idiosyncratic, and painstaking rehearsals
because his imagination had been aroused and had jolted his previous
perceptions of the play. The result was that he was able to sense the
"ghosts of Freud and Jung inhabit[ing] the production" and to find a
"liquidity in the text" that Shakespeare wrote centuries before (119).

One thought must occur to any reader: could not these perceptions have derived as well from a present-day reading of the text by
someone who was familiar with the same books and had had much
the same "lived experience" as this director and his designer? We
shall never know, but the production had given their ideas a palpable
quality, a "local habitation and a name" for those who witnessed it
without too much resistence to its innovations. Theatre is a place for
seeing and Halio is claiming that this production showed its audience
qualities that have always been inherent in the text and had illuminated it for them at this time.

The very new, especially in scenic and extravagantly non-realistic
stage activity, is the easiest part of any production to document and
critics often give most attention to it, even when they disapprove of
the treatment of a text. As chronicles of Shakespeare's plays on the

stage in our time, such writing about performances has its value, even at the cost of considerable length as its words limp behind the spectacle they try to describe. Of course, a stubborn question remains: is this, indeed, "our" *Dream* or is it, less interestingly, that *Dream* which a few theatre people had judged appropriate for themselves and their particular kind of theatrical pleasure? The critic cannot sufficiently answer that question by asserting a personal interest in the contrivance. The task of writing about performances of Shakespeare is not complete until the critic has taken into account their effect on audiences. Any striking invention should be judged according to its particular value as entertainment or as an illumination of life or thought outside the theatre.

Other critics are wary of new and obviously contrived stage effects and take refuge in fixing their attention on the words of the text, noting what the actors make them "mean" for a hearer, as if reference to a printed edition provided sufficient understanding of any effect and was a mark of authenticity in performance. Others try to "look" beyond words at what the actors do, pretending that they are performing on some unlocalized Globe-like stage, without twentieth-century embellishments and trickery. They pay heed to the "presence" of actors and assess the individuality and interactions of the play's characters. Both kinds of discourse have a great deal to document and many small details to compare between one production and another. So extensive and so various is the material to be dealt with, that criticism of this kind can never be complete and, therefore, seems incidental, governed by accident in choice of what it considers and, consequently, in any judgement that it makes. Not surprisingly, these critics tend to write at length and in conclusion are liable to note the "infinite variety" of interpretation that Shakespeare's "characters" give rise to in performance, forbearing to express any preference between them. This does not take their readers very much further than a slow and thoughtful reading of the text itself might achieve, although descriptions of actual behaviour can awaken sense-responses and so be a spur to fresh perception.

Any writing about how a performance deals with the words of Shakespeare's text is an endless task, always limited by its author's selectivity. Even Marvin Rosenberg's huge accumulations of careful detail in his books about four of the tragedies are limited in scope, as he has been the first to confess. As the volumes followed each other over the years from 1961 to 1992 comparisons were supplied ever more generously and scrupulously together with frequent and minutely careful reference to Shakespeare's texts. But their principal shortcomings are those of selectivity and not incompleteness: Rosenberg is star-struck and so pays attention only to leading actors or, for present times, to what directors have encouraged their actors to do. His scope includes star performers from all centuries since Shakespeare's and from theatres other than the English-speaking, but he does not give to any one performance of a play an attention that follows its entire action, and so he is unable to consider its overall shape and impact. He tells readers what his chosen performers have done to bring their roles alive on stage but only at one moment and then at another. While he uses every possible means to say how they spoke particular words of the texts and what they did while doing so, much is inevitably missing. The more ground he has been able to cover in his studies of single plays, the more inadequate has become the engagement with any single performance as a response to the whole play in one unique time and place, his concentration on the leading actors notwithstanding. Because his method is to create a patchwork out of small observations, he has no scope to consider either the material substance, shape, or impact of any one of the productions from which the shreds and patches have been taken.

Rosenberg's latest volume on *The Masks of Hamlet* is exemplary of much other writing about performance when it centers attention on the actors of the principal characters of a play. The "Prologue" tells us the reason for undertaking this task:

> the words [of the text] were written to be clothed in the unmistakably physical, recognizable human forms of Shakespeare's players. Live people. Hamlet is only part of himself on the page; he is complete only as realized on stage or in the imagination.[4]

In line with this approach, the book's last section spends thousands of words on how various Hamlets have, or might have, said "The rest is silence" and, possibly, the Folio's "O, o, o, o." as well. An earlier section considers the other figures on stage in this scene, but briefly, and mostly in their relationship to Hamlet. The focus of the book is unmistakable: "What may Hamlet be trying to convey?" (924). That the critic cannot answer with any certainty is the message that he reiterates time and again; for example:

> All the words about Hamlet, almost three centuries of words, and as many of stagings, and the adventure into the depths of the play has hardly begun. (924)

But we should remember that this play has width as well as depth because it mirrors life as Shakespeare lived it and thought about it in the context of an entire nation and among people in all their variety of mind, feeling, and activity. These social and political concerns are expressed in narrative, action and interaction, dramatic structure and timing, stage images of all kinds and in many combinations, whole casts of characters and supernumeraries, and the entire text of each play—which all together needs a "fellowship" of actors to perform and not just a few star actors. Rosenberg's star-centered observations about moments of performance do not take his readers very far towards an understanding of these essential aspects of the plays.

This form of study—the creation of a patchwork from details about how Hamlet and others around him behave—has other shortcomings. Because no one performance is considered as a continuous action, description always lacks an important ingredient: the actor's response to his or her whole journey through a play, which involves changes in relationship to other characters and actors, and in self-awareness. How any one moment is arrived at will always be part of that moment in theatre performance. In outwardly visible and audible signs, the past is always marked indelibly in the present on the bodies and minds of the performers and so no moment can be fairly judged in isolation. Moreover, as expectation changes, so does the actor's very being and the audience's attention. From manifestations of these facts stems much of the excitement of performance—an excitement which falls through the net of descriptions of performance that focus on single moments. But perhaps the greatest difficulty of this form of writing about Shakespeare's plays is to know what to emphasize in any brief description. Often it is only those details that the critic finds to be unexpected and also describable that find their way into the reckoning; and these details may not always represent the full force of a production or the reasons for its appeal or failure.[5]

Hamlet's encounter with Ophelia in Act 3, scene 1, may serve as an example of Rosenberg's detailed accounting, as he piles up conflicting "treatments" of "Ha, ha, are you honest?":

Calvert assumed that the laugh indicated that Hamlet was to put on the "antic" role here—he suspects the plot…. With the tense Kainz who had turned his back to Ophelia "… [it] is an attempt to regain composure: laughing nervously, he suddenly turns round…." Warner "falls back shocked and fumbling" … Kachalov's subtext [was]: "I want to show her to his face that I know all." Booth took the gifts in his left hand, but with his right he seized Ophelia's wrist, and gripped it even though she cried out; Olivier stared at her; Evans seized her and held her before him; Gielgud grasped her by the hands; McKellen held her face, and studied it—she had to turn away. (507–8)

From this bombardment of "facts," a dazed reader will gather little more than many incomplete and conflicting impressions.

The effect of a critic's predilections can be seen most clearly when he or she writes at much shorter length, as in the accounts of performance included in many recent one-volume editions of the plays. In his Oxford edition of *Macbeth,* Nicholas Brooke heads the relevant section of the Introduction "Staging," which is as revealing as Rosenberg's repeated use of the plural "Masks" in the titles of his books. In a Preface, the editor explains more: during a visit to Munich long ago, in the church of St. John Nepomuk, he

> experienced a conversion, not of a religious kind, but to a perception of baroque art. What was most strange was that it was *Macbeth* which came so powerfully into my mind: for better or for worse, my debt to that occasion will be obvious in this volume.[6]

So, it would seem, the attention to "performance" provided in other volumes of this edition is replaced here by a care for "staging." Brooke gives a high proportion of his four or five thousand words to operatic versions of the play. He notes that the Folio edition has numerous calls for music and quotes Frances Shirley's opinion that when the text speaks of "horses' hooves, the mew, croak, and whine of the witches' familiars, the owl's screech, the bell, and more certainly thunder," these sounds were all heard in the play's first performances. He records how the supernatural episodes were staged over succeeding centuries and the text reduced accordingly. He notices that Lady Macbeth came to have more sway in the theatre than her husband, but quotes Mrs. Inchbald to the effect that "spectators return again to their childish credulity, and tremble, as in the nursery, at a witch and a goblin" (43).

Coming to the present century, Brooke seeks to explain why "though quite often played, the play has so seldom been successful in modern theatres" (47). He notices Laurence Olivier's *Macbeth* at Stratford upon Avon in 1955 as remembered "chiefly (it seems) for his resemblance to Edmund Kean in dynamic presence and blazing eyes, together with his own characteristically eccentric locutions" (47)—an opinion that can easily be countered by the recorded effect of this performance in the minds of other theatre-goers, actors, and numerous writers about Shakespearian performances.[7] No other twentieth-century production gets more than glancing attention, except Trevor Nunn's at the intimate Other Place theatre in Stratford (1976):

> The odd stress on religious rituals which had been tedious in the main theatre [in Nunn's earlier version] was neutralized here because it seemed to be a convenient device to organize the play in what was very nearly a round space; Ian McKellen and Judi Dench gave fine performances, but they were not what made the play so memorable. (47)

Here, with the almost endless "evidence" of a film to choose from, this editor gives no more than this generalized, and consequently dismissive, appraisal of "fine" acting.

Gary Taylor's *Henry V*, also for Oxford University Press, gives attention to more of the multitudinous facts of performance and adds some weight to the stage-history by splicing his account of it into the general critical Introduction of the play. But his focus is narrow and he refers to the theatre only when wishing to debate some problematic intention of the dramatist. He writes as if very sure of his own opinions, so that reference to performances is primarily a way of reasserting previously held views. One actor catches the attention of this critic when he presents a dogged and pugnacious Henry the Fifth, "shorter and less impressive physically than many of the other actors around him," and another when he "may have exaggerated Henry's own uneasiness with his role." Judgement follows decisively:

> the demotic, complicated Henry of these recent productions takes us closer to the play than has any production since the Restoration.[8]

Taylor makes no apology for selectivity and no attempt to give a comprehensive account when judging performances but, at his best, he uses stage-history shrewdly, showing how the play's minor characters have made a greater mark in the theatre than is obviously indicated by the words they speak (59–62) and how the theatricality of the Chorus has been vindicated in many very different ways (56–7).

By virtue of their small scale, accounts of performance in editions of the plays cannot demonstrate all the ways of writing about performance. They do however exemplify the most common methods in relation to other forms of study and criticism. When two new editions of the same play are published simultaneously, as happened when the Oxford and New Cambridge editions of *Measure for Measure* appeared in 1991, comparisons between them can illuminate their different usage of identical material. The very strategy of writing about performances when presenting a text is different in these two cases. In N. W. Bawcutt's Oxford edition, the section on "The Play in Performance" precedes that on "The Play," as if such matters are to be dealt with before giving attention to the main task in hand. In Brian Gibbons's edition for Cambridge, "The play on the stage" is promoted to be the concluding section of the Introduction.

These editions have much in common, most notably the inclusion of many undebatable facts about the various cuts and additions that have, at various times, been made to the text. However, when acting is their concern, they are very different. Naming the actors in principal roles or describing specific pieces of stage business is usually as much as the Oxford provides—although the "real, sombre splendour" of John Emery's "depraved, abandoned" Barnardine gets a long descriptive quotation from 1846—while the Cambridge seldom cites any performer without being precisely descriptive of some element in performance and attempting to characterize its style. While Bawcutt comments that Sarah Siddons was forty years of age in 1795, Gibbons notes that in 1811–12 at Covent Garden, she was "so weakened by age that when she knelt in the last scene before the Duke she could only get up again with his help."[9]

The Cambridge edition is also more ambitious in trying to put each piece of information into its context. While both editors retell the story of William Poel placing an "Elizabethan stage" within a picture-frame stage, it is Gibbons who notes that, in 1908 at Stratford-upon-Avon, Poel's actors were playing "constantly to the front" and that the stage projected "beyond its usual limits" (59). While both note the long pauses that have variously been introduced in modern productions, it is the Cambridge edition that is the more helpful in showing the effects that have been obtained. The silence that Peter Brook asked his young Isabella to hold before pleading for her brother's life is noted by both, but only Gibbons tells how, afterwards, her "words came quiet and level, and as their full import of mercy reached Angelo, a sob broke from him" (64). Whereas, for Keith Hack's production at Stratford in 1974, the Oxford edition notes that, at the beginning of Act 5, the Duke "descended from the flies on a bar labelled 'deus ex machina'" (40), the Cambridge explains that the director was an admirer of Brecht and had conceived the play as a "fable of social oppression." His Duke was the actor-manager of a jaded and underpaid company of actors:

> For the final scene the Duke with golden hair descended on a ramp labelled "deus ex machina"; his over-acting was intended to undermine the audience's belief in the happy ending. (70)

"It was ironic," the editor adds, "that this production failed to give the low-life characters substance: [they] were mere caricatures without conviction."

While the Oxford edition describes performances in moments, leaving the reader to think of the consequences, its Cambridge rival attempts a wider and more sustained view and gives attention to a production's physical and ideological context. The concluding paragraph of the former begins, dutifully: "Outside the British isles the play has had a rather limited stage-history"; that of the other edition:

> The play's rhythms, the scale of emotion and the texture of the language, the development of thought and argument, can be damaged or obscured by unsuitably dominant settings.

★ ★ ★

Writing about performances of Shakespeare's plays should not be limited to a collection of momentary details about what individual actors have said and done so that they can be used to support, without defending, the writer's own critical views. Nor should it be guided solely by an uncritical acceptance of the writer's own predilections. The pleasures of recounting a number of new and amazing stage inventions or a wide range of unexpected on-stage activities should also entail some adjudication of their interest and value. These are some standards that could usefully be applied and would be in keeping with recent developments in Performance Studies.

By asking what is entailed in any performance in a theatre before an audience, scholars in this new discipline have come to recognize certain basic elements that are often neglected by writers about Shakespeare. First, a performance provides a progressive experience for both actors and audiences. The passage of time should be involved in any description of a theatrical event: sequence, development, growth, and possibly change is happening at every moment in a play. Neither actor nor audience remains the same throughout a performance. Second, during a performance, the actors as the persons in a drama pass through various imagined, and sometimes partly realized, locations and so arrive at a conclusion or, occasionally, come to a stop. On stage, the play is like a journey in which various places are visited and so, to describe its performance, space as well as time must come into question. The journey needs to be noticed, at least its beginning and its end, and what gets lost in the process, and what is retained, newly discovered, or created. Describing both these basic features of performance, and so involving time and space, should encourage critics who write about any play of Shakespeare's to keep its whole effect in view and dissuade them from dealing only with momentary perceptions.

Performance Studies insist that what happens on stage is only one part of a theatrical performance. In theatres within European traditions, audiences are usually kept sitting comfortably in the dark, their attention held by what happens in the bright and other "world" on the stage. But even under these un-Shakespearian conditions, the actors, if not the audience, know how much they are affected nightly by the behavior of the audience and how, in consequence, what they do changes as well. This effect is heightened when performances are given in close contact with an audience that is free to move and talk in the same light as the actors. Under those conditions, many more of Shakespeare's lines can be addressed to the audience than may at first appear to a reader and, it will also be found, that the audience is likely to respond with surprising freedom. A critic who wishes to view the plays on stage in something like the conditions for which they were written, should seek out performances in which the actors and audience are not kept apart from each other by lighting or the physical conditions of staging and where the imaginations of neither party are confined by restrictive predetermination. Even with minimal contact between stage and audience, theatre is a social occasion and the nature of that meeting is part of what the enactment of a play achieves at any moment. A performance has not been fully described if its audience has not been given careful attention.

A writer who wishes to study Shakespeare's plays in the theatre— for whatever reason—should remember that each performance is unique. Not only does it include much that could never be under a dramatist's control because of the many other agencies at work and the complexity of the human participators on stage and in the audience, all of which will change from one occasion to another, but a performance will not be the same for every member of an audience, no matter how fully shared is the pleasure that is given. Writing about performance, it is prudent to remember Marvin Carlson's advice that its nature is to resist conclusions, definitions, boundaries, and limits. In a theatre we view Shakespeare's plays as they give rise to an endless series of new manifestations in which each instance has unique qualities. Descriptions should be specific about date and place; their writers should be aware that the finer details of any one moment may well be ephemeral and their wider significance open to doubt. On the other hand, insofar as the plays become the mirrors of our age and of ourselves, those unique and temporary qualities, dependent as they are on the lives outside of the theatre of all participants, may well be among those that are most worthy of attention.

Writing about performances of Shakespeare's plays is a complex task, but worth attempting because each three or so hours in the theatre are like a glass through which we are able to see Shakespeare's imagined creation coming to life in more or less its full context. We also witness how the play's effect as performance draws upon the experience and sensibilities of actors and audiences of later ages, including most revealingly, our own.

Notes

1. Elam, *The Semiotics of Theatre and Drama* (London: Methuen, 1980).
2. Marvin Carlson, *Performance: a Critical Introduction* (London and New York: Routledge, 1996), 189. Another introduction to this field of study is Elaine Aston and George Savona, *Theatre as Sign-System: a Semiotics of Text and Performance* (London and New York: Routledge, 1991).
3. Halio, *A Midsummer Night's Dream* (Manchester: Manchester University Press, 1994), 118–19.
4. Rosenberg, *The Masks of Hamlet* (Cranbury, NJ: Associated University Presses, 1992), xiii.
5. The present writer had prolonged experience of two of the productions referred to in Professor Rosenberg's study, directing one and being present at many rehearsals of Peter Hall's with Albert Finney at the National Theatre in London, and can report that neither account mentions any details from the scenes which he would chiefly speak about in assessing the achievements and failures of these productions. This is not to argue that closeness to a production will give a truer view of its qualities, but to illustrate how far one judgement may vary from another.
6. Brooke, Preface, *Macbeth* (Oxford: Oxford University Press, 1990), vii.
7. See, for example, Gareth Lloyd Evans, from a careful account of the performance, in *Focus on "Macbeth,"* ed. John Russell Brown (London: Routledge, 1982), 97: "Olivier created an overwhelming sense of growing spiritual fatigue in a man haunted by some of the very questions the play leaves us wondering at" or Dennis Bartholomeusz in his comparative stage history, *Macbeth and the Players*

(Cambridge: Cambridge University Press, 1969), 259: "Olivier seems to have caught unerringly the sensitiveness intermingled with the evil in Macbeth." Samuel L. Leiter, in the compendium he edited, *Shakespeare Around the Globe: a Guide to Notable Postwar Revivals* (New York: Greenwood Press, 1986), writes of Olivier's "momentous performance" as Macbeth (356) and brings together the testaments of numerous critics, such as "that rare Macbeth who was outstanding both in speaking the poetry and conveying the sense of a dangerous warrior" or, more briefly, a Macbeth who was "strenuous, lurid, unforgettable" (368–69). Perhaps the most affirmative review was by Harold Hobson in *The Sunday Times,* concluding: "Macbeth is notoriously one of the most treacherous parts in the entire realm of drama; but Sir Laurence's performance is such that I do not believe there is an actor in the world who can come near him." The value of this review is considered in the context of Sir Harold's other reviews by Dominic Shellard in *Shakespeare Survey 49* (Cambridge: Cambridge University Press, 1996), 225–34.

8. Taylor, Introduction, *Henry V* (Oxford: Oxford University Press, 1982), 51.

9. Gibbons, Introduction, *Measure for Measure* (Cambridge: Cambridge University Press, 1991), 29, 56; Bawcutt, Introduction, *Measure for Measure* (Oxford: Oxford University Press, 1991), 29.

2

Research in the Service of Theatre*

It seems obvious to me now that a study of Shakespeare's plays in perform-ance involves a wider and parallel interest in theatres and audiences but it was some time before I was aware of the consequences. In this article I look at how I started out, drawing on what was familiar and mapping territory that was new to me.

Masterpieces of theatre are tantalizingly inaccessible, except in print.[1] Before we can see or hear the great plays of past ages, a theatre com-pany has to learn how to produce them in a very different world from that in which they were written. Directors, designers, and actors who are available today are very different from the people first responsible for staging the plays. The buildings and equipment of newly-built theatres make their own distinct and irresistible contributions to any production. Before old texts can be staged, problems of meaning, characterization, convention, and statecraft have to be tackled. How can classics become fully and engagingly alive under such changed conditions? Any responsible theatre should consider establishing its own laboratory in which to conduct the necessary research.

But productive theatres will not provide the right setting for research. Each new production finds its own identity by other means, by using the imagination, instinct and active collaboration of many and very various persons: this process is essentially different from scholarly investigation and is the proper business of theatres. No busy

---

*First published as 'Research in the Service of Theatre: the Example of Shakespeare Studies', *Theatre Research International,* 18, 1 (2000), 25–35.

19

theatre has the additional time or resources to invest adequately in disinterested research, to collect evidence and pursue conjectures.

Yet a theatre which works in ignorance of the problems that the passage of time has brought is taking unnecessary risks when it seeks to keep alive the work of previous ages. And if a theatre does not tackle the classics, but speaks only in contemporary voices, it is neglecting one of its most amazing opportunities: our present-day consciousness *needs* the stimulus of other times, and their different perspectives on what we are now. Even a theatre dedicated solely to contemporary drama could benefit from research as it tries to respond to the most adventurous and deeply persuasive writers of the present time— artists whose imaginations are best employed when free from current convention and theatricality.

But fortunately, theatres do not need to establish research institutions within their own organizations: they are already in existence elsewhere, and subsidized from other sources. The true problem is how to develop and maintain good communications between theatres and the centres for research in universities, so that both parties may thrive in full knowledge of each other.

★   ★   ★

In some ways, this is an unnatural alliance. Theatres and universities have totally different rhythms of work, the one organized in periods of a few months around a series of crucial operations dictated by the 'first nights' of each season, the other committed to weekly teaching-schedules planned in two or three year cycles and to research enterprises which take years or even decades to complete. The two organizations are inhabited by individuals whose ways of thinking are dissimilar and deeply ingrained. Impatience often goes with creativity in the theatre, as well as an ability to maintain a large vision, to use and trust many other persons, and to take risks. On the other hand, patience is essential for research, as well as an ability to concentrate attention on particular issues over long periods of time, to analyse precisely, and to reject the results of work that cannot withstand the closest scrutiny. The two activities are different to the point of incompatibility.

Mismatches are often very evident. When a production does take account of scholarly writings, it is commonly found that only a part of the message has been received, or that it has been received, or that it has been heard and almost wholly misunderstood. An example is a

Royal Shakespeare Company's *King Lear* for which the director had listened to the Oxford editors and other scholars, and had prepared a production-script based on the Folio text of 1623, rather than on a conflation of the Folio and earlier Quarto. But he did not go all the way in accepting the Folio's deletions: the Arraignment Scene (III.vi) was played in full, according to the Quarto. An opportunity to assess the effectiveness of a later reworking of Shakespeare's script was missed because instinct, not logic or respect for scholarship, had been the final arbitrator.

But the theatre does sometimes show that it is looking for help from scholarship. When Gordon Craig returned to London in 1925 to set about a production of *Macbeth* which he would design and direct, he turned to a young and recently-appointed Professor of English Language and Literature, Allardyce Nicoll, who had already published extensively on English poetry and the history of dramatic literature. Craig was enthusiastic and eager to respond to both facts and insights; but he demanded a great deal, and insisted that his young dramaturge should give up his university post in order to give sufficient time to this important project. Allardyce Nicoll was not prepared to do that, although he respected Craig more than any other director working at that time.[2] And it was fortunate that he did not, because the *Macbeth* project came to nothing, beyond making some contribution to a New York production several years later, the designs for which Craig signed 'C.p.b.', that is 'Gordon Craig, pot-boiler'.[3] Theatre often issues imperatives which seem of overwhelming importance one week, and can be forgotten or derided a week later; scholarship is naturally more tenacious.

Encounters like this do not imply that any alliance between research and production is impossible. Rather they illustrate the need of the one for the other, their complementary virtues proving fruitful whenever bonding does not attempt to be total or restrictive. Difference, which seems at first to be threatening, can often prove stimulating, if not essential, for active and productive partnerships. But it is wise to be prepared for the more obvious occasions when conflict of interest and activities will occur.

In some way, mutual respect must be gained, and time made available for easy exchanges of opinion and enthusiasm. The collaboration between Allardyce Nicoll and Sir Barry Jackson, which influenced theatre productions at Malvern and Birmingham over many years, and briefly at Stratford, is a notable example of a productive association between theatre and research. Both men had a gentle courtesy in common, as well as wide-ranging minds; and they clearly enjoyed each other's company. Strong disagreements were quietly resolved, because there was no formal association, no question of one having authority over the other. Neither man was typical of his own world, but both have earned a place in their dissimilar histories, achieving far more than common measures of innovation and sustained influence. While the obvious authority, temperance and financial security of both men seem out of tune with the present time, their collaboration does indicate that opportunities are needed in any such association for relaxed exchange of views and sharing of pleasures. Theatre is so often under threat, concentrating its every conscious thought on extremely difficult enterprises, that periods of enforced inaction seem almost mandatory. When these cannot be achieved, a scholar's comparative freedom from sudden crises and large scale operations might enable him or her to supply some of the reflectiveness and freedom of thought which are necessary for good forward-planning and imaginative health. Then the task would be to find the right time for intervention and innovative suggestion.

In some ways, a scholar in the theatre is like an-old-time fool in attendance at court:

> He must observe their mood on whom he jests,
> The quality of persons, and the time:
> And, like the haggard, check at every feather
> That comes before his eye.
> (*Twelfth Night*, III.i.59–62)

This practice is 'full of labour', and involves responding to sudden and unexpected enquiries, and working long hours at short notice. Sometimes an answer can be given only indirectly, and then the fool's skill lies in allowing director or actor, designer or publicist, to find the sense of the matter for him or herself.

From my experience it seems that a scholar is often asked questions to which there is no simple answer. The phone rang one day, and a director's assistant had been given time off from rehearsals to ask me how the Lords in *Love's Labours Lost* thought of the park in which they were living, and what books they might be studying, and what poetry they were enjoying. In some way, I had to speak of the English countryside, France and Europe, of Sidney's *Arcadia*, Castiglione, Lyly, Lodge, of a dozen poets and numerous painters and miniaturists, of Elizabethan gardens, hunting, dancing, feasting, parading, disquisition, education, courtly manners and country customs. To such questions there are no easy or predigested answers; the best recourse is to promise to phone or fax the following day, and in the meantime try to imagine the needs of actors and director, and the nature of their stage and audience. An earlier question about the same production was difficult for other reasons: 'How old is Armado?' sounds straightforward enough, but it cannot be answered by any convenient quotation from the text. It involves this character's relationship to Moth and Costard, and to Jaquenetta and the young Lords. Literary and theatrical sources for the character will also come into the reckoning, together with a great tangle of possible allusions to Elizabethan persons in this and other characterizations in the play. Theatre history is also helpful: how old were the actors who have shone in this role? Paul Scofield played him when he was only twenty-four; but then the production was by Peter Brook, who was at that time twenty-one. Yet Ralph Richardson could have played Armado wonderfully at the age of seventy. The scholar's task is not to be prescriptive, but to help the director and others find their own answers in the light of as much information as can be provided usefully. The aim should be to give no more in reply than is sufficient to spur the imaginations of those actively engaged in rehearsals under whatever circumstances prevail. The scholar needs to be aware of the context in which questions are asked, and the 'quality of persons' involved.

When answering practical questions, the researcher should also be aware of consequences and constraints. For example, what can be said about the Witches in *Macbeth?* By now many volumes have been written which develop our understanding of what they might be, on stage and in the imaginations of Jacobeans of various persuasions and ways of life. But what are the consequences of this knowledge for casting and costume, and for stage business and stage effects? For a start, what should be made of the Folio's direction indicating that the '*WITCHES vanish*', and of the dialogue which follows:

> —The earth hath bubbles, as the water has,
>   And these are of them. Whither are they vanished?
> —Into the air; and what seemed corporal melted
>   As breath into the wind.
>   (*Macbeth*, I.iii.79–82)

Should the witches 'fly' off above the stage, or descend into traps, or disappear in smoke, which then hangs around as the play continues?

Or should carefully managed stage movements work some trick of focus, and Macbeth's later 'infected be the air whereon they ride' (IV.i.138) say more about his state of mind than about stage business? Then, how should the witches conclude their part in the play? Is the Folio's speech genuine in which the First Witch calls for an 'antic round', or is this one of several corruptions introduced when the players were influenced by Middleton's *The Witch?* How about the Folio's direction *'Enter HECATE and the other three WITCHES'* near the beginning of the 'Apparition Scene' (IV.i.38)? At this point, a climactic dance involving an orchestra and up to fifty witches, some of them flying, was to be seen on the nineteenth-century stage. Some overwhelming stage effect does seem called for as a climax, but what ought it be? Might the witches' most impressive and concluding statement be the long procession of the heirs of Banquo, or is it some weird 'antic round' of six witches, watched by a silent Hecate and followed by aerial exits? Certainly, research can provide a number of alternative readings to spur the imagination of the director, but something more might be added about the wider consequences of this moment: what is its relation to other spectacles in this play, and to the developing use of spectacle in Shakespeare's other plays, and in other plays, court masques, and social entertainments of the Jacobean age? The place of ritual in religion at this time might also be considered when reporting on the stage business implied by Shakespeare's text.

Scholarship's function reaches further than responding to questions, as if theatre had always to administer occasion to research. (The fool should not be gagged or thought to have 'no more brain than a stone'.) The relationship can be active on both sides, and research have its own inspirations and imperatives. The first concern in order of importance is the text itself, because this is scholarship's basic material and the most durable element of the theatre of past ages. How should the surviving texts be edited, printed and understood? Research must have its say about all these difficult and theatrically vital matters. A scholar's obvious duty is to provide good texts, but he or she should then proceed to illuminate those words with the needs of theatre in mind, as well as those of students and other scholars. Every detail is worth an editor's attention from a theatrical point of view: spelling, elision, punctuation, and lining, as well as meanings, wordplay, associations, syntax, rhetorical structure, and metre; sound, texture and rhythm, and more subtle matters still, like tone and idiom—the social and individual differentials of speech. For a verbally brilliant dramatist like Shakespeare and some of his contemporaries or followers—Jonson, Webster, Middleton, Ford, Congreve—some attempt should be made to distinguish the several styles from play to play, and within each play and, to some extent, within each character. The variety of the dramatist's writing, the deeper harmonies and discords of it, the freshness and surprise of its poetry, the reach of the writer's mind and, at some moments, the dizzying clarity of it—all this is at stake.

After a response to the text, the next most pressing question is casting: how can a play be served best by the actors who are available? Usually such matters are left entirely to the director, the administrator responsible for money, and the actors and their agents, and managers. But research can help in these crucial decisions. Stage history shows what kinds of actor have succeeded in a difficult role, and so can widen the range of possibilities under consideration. Commentary on the text can explain how a certain character functions, what are the personal, local, social, economic or political restraints that should be evident in what he or she does and says; what age, physique and temperament would best suit the words to be spoken; what is the relative importance of family and political relationships; are mental processes fast or slow, deep or shallow? With care 'identikits' can be provided from the text which will help to identify the right actor for each part. Such work will not solve casting problems, but it may make a contribution.

The importance of casting has often been stressed. Richard Eyre, Artistic Director of the National Theatre, has said that 'casting is sixty to seventy per cent' of a director's job: 'not just in regard to type and the suitability of an actor's looks and ability for a particular role, but also that you feel you will have a relationship with the actors and that they will fit into some kind of social group'.[4]

In practice, no play is chosen for production without careful regard to casting: if a theatre cannot find the right actors, there is no point in thinking further about it. If possible the actors should be both suited to their parts and challenged by them; and each new mixture of actors should in some way awaken expectancy and a sense of discovery. A scholar can know nothing about the availability of actors, and an ability to see that Ms X could play Cleopatra, if only Mr Y would play Antony, does not come from any regular kind of study; but perhaps the freedom from direct contact with the persons most closely concerned, coupled with a detailed knowledge of the text

and stage history of the play in question, might give the more distant specialist a useful and unbiased view of the complex situation.

Next in importance in the staging of a play—some would say, first in importance—is to discover how to present in visual terms the world which its characters inhabit. Here the designer has a great influence on any production. Asked how *much* influence, John Dexter replied that it was 'enormous; it's more important than casting the leading role, because it's from the designer's response that you lay out certain guidelines and make concrete your own ideas'.[5]

Every play has its riddles, and none more immediately enjoyable than that of finding out how to unlock its corporate life, its time and place, and its mode of physical being; and so to discover the visual world of the action. Intuition plays the largest part in this search, but research can make its own contribution. What, for example, did Shakespeare imply when he set *Much Ado About Nothing* in Messina? What was Sicily to him, and how did Dogberry the Constable, Verges the Headborough, and the watchmen with those very English names figure in that world? Why did he specify, unusually, an actual date in the earliest scene: 'the sixth of July' (I.i.246)? Should the weather seem as hot and humid as it might be in July in Sicily, or should the characters behave as if in England, where rain is nearly always a possibility? What masked dances are appropriate in this world, and what wedding ceremonies and what mourning rites? How was the banquet prepared, the wedding, the reception of royal guests, the management of a household in the apparent absence of the wife and mother? What was the social relationship between the four women in the play, with special regard to the functions of Margaret and Ursula? These may seem unimportant questions to scholars, but if the play is to be created in our modern scenic theatres and be in sympathy with Shakespeare's imagination, the text and its literary and theatrical backgrounds should be studied with care to interpret its stage directions and to observe whatever clues to an appropriate visual realization may be hidden within its dialogue, in its various characters' choice of words, turns of phrase and, even, rhythms of speech.

Indications of a historical or actual location, or references to Elizabethan or Jacobean behaviour or stage practice, will not provide sufficient elucidation to help designers and directors reach crucial decisions. For one thing none of these could be reproduced today without changing their effect and, sometimes, their very nature. It is more important to seek the imaginary setting of a play's action, how it seemed to take place in its dramatist's mind; and then to find some way to translate or transform that into stage images which produce something like the same effect in our modern minds. Imagination, inventiveness, sensitivity are all needed here, and the theatre provides them according to talent and opportunity. But research and careful, textual analysis can discover further clues which may stimulate creative thought, while not replacing it.

Again *Macbeth* may provide examples. Is Scotland that primitive society of independent and hostile thanes, as described in Holinshed's *Chronicles*? The election of its king and the bloody nature of its warfare, suggest that it is. Or should the various allusions to Jacobean life be given precedence, so that the play becomes a glass held up to show a contemporary image for Shakespeare's audiences? In either case, how shall we best serve the play when staging it at this present time, which is neither primitive nor Jacobean? It is not helpful to answer that it should be staged in the round or on a very simple platform in a small auditorium, so that the figures of the characters will dominate every visual impression, for then costume becomes the crucial design-factor. Trevor Nunn's production at the Other Place and now available in video is indeed set in a kind of limbo; but the costumes do locate the action firmly in two distinct and oddly contrasted realities: an ancient sacredotal kingdom and a modern 'World at War'. The play, in this production, was presented as an irregular nightmare. What were the consequences of such spectacles on the impact of its words and actions? In the theatre, I had the impression of a team of young men playing some sort of brutal game around a resolute mother-figure, in the course of which one of their own kind grew into a monstrous predator—so that he became increasingly isolated, until he collapsed. Does this serve Shakespeare's text, as well as any other 'world' that might be realized with stage-business and costume? Or might such an unlocalized setting be taken still further into fantasy, or be governed more strictly by a single visual reality?

One particular textual crux demands that a director of this play knows precisely what kind of world he is creating. After Malcolm has been named Prince of Cumberland (I.iv.35–42], the king continues simply, promising 'signs of nobleness' to 'all deservers'. No verbal response is provided at this point, but is Duncan heard in total silence? A few lines later Macbeth acknowledges the significance of such change from ordinary Scottish methods of ensuring a succession to the throne; so if the other thanes say nothing they will appear either too dutiful or too timorous to expostulate. Or should they combine without debate to honour the king's eldest son with silent acts of fealty?

Whatever they do, their actions will give a large-scale visual impression of the nature of Duncan's kingdom, and a director has to know what that is. In most modern productions, there is an orchestrated cry of 'Hail!', and some kneeling; saluting or brandishing of weapons. Unfortunately this often speaks only of tired, old-fashioned theatrical convention, but even that establishes one kind of 'world' in which the play takes place. Holinshed tells the story so that it is very clear that Duncan was appointing his own successor: did Shakespeare omit this, adopting the more ambiguous, 'We will establish our estate', in order that Scotland should seem less easy to understand, and Duncan a more devious king than suggested by the verbal tributes which are paid to him elsewhere in the play? Thematically, as well as visually, the political society that is evoked at this point, by dress, stage properties, behaviour or interpolated words, is of great importance to the effect of the play in performance: do flags and trumpets dominate formal proceedings? or should loud cries, clanging weapons and military movements take over from words, or is there only a muted response and hurried disarray? *Something* must be said visually at this moment, or Macbeth's subsequent comment will not be comprehensible to the audience, but will sound unmotivated and pass with little effect. Research should investigate the visual and practical consequences of a text as it is realized in performance and production, and it should maintain a critical discourse with theatres about them, even if it has no direct influence on theatre practice and has to acknowledge that there are many different answers to such riddles.

In considering the visual worlds of the plays, research will also be continuing the exploration of themes and meanings which has been in progress for most of this century. Scholarly and critical preoccupation with new 'interpretations' has indeed encouraged several generations of theatre directors to take hold of a text in order to propound their own concepts about its meaning and about the world in which we live, and it is, perhaps, on this rather reductive level that research and theatre will always co-exist and help each other most readily. But 'concepts' and 'meaning' are less revered today than a decade or so ago. Now in the theatre the 'exploration' of a text with a 'group of actors', or the 'testing' of a number of contrary interpretations, or the 'privileging' of what is avowedly an undercurrent in the writing are all more in favour. No longer is a single intellectual concept supposed to do all the work of creating a novel production: a director's 'interpretation' is often relegated to serving as a rallying point whenever the actors are at a loss in rehearsal; or it may be used, like a long spoon, to stir the mixture in the cauldron so that still more flavours and potential meanings are released.

But research must continue to ask about meanings—not only the meanings of speeches, images and arguments, but also of narrative and action, of repetition and changes of tempo and focus, and of the nature of the visual world on stage. When a text provides many passionate arguments for characters to speak, about politics, morality, philosophy and psychology, it would be very strange if the dramatist, behind the motley of performance, did not himself have ideas which he wanted to explore and express. What these were and how they are present in the action and visual appearance of a play in performance, are questions which should occupy both theatre practitioners and critics in a 'joint operation'. For dramatists less intellectually alert than Shakespeare, the same tasks are to be done, but with greater difficulty and perhaps more need.

Another basic task for research is to keep reading all the playtexts which have survived from the past but are seldom or never revived, with an eye to finding those which should be brought back into the repertoire of our times. Often this will entail grappling with obstacles which are more negotiable by a scholar than a theatre director. For example, the dramatic effect of the Ghost of Andrea appearing with the allegorical figure of Revenge as they preside over the main action of *The Spanish Tragedy* may not be comprehensible until the physical loathsomeness and moral danger associated with Revenge in Kyd's day become recognized: given an appropriate visual enforcement in costuming and behaviour, this stage character without any individualization makes a potent and challenging contribution to the whole play. Marlowe's *Tamburlaine* may have been held back from our stages because the text seems to require a cast of hundreds, making it too expensive a show for most theatres to contemplate; but once the size and organization of an Elizabethan acting company have become better understood, a less expensive production style immediately suggests itself and doubling becomes part of the play's eloquence. The anonymous *Arden of Faversham* has been less frequently performed than its quality deserves, largely because of modern editorial procedures. The Quarto of 1592 was printed as if a very high proportion of its lines had been written by someone with a tin ear for verse. Editors, schooled in a 'conservative' tradition, have not used their knowledge of printing house practices and of Elizabethan language and prosody to emend the Quarto's wayward use of elision, particles of speech, and orthography. The precept of Fredson Bowers runs:

> We can often be aware of corruption in the 'bad' text (though not always), but we may have no concrete evidence at all about the autograph reading which has been memorially corrupted. To attempt, therefore, to reconstruct a purely hypothetical text by metrical smoothing and verbal emendation is sheer folly except in isolated cases.[6]

These words were enough to excuse a recent editor from using his expertise and sensitivity. For fear of being wrong in any particular and so being accused of 'sheer folly', he left the text as clumsy as it was at first, so that anyone who wishes to read this play with any pleasure must make rapid mental adjustments at almost every line and so refine the play's poetry as it is being perused.[7] With every modern editor agreeing with this procedure, it is no wonder that *Arden* is not often produced; and yet careful restoration, without altering meaning in any significant way, can reveal the poetic sensitivity and muscular eloquence of the anonymous writer, and restore a versification which is as firm as it is refined.

Scholarship has had considerable success in recommending the lesser known plays by Shakespeare to the attention of theatre directors—partly because Shakespeare is a name that sells well in the market-place—but there is more work to do on plays by his contemporaries. If these are to regain their viability on the stage more persuasion will be needed, and more theatrical awareness in that persuasion.

If theatre research does enter the service of living theatre, it will find that theatre will make increasingly significant contributions to its own work. In a general way, productions of all kinds help to train scholars and critics to experience the plays in performance as they sit down to read scripts in solitary study. But research in the service of theatre develops a capacity to think behind and around the lines, to ask questions about structure and action, about performance and interaction, about visual elements of staging and all the manifold complexities which are involved with a play in performance. As scholars and critics *see*, and perhaps 'feel', the consequences of any ideas which they propound, they experience a feedback which stimulates fresh thought and better definitions. More than this: when scholars interact with theatre people, they receive lively criticism from those who know the texts at least as intimately as they do, and yet in different ways.

Notes

1. This article is developed from a lecture given to a conference on 'Drama and Theatre', at the Shakespeare Institute (University of Birmingham), 29 November 1991.
2. Allardyce Nicoll, in conversation with the author, summer 1973.
3. See Denis Bablet, *Edward Gordon Craig,* tr. Daphne Woodward (1966), pp. 187–89.
4. Judith Cook, *Directors' Theatre* (1989), p. 29.
5. Judith Cook, *Directors' Theatre* (1974), p. 39.
6. *The Dramatic Works of Thomas Dekker,* I (1953), pp. 309–404.
7. See *Arden of Faversham,* New Mermaids, ed. Martin White (1982), p. xxxi.

3

Writing about the Plays in Performance*

Some ten years ago I began to edit a series of Shakespeare Handbooks and wrote three of the early volumes. These book-length studies were significantly different from other existing series about Shakespeare in performance that evaluate individual productions, directors, performances and actors: they do not try to describe a few specific productions by reference to the texts, in the manner of other commentaries and extended studies. Knowing that all performances die as soon as they have been given, I concluded that a responsible attempt to understand what happened on stage involves describing productions that no longer exist and contextualising the theatrical events of which they were once a part. To describe any theatrical performance is a skilled and, ultimately, unsatisfactory task; many factors must be considered and description, at best, can only be the impressionistic and personal view of the writer.

In contrast to other studies of the plays in performance, the Shakespeare Handbooks are designed to help their readers imagine the plays in performance for themselves by providing commentaries that, moment by moment, describe the tasks that the texts require all actors to undertake and, at crucial moments, to consider some consequences of the choices that they can make. A reader needs no special theatrical knowledge to understand the actors' tasks because the plays mirror life and not theatre: the commentaries show what can be seen in that mirror once the texts come alive in performance.

I want to blow a whistle and stop the game because studies of Shakespeare's plays in performance have added little to our understanding

* From 'Learning Shakespeare's Secret Language: the Limits of "Performance Studies" ', *New Theatre Quarterly*, 95, XXIV (2008), 211–21, revised and updated December 2009.

of the texts. They tend to be limited in range and small in scale, looking at moments that can be described but telling us no more than how one particular actor or director has made the incident unusually meaningful or effective. Other studies have been about a production's stage design or its director's concept. None tells us much about Shakespeare's plays because scholars and critics do not consider the progressive experience of an audience or seek out elements whose validity extends beyond the context of one production that is now dead and beyond recall. I am blowing the whistle because I question the worth of much that I have written in the past and of many studies by other scholars and critics whose learning and skills surpass my own.

During the twentieth century a succession of highly regarded critics and scholars have argued that Shakespeare's plays should be studied in performance because they were expressly written to be acted in a theatre. Their rallying cries have been so urgent that echoes of them are still heard today and yet the anticipated revolution or revelation has never arrived. At a recent meeting of the Shakespeare Association of America, only two out of forty-four seminars were basically concerned with this branch of study and, in the same year, among nine seminars on offer at the International Shakespeare Conference at the Shakespeare Institute in Stratford-upon-Avon, only one or possibly two centred on the study of a play's performance.

Experience has exposed the difficulties of studying Shakespeare's plays theatrically. Productions are sometimes poorly cast or hurriedly prepared and so not worth serious study. Performances often find new meanings for the text, invent new stage business or tell the tale differently but how can track be kept on all these details and close attention be given to productions of most merit? Many writers, including my younger self, have been so pleased with theatrical moments that we have scrambled to catch the crumbs as they fall from a performance or have concentrated on pulling out one plum at a time. But too little attention has been given to an audience's experience, its changing moods, sensations and expectations, the awakening of curiosity, frustration, or satisfaction. Non-verbal elements are undervalued or neglected altogether: sound, visual effects or on-stage movements, an actor's stage presence and how it changes as the action unfolds, or where, how and when the production has been created, with what intentions and for what audience.

'Performance Studies' has become established as a branch of scholarship and higher education but, because research in this subject is not primarily concerned with play-texts, Shakespeare scholars have paid little attention to colleagues in these departments.[1] This new field of study should be able to sharpen analysis of performances and show how they contribute to an audience's experience but, instead of following this new lead, Shakespeare scholars have continued to describe what is said and done on stage at certain moments in a performance, as if that were all they were able to study.

Theatrical performances will always be difficult to describe and analyse and, when the play is by Shakespeare, more difficult than most. Even now, after years of persistent research and reflection, scholars seldom view what happens on stage objectively or consistently but depend on little more reliable than their own instinctive, textual, or historical judgement on a number of striking moments. Evidence about performances in the past is seldom reliable so in studying them scholars have the additional problem of discriminating between different descriptions of moments that were written by reviewers paid to write interesting journalism rather than give full and accurate descriptions of what happened in the theatre. Even a large collection of insightful observations will never explain how a performance held the attention of audiences for two or three hours. No moment has its complete meaning and value alone but is dependent on its place in the progress of an entire performance and should be viewed in contrast to other moments and in relation to whatever information and sensations the play has earlier provided. Similarly, an audience's experience of a play depends on every element of the 'theatrical event' of performance, including the predisposition and predilections of its members, the place, day and time of performance, the organisation, policies and reputation of the producing company, and events taking place outside the theatre.[2] A theatrical production lives, struggles or dies because of its effect on an audience and that phenomenon should be an important part of the study of plays in performance.

All the difficulties of studying performance are compounded for Shakespeare's plays because they have been performed long after composition without benefit of the author's guidance or the continuance of widely accepted theatrical conventions. As literature, their speeches and, still more, their dialogue cannot be readily or fully understood by readers or actors who live in a very different world than the one Shakespeare knew and drew upon in his writing. The plays are complicated, and narrative and action varied in mood and means: one moment calls for many actors, the next for one or two; a very quiet simply worded passage may be followed by sustained and elaborate speech, half-formed sentences or inchoate cries. After stillness, intimacy, formality or restraint may come activity that is free, urgent, brutal or widely dispersed. Shakespeare's plays have no detailed and authoritative stage directions and are notable for the variety of ways in which they have been staged and for an actor's ability to spring surprises.

All productions of Shakespeare must go beyond what the text requires and depend on the contribution of actors who live in the present time and inevitably draw upon that experience. Students of the plays should ask whether a production's actors serve the story as it unfolds, whether a striking effect originates in Shakespeare's text or in the mental and physical contribution of the actor or the decisions and skill of the director and designers of set, costume, sound and lighting. When, many years ago, critics called for Shakespeare's plays to be studied in performance they were setting a huge task and no one has found sufficient time and expertise to attend to more than a few contributory elements.

★   ★   ★

The revised edition of Julia Hankey's *Othello* in the *Shakespeare in Production* series (Cambridge University Press, 2005) gathers details and quotations about moments in the play as if they were collectible curios or odd pebbles taken from the seashore. They are printed as annotations alongside the full text so that a reader can see where they belong but little help is given to relate these moments to the on-going action or the development of individual performances and the progressive experience of an audience. Variety seems to be prized, rather than suitability to the text and individual performances. Here, for example, is Othello's return to the stage to encounter Iago in Act III, scene iii:

> Kean 'entered with the abrupt and wandering step of one to whom the grace or dignity of motion were new things, and swallowed up in the fearful bewilderings of a heavy heart' (*T*, 14 May 1814). Salvini 'seems to enter as if his inner soul is red-hot . . . he suffers not only mentally but physically also' (Stanislavski, *My Life*, p. 271). Olivier returned sniffing his fingers 'as if they were tainted by contact with [Desdemona's] body' (Tynan, *National Theatre Production*, p. 8). John Kani sobs and groans in the Suzman video (p. 209).

In this form of study much depends on the impression made on individual observers, except where a film, video, or document can be cited to verify the facts of what happened: for example, 'Nunn's

Bianca sniffed the handkerchief here (promptbook)' or 'In the video, Imogen Stubbs [as Desdemona] giggles again' (pp. 227, 258). When critics and scholars study a production that they have seen, the same isolating and diminishing factors are at work. Catching an impression or an innovation needs close observation and tends to keep out of the reckoning its effect on an entire performance or production. Almost always the moment is associated with what is novel in a setting, costume, stage business, or the 'reading' of a particular line of text. Reviews in academic journals furnish many examples. They crowd, for instance, into Michael Dobson's four to five thousand words in *Shakespeare Survey, 60* (2007) about the Royal Shakespeare Company's *Antony and Cleopatra* of the previous year. For example, Patrick Stewart's Antony:

> a smirking bare-chested figure in white harem trousers holding an ornate leather whip comes dashing stealthily up through the front stalls. . . .

> he decides his overall battle-plan at Actium . . in mid-sentence: 'Candidus, we / Will fight with him by. . . [*slightly extending this monosyllable while he looks upward as if mentally tossing a coin*] . . . sea.'

> for the encounter with Thidias in III.xiii, . . . he is filled with all the neurotic energy of complete despair, displaying a ranting, twitching state of alternating reckless bravado and unbearable self-loathing,

> sending his angry challenge to single combat, he is on the edge of complete incoherence, scarcely able to hold the shape of a whole sentence in his mind (pp. 294–5).

Here the play in performance is reduced to a number of incidents in which an actor's, director's or designer's invention is more notable than any response to the text being acted. In most studies of Shakespeare an audience's progressive experience of an entire play is seldom the critic's main concern; nor is the theatrical presentation of general themes inscribed in the text, such as, in this example, the course of history, the loyalty, responsibility or egotism of individuals, the effect of power in politics, military heroism, nationalism, ethnicity, fate, supernatural agencies or superstition, and so on and on. A very basic question is often ignored: 'How is the theatrical experience made and used?'

In response to performances a Shakespeare scholar-critic tends to make each production a test for the principal actors. This emphasis is most useful when comparison is made with performances by other actors and attention paid to the final cumulative effect. Here, for example, is Robert Smallwood in *Shakespeare Survey, 53* (2000):

> Zoë Waites' Desdemona [was] a proud, strong-minded young woman in her smart Mrs Pankhurst suits, perfectly capable of the 'downright violence' of the decision she had made, as uninhibited in her physical desire for him as he for her. Some Desdemonas have seemed more vulnerable, but the great benefit of this interpretation was to present the relationship between Othello and Desdemona as absolutely reciprocal and fully self-aware, its destruction a terrible undertaking (p. 256).

The consequences of this mode of study is clearly shown when it is adopted for a school edition of a play. It will quote numerous opinions, ask a string of questions, point out 'problems,' give instructions for practical explorations and add photographs to its text, all of which results in a rich but indigestible brew of information. Following only half the suggestions is likely to spread over months of search and endeavour; for example, the *Cambridge School Shakespeare* edition of *Romeo and Juliet* (3rd edn, 2005) prints four notes about the first fifteen lines of Act IV, scene iv, organised under four headings, three of them ending with question marks:

1. Angelica – is that the Nurse's name?
2. Who speaks the lines?
3. Husband and wife – a distrustful relationship?
4. Watching.

The Sourcebooks Shakespeare (Sourcebooks; USA, 2005 and A.C.Black Publishers; London, 2007) poses fewer questions but provides rather more photographs and comes with an audio CD of twenty 'classic scenes'.

Study of 'Shakespeare in Performance' in both universities and schools is in danger of too much industry and too many dislocated and personal observations for any well-grounded view of a play's theatrical possibilities to emerge. Marvin Rosenberg's large compilations about the major tragedies, published from the nineteen-seventies onwards, were to become models for this mode of study.[3] He set himself to consider every account he could unearth of what had been seen and heard on stage before recording those he thought most interesting and sometimes adding his own comments on their effectiveness and validity as a representation of Shakespeare's text. Here is his account of the entry of Lady Macbeth for Act III, scene i:

> Siddons felt burdened. The golden round of royalty now crowns her brow and royal robes enfold her form; but the peace that passeth all understanding is lost.

> Siddons armed herself in dignity. With other Ladies the stress would show more. Ziegler tried to hide her torment behind a smiling mask, but a German observer saw the muscles of her face resisting her intentions, cramping her face, half-closing her eyes. Faucit's first splendid, aggressive power seemed to desert her under her golden crown; she seemed heart-stricken. Ristori, for all her control, projected an awareness that their new power was not secure, her attention dividing between the court and a distant fate she listened for. Modjeska walked like one in a dream. Modjeska's sensitivity had long ago surfaced; the neurotic [Diana] Rigg had, until the murder discovery, been impassive in her control, now what was insecure and fragile beneath it showed.

> She looks desiccated, broken, and walks like an old woman, inter-mittently emerging from self-absorption to present . . . a grin the more ghastly for the rouge she has hopefully daubed on her sunken cheeks.

Rosenberg's book was well received but today it can be seen as a tombstone set upon one way of studying Shakespeare's plays. This passage alone raises large questions. Why did this scholar choose these productions to record? Would any of another dozen give as much or more information or the next dozens following them? How did he choose these descriptions in preference to others by other specta-tors? How do these moments function in the rest of the production? How did these individual performances collude with others in other major roles in the production or contrast with the work of another theatre company? What else was seen on stage or heard at the same time? This way of studying Shakespeare's plays can never be either complete or completely reliable.

Alternatively, a scholar will choose a comparatively small number of varied productions and give impressions of their overall effect, either gleaned from reviews or experienced at first hand in the theatre. Interviews with actors or directors are often used to explain how performances have come about. For a student of Shakespeare these studies are chiefly valuable for demonstrating the range of interpreta-tions that directors and designers have given to the texts but a sense of the play's enduring potential in performance is rarely communi-cated because much of the available space is needed to describe a number of discrete productions and explain the directors' concepts and the sensations conveyed by the stage settings.

At their best, accounts of plays in performance combine these two approaches. Antony Dawson's account of Michael Benthall's 1948 production of *Hamlet* in the *Shakespeare in Performance* series (Manchester University Press, 1995) repeatedly relates Paul Scofield's performance as Hamlet to the progress of the plot, action and production. For example, at the end, 'despite the bloodshed, . . . his death was quiet and noble,' but then attention returns to the director's invention and concept by noting how an un-named page wept in 'in a mutual silence, . . . a wordless but eloquent chorus' (pp. 131–2).

The difficulties of retrieving a sense of performance from the past are fully recognised in this book:

> I am engaged in reconstructing the meanings generated by past perform-
> ances of a text that makes the play of meaning one of its primary subjects.
> And 'reconstruction' is itself a slippery process, since it depends on docu-
> mentary sources, such as reviews and prompt books, that are themselves
> culturally mediated. The result is an approximation that I want to make
> accurate, but which itself derives from a constraint associated with the
> responsibility of writing a book like this one – the need to produce a
> meaningful narrative, to offer more than just a lot of loose details to my
> readers (p. 3).

The difficulties are even greater than that because a theatrical event cannot be fully described and appreciated without an account of its context: the theatre building and equipment, the theatre company and its organisation and history, the occasion and location of performance, and each actor's earlier career, training, rehearsal techniques, stage presence and personal characteristics. The moment in time and in the history of a nation and society will also have influenced performance and its audience's response.

The effect of these critical and scholarly difficulties has been complex, confusing, and often dispiriting. Yet from the struggle, a new reason for engaging in this form of study has been identified and has inspired a number of cultural and sociological studies. Journalistic accounts of performance and descriptions of innovative settings, concepts and 'readings' can help to identify the spirit of the times, the vision of a director, or the effect of living in a technologically adventurous age. Evidence is scattered, biased and incomplete but students of culture and society are practised in the use of statistics, histories and individual observations. What has become of Shakespeare's texts in a theatre may be seen as no more than one straw in the wind of change but one that provides an exceptionally detailed and illuminating insight into wide reaches of culture and society, and one that is entertaining and informative to encounter.

Robert Shaughnessy's *The Shakespeare Effect: A History of Twentieth-Century Performance* (Palgrave Macmillan, 2002) tells the story of Shakespeare's plays in performance 'because it offers a way of seeing cultures' (p. 194):

> My concern is not just with what happened in the places and at the moments in time . . . but with how the exchanges between texts, spaces and bodies might have conveyed meanings above or beneath those apparently contained within the remit of Shakespeare. The divers appropriations charted in this study are examined less for their success in realising the Shakespearean dream than as compelling evidence of the theatre's productive capacity for misreading, for accidents, coincidences, mistakes and for failure. The tendency for performance to fall short of (or move beyond) its official function might be considered its fundamental weakness, but for my current purposes it is its greatest virtue (p. 14).

What happens on stage in a performance stems, at base, from the conditions of production, the lives of those engaged in it and the mood and ideas that are 'in the air' at the time. Such influences are hard to discern but viewed in relation to an unchanging and complex text their effect and potency become more apparent.

Recently a group of critics have investigated Shakespeare's plays in performance, 'both at the first and now,' for their cultural interest. Barbara Hodgdon's 'Bride-ing the Shrew: Costumes that matter' (*Shakespeare Survey*, 60; 2007) shows that the clothes the text requires Katharine to wear express the culture and social mores of his time and, in new productions, those of our own generation:

> Kate's clothes -- those worn by [Alexandra] Gilbreath and by other Kate-actors – play with the most serious theme of human, and theatrical, consciousness – *Who am I?* -- to perform the double dream of identity and play which lies at the heart of *Shrew*'s theatrical self-fashioning (p. 72).

Douglas Lanier's *Shakespeare and Modern Popular Culture* (Oxford, 2002) is among a growing number of books that show how plays have migrated into forms of expression, performance and consumption that their author could never have envisaged. In cultural studies the plays themselves are not the main focus of attention and contention.

★   ★   ★

Old questions call for new answers:

1 *If scholars and critics seek a better understanding of Shakespeare's plays why should they study how individual actors have enacted their roles?* The distinctive nature of an actor's achievement will depend on talent, earlier experience and personal choices, as much as on the play-text; and each performance will be influenced by the occasion and the response of an audience, both of which are temporary, hard to describe, and harder still to relate to either text or performance. The actor may be skilled and imaginative but neither quality derives from the play and may be surpassed or at least superseded by the next person to take the role. Studying an actor's performance will reveal much about the actor and the theatrical event in which he or she is involved but comparatively little about the permanent theatrical qualities embodied in the play text.

2 *How can a past performance be worth studying when we have no direct and unmediated evidence about it?* A description and critique of a former performance, although incomplete and inaccurate, can extend what we are able to visualise when studying a play text. No one is able, any day of the week or year, to go to a theatre and see a well-mounted and inspired performance of a play by Shakespeare but descriptions of a number of past performances will establish a wide range of possible enactments and so spur the imagination to envisage other ways of staging and acting the play that would reflect and illuminate life at the present time.

3 *How useful for studying Shakespeare's plays are present-day performances?* Talented and experienced actors will often reveal possibilities and meanings in the texts that otherwise might not be recognised. Although experiences in a theatre will be ephemeral, hard to remember, still harder to describe, and less open to scrutiny than a play-text, when we *see* almost any production we actually experience the play consecutively as the story unfolds, which is one of the conditions in which Shakespeare expected his plays to be received.

One response to all these questions is to cut through the temporary features of performances and ask what can be learnt about the heart of the matter – what Shakespeare wanted to be seen and heard on stage and what, moment by moment, the speaking of his words requires from any actor. Numerous cues can be found in the texts telling what should be done as well as said and these a reader can seek out and, in his own mind and his own way, begin to respond imaginatively to their physical and vocal requirements. By learning to read what may be called this 'secret' language in the texts, a reader can begin to visualise what might happen onstage and represent real and tangible life.

*   *   *

A practicable way of studying a play in performance – rather than performances by individual actors – is for the reader to use himself or herself as both actor and audience and in his own mind bring to the task whatever the experience of living and an active imagination can supply. In plays that stage the acting of a play, Shakespeare identified imagination as the agent whereby the text comes alive in the actors' performances and spectators are shown responding according to whatever they can imagine and have experienced in their lives.[4] Such an open and varied response is not usually associated with scholarship and, as a glass through which to view the plays, it is obviously limited and peculiar to each reader, but it is the response that Shakespeare foresaw when he wrote for the stage.

Inscribed in the texts is what may be called a 'secret' language because it needs to be decoded before it reveals the numerous cues for the performance that Shakespeare supplied. Individually its details will seem insignificant but they are present throughout each play and together can shape performances and help a reader to respond as if a member of an audience. While actors instinctively become aware of this secret language as they explore the dialogue in rehearsal and shape their performances, readers have to seek it out within the words of a text.

The plays' secret language does not require actors to conform to a single and authoritative way of presenting their characters but allows them to develop performances in ways best suited to their individual talents and imaginations. No reader could consider every possible way of acting and staging a Shakespeare play but to study what is, unequivocally, in the text for actors to use in performance is a much more attainable task. The commentary in each volume of the series of *Shakespeare Handbooks* (Palgrave Macmillan, 2005, etc.) sets out to do just that by replicating the actors' encounter with the text so that readers are helped to bring the play to life in their own minds as it would on stage.

Some of the *Handbook* authors give special attention to narrative and exposition, noting the handling of entries and exits and the change of attention they bring. When the dialogue gives the necessary information, an audience can become fully aware of what is about to happen and watch for its effect; when it explains little or nothing an audience will be surprised, perplexed, kept waiting to know more or made aware that some unknown force has taken the play's story forward. This means that certain questions recur. What does an audience need to know or not wish to recognise? When is an audience taunted or thoroughly unsettled in mind? Why does a person in the play give this information now and not earlier, and why in this oblique or striking way? Why does an entry or exit happen at this particular moment? Should an entry or exit be at speed or unhurried; is it for a stated purpose or without any particular intent? To these and other practical questions an actor needs answers and, very often, finds them in the text; when acted upon, they affect both performance and the response of an audience. Rosencrantz, Guildenstern and Osric in *Hamlet* are examples of characters whose relevance is not fully known on first entry and a commentary can trace the steps by which an audience's curiosity is aroused and ultimately satisfied as they become pawns in the operation of what Hamlet calls the 'villainies' by which he is surrounded (V.ii.29).

For moments of hesitation or silence, marked by incomplete verse-lines, broken syntax, or a sudden halt in speech, an actor must find other means than words to hold an audience's attention: stage presence becomes more significant or, perhaps, some gesture or movement. Holding or relinquishing the lead in dialogue also sets problems that actors must answer wordlessly by turning away or moving closer together, or by an involuntary sound, laugh or wordless exclamation. Sometimes a lessening or heightening of mental awareness is sufficient to mark the change and alert attention. In all these ways physical action or movement makes a potent contribution to the play and an audience's response changes, its comprehension being challenged or clarified.

If we wish to respond to a play-text as if in performance attention must be given to small actions (the turning of a head, hand-movements, a stiffening of the body) and to small words (conjunctions, prepositions, pronouns, negatives, incoherent sounds): all these can contribute to what is happening on stage by changing meaning, emphasis or the focus of attention. Anything an audience sees can become a significant element in performance. Small elements can work together and grow stronger, as many threads become a rope or a number of unremarkable words an undeniable statement.

References to the time of day or season of the year, the weather, location or surroundings are not only matters of a moment but influence the acting and tone of an entire scene until further change is signalled. So, too, a stage property, the persons on stage or what happened in the preceding scene may contribute to the effect and meaning of any moment without a word being said that takes note of this. Nothing in a play exists alone and to grasp a single moment of performance or understand the effect of even a short speech may call for a considerable accumulation of information. Words or actions that make a strong effect when watching a play can fail to register in the text unless the reader is constantly aware of Shakespeare's secret theatrical language and the effect of seeing and hearing a performance.

Attention paid to an audience's progressive experience – the continuous building of response towards the play's conclusion – is an element of Shakespeare's writing that can best be studied in a continuous commentary that gives attention not only to meaning and intention but also to underlying sensations, changes in the focus of attention, recurrence of ideas, physical gestures or groupings, to moments when silence is more dominant than either verbalised meaning, conscious intention or physical effort, and to times when clarity, strength, ease, wonder, simplicity, pleasure, fear, laughter, grief, pride and many other spontaneous effects and reactions are introduced, established or withdrawn. Considered as isolated phenomena these may have little weight or significance compared with the speaking of Shakespeare's words but they are instantly accessible to all audience members because, unlike many speeches and quick interchanges of dialogue, little or no aptitude or special knowledge is needed to respond to them. The cumulative effect of something apparently so simple as an actor's physical presence on stage can influence every other ingredient of performance and stay in the mind when the play is done. None of this is easy to describe and will vary with each change in casting and the accidents of each performance, and with each spectator.

To deal with all these elements of a play that cannot be considered by quoting the text, some authors of *Handbooks* draw on interviews with an actor or director, or recount discoveries made in workshops that explore Shakespeare's choice of words by questioning their meaning or seeking appropriate phrasing for metre and clarity. Others reflect their attendance at rehearsal during which actors have discovered how to speak their words as if they were necessary to the persons they play or have found appropriate responses as the story moves onwards and situations change. Some *Handbook* authors have watched as actors and director experiment to find when and how performance should replicate life or when to re-create it in a more amazing or meaningful form. They will have seen how actors slowly develop full performances and together shape what happens on stage so that it holds attention and continues to develop an audience's understanding. The authors' objective has not been to describe an authoritative performance – there can be no such thing – but to explicate 'secret' theatrical messages in the text and so help readers to hear and see what could and, sometimes, must happen on stage.

As a substitute for seeing many productions, searching many reviews or reading an account of a play's past performances, a study of the theatrical implications of its dialogue with the help of a *Handbook* commentary will encourage a reader's imaginary and first-hand engagement with the text. Armed with this experience the play can be set in action in the mind's eye and so encourage an appropriately sensuous, intelligent and progressive response. This form of active exploration is bound to be limited in definition and clarity but it will be intimately and imaginatively involved with the words that Shakespeare used to guide his actors and give theatrical form to his innermost thoughts and experience of life.

The *Handbooks* were designed for student use and that will always be their primary purpose but their authors have also been developing a new form of study for Shakespeare's plays in performance that is not based on what individual actors have done in present or past times but on a close scrutiny of the texts for their theatrical potential. This approach is in accord with Elizabethan theatre practice because, in the absence of a director, there was no alternative to accepting what individual actors could make of the dialogue. Shakespeare must have written accordingly and developed a language that was as theatri-cal as it was intellectual and poetic. Much could go wrong in these conditions but by offering this freedom to actors Shakespeare pro-duced texts that over the course of four hundred years have drawn highly skilled actors to perform them and audiences to see them in many different countries and circumstances. When twenty or more

Handbooks have been published and can be compared with each other, it might be possible to write a grammar or dictionary for what has here been called Shakespeare's 'secret' theatrical language.

★   ★   ★

Shakespeare's plays would be much easier to study if they could be read as works of literature, but they were written for performance. Lukas Erne's *Shakespeare as Literary Dramatist* (Cambridge University Press, 2003) argues differently and asserts that Shakespeare positively wanted readers for his plays and wrote accordingly. A wish to escape the impermanence of theatre seems to have been father to this thought since no existing evidence shows that Shakespeare encouraged or aided publication in book form. He neither visited the printers to help with press-corrections as did Ben Jonson and John Webster, nor did he write dedications or commend his own works to readers, as did Barnaby Barnes, John Fletcher, Thomas Heywood, Ben Jonson, John Marston, Philip Massinger, Thomas Middleton and John Webster. If Shakespeare had cared about readers other than those who staged his plays, he could have taken one of several options open to him that would have helped to secure them. Nor does anything suggest that he tried to stop the publication of imperfect texts, although the acting company almost certainly did at the start of his career while his name was still gaining recognition. Lukas Erne argued that Shakespeare sought a literary appreciation because several published texts are too long to be staged in the regular way of theatre at the time but in doing so he forgot that dramatists, poets, novelists and almost anyone who seeks the most effective verbal expression of thoughts and sensations will over-write early drafts before cutting what is unnecessary, confusing or does not pull its weight. Lengthy early versions of Shakespeare's plays could have been sent or taken to the printers because they were the manuscripts that the players could most easily spare and would not guard as carefully as others.

In a preface to the 1623 posthumous edition of his collected works, Shakespeare's fellow actor-sharers in the King's Men, John Heminge and Henry Condell, considered it necessary to tell readers who failed after several readings to 'understand' the plays, to get help from persons who could. (This might have been a way of telling readers to consult fellow actors.) As literature the surviving texts are not always easy to read but, after rehearsal, the words will be readily appreciated and understood in performance. Although by turns lyrical, eloquent, grand, reverent, sensuous, sensational, subtle, simple, discursive, conversational, argumentative and, often, multiple in meaning and association, in the mouths of actors Shakespeare's dialogue can, nevertheless, seem to be the natural idiom of its speakers. What then must be done if the plays are to be studied as if in performance? First, readers must be patient and collaborative. Seeing a play in almost any conditions will almost always be instructive but students must be prepared to reach beyond what individual actors have effected in performance and behind what a director and designers have contributed to a production. They should not hesitate to engage theatrically with a text on their own account and try to consider the progressive experience of audiences. Rather than relying on reviews of performances, they should go to the text and ask themselves what it demands of actors, directors and designers. Failure to heed a play's 'secret' theatrical language is as eccentric as a performance that omits significant passages of dialogue and story.

The interest, authority and force of even the most talented, original or responsible performances will be temporary, as all theatrical events are temporary and unrepeatable: the text alone has permanent value, deriving from the author and capable of affecting all elements of performance, both words and action, time and space, actors and audience. Ironically, it follows that when study is concerned with Shakespeare's plays in performance on a stage, rather than as literature in a book, it has proved necessary to turn back repeatedly to the texts to discover, through their secret theatrical language, those elements of performance which the author would have had in mind as he wrote and are implicit in the text. From this base it should be possible to build an impression of the theatrical life a play could have in any context and at any time. Rather than trying to describe and analyse what very different actors, directors and designers have made of the plays in very different circumstances and at various times, we can best study them in performance by attending to their secret theatrical language and seeking their theatrical potential for ourselves, even though this means they are bound to reflect our own lives and preconceptions. Their ability to do this is one of Shakespeare's greatest achievements.

Notes

1. An exception is W.B. Worthen but he was more interested in critical theory and history than in Shakespeare's play-texts, as the titles of his books indicate: *Shakespeare and the Authority of Performance* (Cambridge University Press, 1997)

and *Shakespeare and the Force of Modern Performance* (Cambridge University Press, 2003).

2. See *Theatrical Events: Borders, Dynamics, Frames*, ed. Vicky Cremona *et al.* (Ropodi, Amsterdam, 2004), especially Hans van Maanen's 'How Contexts Frame Theatrical Events' and its diagrams that show the many elements of a theatrical event and their relationship to performance (pp. 243–77).

3. *The Masks of King Lear* (University of California Press, 1972), 431 pp., was followed by larger volumes in the same form.

4. See, for example, 'That's good' and 'that's wormwood' (*Hamlet*, II.ii.498–9 and III.ii.176).

Part II

Words and Actions

4

The Nature of Speech in the Plays*

In common with many others, I had become interested in Shakespeare's plays by reading their texts when I could not see them in performance. They were more akin to the poetry I was reading than any other form of literature and so I started to study them as if they were poems that demanded my close and very personal attention. When I could see them in performance, however, much that engaged and moved me left me wondering what had happened and why this was so different from reading the texts. I wanted to know how speeches affected an audience and, more basically, how actors turned text into speech and poetry into theatre, and what were the consequences of these transformations. I was grappling with fundamental and difficult questions for any student of the plays.

The two words "Shakespeare's plays" can signify many things. They may cause us to think of a single, fat, and familiar volume or of a row of uniform paperbacks, some more thumbed than others. There, in small space, is "the text;" one of the most fabulous treasure houses of the past; there we can roam at will and appropriate whatever catches our fancies. We take speeches from this great hoard of words and reflect upon them, changing them according to our own individual thoughts and desires. Of course, we are troubled by problems of obscurity, authenticity, punctuation, and spelling, and by doubts about the reference, definition, and interpretation of individual words. But

---

* First published as 'The Nature of Speech in Shakespeare's Plays', in *Shakespeare and the Sense of Performance,* ed. Marvin and Ruth Thompson (University of Delaware Press, 1989), pp. 48–59.

"Shakespeare's plays," in the physical sense of type on pages, is a palpable, basic, and limited thing, a constant point of reference. But in another sense "Shakespeare's plays" is much less manageable. The phrase can awaken a whole world of still-breeding thoughts: teeming theatrical images that have been introduced to our minds, selected not by ourselves but according to opportunity and chance. Shakespeare is not solely responsible for his plays in this sense. He has many collaborators who create in our day—and not in his—effects of their own by a variety of means: designers of set, costumes, sound, and light; carpenters, technicians, and stage managers; together with the actors who take his words upon themselves and the directors who control each evolving production. The plays in performance provide a multitude of interlocking sensations, all highly variable in origin, effect, and stability. "Shakespeare's plays," in this sprawling and spawning sense, cannot be defined or confined; they are shadows of the mind that resist our predatory grasp.

Between these two extremes of meaning, there is a great divide. On one side, it is proper to speak of the plays' language, vocabulary, images, gestures, style, syntax, dialogue, text. On the other side, other words can be added to our critical discourse: *delivery, action, play, performance, personification, perception, reception,* and *interplay,* together with *entertainment, celebration,* and *discovery. Interpretation* does not offer a crucial distinction between the two opposed meanings of "Shakespeare's plays," because the text and its theatrical enactment are equally hospitable to many different readings; both await our differing attempts at decoding. Nor does *speech* or *dialogue, discourse* or *speech-act,* with reference to words allocated to particular characters in a certain sequence, take us decisively away from the comparatively secure world of the printed word. Only *Speech* as the act of speaking and a part of performance provides the crucial distinction. Speech, in this sense, identifies an element of Shakespeare's plays that is close to the text and yet also releases a seemingly unfettered theatrical life.

Speech originates from words on a page, but it also introduces the individual performer, idiosyncratic, specific, and always changing. Speech involves us as members of an audience and not as independent readers. Of course, speech does not account for all that happens in a theatrical event, but it is such a crucial element, dividing and yet connecting a text and its performance, that we should think as clearly as we can about its nature. Such inquiry might help us to respond more fully and perhaps more suitably to the plays as they lie inert and ready for our reading on the printed page.

There is no need to call for more study of Shakespeare's speeches in a textual sense. The words spoken by individual characters have been studied with great finesse, especially in recent decades. We have become increasingly interested in what words *do*. We can now understand how rhetoricians in Shakespeare's day manipulated the minds of their auditors by varying their methods of exposition, the structure of their speeches, and choice of words, figures of speech, and modes of address. We have learned how Renaissance poets were aware of subtle influences of meter, rhyme, assonance, and all the musical effectiveness of sound, how silence can be given meaning over against the spoken word, how text can suggest subtext, how words mask and disguise thoughts, how questions may be answered by avoidance of a direct response. We have studied, too, how speeches in Shakespeare's plays imply gestures and actions that add visual effects to the auditory operation of words. We have begun to understand how meaning is never fully present in any utterance but depends also on what is *not* said, on the difference from other possible words and sets of words. We look beyond an editor's annotation that offers a single definition or paraphrase and would like to know what words Shakespeare did *not* select. We recognize that a subversive use of ordinary means can effect huge changes of understanding; and so familiar words have become as interesting as those "hard" words which Shakespeare forged for the very first time or borrowed from obscure sources. Personal pronouns—*us* and *them*, and, particularly, *she* and *he*—auxiliary verbs, exclamations, the most routine modes of address and reference, now seem to leap forward for our attention as they signal innovative thoughts.

Words swim in our minds, assemble together, and break apart. They change as we study them; they float and sink and get carried downstream into other regions. Words are stimulating and elusive, mocking and bewildering. We realize now that we shall never pin down the effect of Shakespeare's text in our minds or in those of other readers and audiences.

This new awareness is changing our view of Shakespeare's plays while older methods of study continue to grapple with the words in print. Verbal and visual images, ambiguities and associative subtleties, repetitions, variations, and other devices to refine and extend meaning; semantics, syntactics, pronunciation, and morphology: all are being considered and reconsidered. Calling attention to the nature of speech in Shakespeare's plays may well seem unnecessary, because so much investigation is in hand at present that few students can keep up-to-date with all that is being discovered.

But speech is an individual human activity as well as a collection of printed signs to be listed, described, and decoded. Speech is physiological and therefore as complex as a living organism, and in each manifestation it is unrepeatable. Even when an actor has prepared for speech with the utmost care and efficiency, he or she will respond in a highly instinctive, unconscious manner to the exigencies of each moment in each new performance. Speech in theatrical terms is part of a continuous activity in space and time, within the speaker and without; and every single sound has special qualities not shared by any other.

For example, it is not enough to disentangle by temperate study the signs encoded in the words "To be or not to be...." What that speech communicates in performance depends a great deal on the set of mind and body in the actor who speaks it. To whom does he speak? In what direction or at what distance? Is it to himself, or to a real or an imagined audience, or to a mixture of all three? Where does he breathe in the course of uttering all those words? What quality of sound is natural to his voice, and how is this altered by his speaking within this particular dramatic context? How loudly or quietly does he begin and continue and conclude? What is his pulse rate, how steady his tempo, how insistent or hesitant his inflections? Beyond all this, what happens within the actor as he attempts to present Prince Hamlet at this point in the play? How the actor has fared in the performance before this moment will influence very strongly—and sometimes in unexpected ways—the game that he now plays with the text, with his fellow actors, and with his audience.

A crude indication of what is involved physiologically in the performance of such a speech can be obtained by memorizing it and then speaking it loud and clear for at least one auditor some thirty feet away. Four or five attempts to make the speech communicate will demonstrate an actor's need to gather and control the expenditure of energy, to choose moments for emphasis, to maintain an intelligible phrasing of the words, to follow through from one moment to another, to make the speech his own. This speech is a challenge, and the chance of winning or losing in the game is part of the excitement and meaning of the play.

All attempts to evaluate the nature of speech in Shakespeare's plays that do not take into account the actor's contribution to the exigencies and pleasures of performance are grounded solely in textual matters and confined to the page. Studies with titles such as *Littérature et Spectacle, The Semiotics of Theatre and Drama*, or *Reading the Signs*, promise to engage with this problem. But they exact a large price by insisting on specialized jargon, parenthetical references, and exhaustive enumeration; and then these scholarly works deliver very little to our purpose. Keir Elam's study of Shakespeare's *Discourse* (1984) speaks of the "presence of the voice" without considering the actor responsible for it.[1] (The phrase "presence of the voice" is somewhat ridiculous because it is the actor who has "presence" and not a disembodied "voice.") Professor Elam considers "the body," but only as a "sign-maker," not as something made of flesh and blood; he is content to list textual references to bodies and physical gestures but bypasses without comment the living, breathing, feeling person who is doing the speaking or making the gesture. "Speech production" is here a convenient heading for listing textual devices for referring to an actor's art and craft. Similarly "units of deictic orientation," discussed in a recent study by Alessandro Serpieri, are defined by the text alone and stand well clear of the ambiguity, excitement, and pleasure of performance.[2] The gestural resources and conventions— the participation frameworks and embedded quotations—that enable Erving Goffman to describe "forms of talk" show that dialogue is like a game with various possible moves but one that seems to be played without physical commitment.[3] All these scholars consider the speaker as a disembodied functionary, rather than as an individual human being who is alive in thought and action and involved in processes of change and chance.

The result of this new research is an old-fashioned rhetorical enumeration, tricked out in a quantity of curious categories. It is scholastic not theatrical, concerned with text and not with play. So Professor Elam writes in the concluding section of his latest book:

> There is quite a distinct kind of dramatic 'dispersion' of the proverb in its citation form (the codified wording, that is, in which it is normally quoted and collected): the paraphrase containing no specific lexical clues to its own proverbial status. What is retained, rendering the transformed saying recognizable, is no longer the key word but the *kernel proposition*. And the audience's cognitive or re-cognitive task is not so much a 'filling-in' as a 'translating back.' The effect is still, however, that of a defamiliarizing estrangement of the codified proposition as such.[4]

The numerous quotation marks and parentheses and the italicization in this passage, together with its curious syntax and punctuation, show how ingeniously this new rhetorical theorizing has been applied to some few words given by Shakespeare to Orsino in the text of *Twelfth Night*. But the effort of mind needed to follow such exposition does little to further our understanding of the speech in performance. The concern here is limited to the content and organization of some words upon the page.

Any inquiry into the nature of speech in Shakespeare's plays must also consider what happens when actors assume the personages of the drama, perform their actions and speak their words. We must try to follow as this activity calls upon an individual's resources and involves him or her in a passionate, intellectual or fantastic game. We should observe how a company of actors are taken out of their ordinary selves in exploration, contest, and discovery. We must notice, too, how actors are able to satisfy and amaze an audience, who will in return influence the way in which the game is played.

When we go to the theatre, we know that Macbeth will die, but neither we nor the actor can know exactly *how* he will die. We know that the pipers will "strike up" at the end of *Much Ado* but not how far that music will seem to resolve outstanding issues, change the behavior of the dancers, or influence the way in which we perceive the concluding action.

Performance is a complicated phenomenon and hard to study seriously. It is very tempting to conclude that performance is so out of our control that we should be content either to study the text on a page or else to enjoy, without interruption, whatever performances we find to please us. But I want to argue that speech, that element of performance which is most closely entwined with the smallest details of the text, does hold some clues that can be followed and help us to a greater understanding of the plays in performance.

★　★　★

Shakespearean critics and students should observe actors at work and learn about the nature of acting. They have suffered by being confined to university departments of English where plays are never seen in performance by skilled and practiced actors.

I do not think that the variety of acting styles in evidence today or the difficulty of knowing how Elizabethan actors practiced their art should stand in the way of such inquiry. Nor should an actor's reliance on instinctive reactions cause a critic to undervalue his or her contribution to performance. A company of experienced actors in rehearsals for a Shakespeare play will show an observer how they discover each day new qualities inherent in the text and respond to demands that they had not recognized before. The play seems always to move ahead of the actors' understanding, exerting its own influence more and more as the words become realized or substantiated in performance. Such an impression of progress toward a distant target could be merely an illusion, a product of the actors' need to trust the material on which they are working, but when theatre people speak of Shakespeare directing them through his text, as they frequently do, they are scarcely aware of using a metaphor; this seems to be no less than the literal truth. As John Barton says in his *Playing Shakespeare*:

> if you want to do [Shakespeare] justice, you have to look for and follow the clues he offers. If an actor does that then he'll find that Shakespeare himself starts to direct him.[5]

When all rehearsals are done, on the first night when the whole play is performed before an audience, good actors go further and give every appearance of growing in power and subtlety, as if summoned by what unfolds before them. How does this happen? How can actors encourage it to happen? What can we learn about Shakespeare's plays from the actors' attempt to give life to the words?

Barton's book, based on a number of television programs showing the rehearsal methods of the Royal Shakespeare Company actors, is a rare attempt to describe how actors work on a text. It reveals some of the questions actors ask as they explore a play and provides some examples of how willfulness or playfulness may carry them toward sufficient confidence to stand up and perform upon a stage. It could serve as an introduction to a study of the nature of speech in Shakespeare's plays. One of its great virtues is that it raises as many questions as it seems to solve for those who had taken part in the studio rehearsals.

John Barton shows how actors can "listen" to versification and to Shakespeare's choice and arrangement of words, and how this leads on to further problems: what words should be stressed? when should there be a pause? how should a speech or phrase be inflected? Barton encourages his actors to find what he calls the "verbal energy" for a sustained passage in *Love's Labour's Lost*, because without this supercharge it would be "hard to follow and difficult to listen to."[6] He asks each actor to "serve up the key words for the others to play off

them"—as if the play were a game of tennis. They must be sure to
"play with words, to give the audience the right information," and
to "relish" the sounds of resonance and onomatopoeia for the same
purpose.[7] Actors must not "fight shy" of rich and vivid language, even
if the effort to respond leaves them, at first, breathless and bewil-
dered. They must make the unusually demanding sounds and yet be
"real": "it's a question of balance" between these two demands, as he
admonishes repeatedly.

Barton's book shows actors being stretched and excited by the
sheer energy needed to make these speeches their own and at the
same time being exhorted to use their discretion and judgment in
order to maintain close and watchful attention to small details of the
text as it surges into dramatic life—and sometimes resists their hold.
An army of students could find pretexts for their essays in the short
compass of this very practical book.

But an exploration of "the nature of speech in Shakespeare's plays"
can be taken further than this. Barton's repeated injunctions to "find
the language and make his listeners feel the words"[8] are too incidental,
too piecemeal, to cope with whole sentences. He pays little attention
to syntax and the shape of thought. His actors can sound precious,
unreal, and overheated, because they are not taught to seek out the
main verb of every sentence and to organize all its words around this
central activity of mind. Speech should be more than interesting and
effectively colored; it should develop from the motive force or action
that has formed the sentence as a whole and in a particular order.
The only way to make utterance convincing is to balance its parts
and find an appropriate rhythm from the needs and forces within the
character in the dramatic situation as it develops throughout the play.
"Relishing" words and "feeling" the language can become an almost
mindless mastication.

In the television series on which his book is based, Barton was
content to leave problems of character to the actor's instincts, but it is
noticeable how often the actors pull him back to consider why certain words are spoken in a particular context by a particular person.
Occasionally, Barton helps to make a speech sound more forceful by
calling for some generalized emotional charge—as when he encourages the speaker of the Chorus in *Henry V* to be more "excited"
within himself and then rewards the new rendering with "I thought
the first half of that was great"[9]—but too often, in my opinion, he
deals with speakers and not with characters or persons in a drama. He
seems content with an actor's intellectual understanding and does not

lead forward from this into the expression of a total and individual involvement in the play. He asks actors to "make the images more concrete," not to look for ways to make the words necessary to their characters in performance at the moment of utterance.

Barton takes time off from the plays to set actors working on Shakespeare's sonnets where he can avoid problems of interplay between speakers and their response to the drama's developing action. This also avoids questions about the nature of a character's involvement in words with the idiosyncrasy of a particular physical human being. But his exercises on the sonnets, with their regular form of fourteen rhymed lines, does permit him to develop the actor's ability to shape a whole speech, a task that is often missing in his other rehearsal sessions.

The Royal Shakespeare actors have to project Shakespeare's words out into the far reaches of the Stratford Theatre or the broad expanse of the Barbican Theatre in London, and this has led them, in my opinion, to simplify and exaggerate. It is important to realize that actors not trained to act in the classical repertory, those used to the close scrutiny of the camera and inspired by its ability to direct attention to small signs of unspoken thoughts and sensations, can also find appropriate ways of acting Shakespeare, and they may well be more able to create characters that live intensely on the stage. I have seen a film actor, unused to Shakespeare's plays, seek to make the movements of Polonius's mind, as expressed in his convoluted prose, a part of a complete personification. The words came very slowly at first, but so did the amazing complexity of a man who was father of Ophelia and Laertes and also the chief counselor of the King. The shape and rhythms of speech governed the inner workings of the actor and his physical activity; there was no contradiction between what was heard and what was seen and sensed. The result was a character made wholly visible, palpable, true, and arresting. Polonius's speech stopped the rehearsal once the actor had achieved the connection between text and being; so strong an impression of reality had been created that the other actors in the scene were not ready to respond.

Reading the signs in a text is not enough; we need to cross over the dividing line and ask how these words can be spoken and how they can best become part of an image of fully lived experience. Experimentally, in rehearsal with trained actors, we can learn more and become skilled at reading the multitude of clues that lie implicit within a text and which actors thrive upon. It is from the text that the whole play springs to life so that our study of performance will in turn lead to a fuller understanding and, perhaps, a revaluation of the most familiar plays.

★   ★   ★

Three brief examples will serve to indicate some of the possibilities that a study of speech may open up. The first is from *Othello:*

> Strumpet, I come.
> Forth of my heart those charms, thine eyes, are blotted;
> Thy bed, lust-stain'd, shall with lust's blood be spotted.
> (5.1.34–36)[10]

The rhythms, syntax, and vocabulary of this soliloquy are so difficult that most directors have pity on their actor and cut it from the production script. The words are in starkest contrast to the Moor's previous utterance, which was still under control for Lodovico's sake. And the tone of his next words changes yet more surprisingly, as he is rapt in wonder and contemplates "the cause" that draws him toward murder and suicide. I have seen Paul Scofield in the pauses of rehearsals moving around and flexing his body, as he spoke these words to himself, seeking the bodily changes that could draw forth and give credibility to their emphatic, lurid, and crudely vindictive qualities, and to the syntax which piles up epithets within each line and moves from present to past, and to future without transitional phrase. By watching the actor I realized that here the whole person of Othello passes through a dark and violent experience: it comes upon him and the audience with a sudden shock and will radically alter the way in which he approaches the final scene, when his repetitions are not violently charged and when delicacy, tenderness, and far-reaching images have repossessed his mind and made his body hesitate and remain poised above his sleeping wife.

Any one speech tends to influence others. Consider Claudius's words to Laertes, in the middle of their plotting to assassinate Hamlet:

> There lives within the very flame of love
> A kind of wick or snuff that will abate it;
> And nothing is at a like goodness still;
> For goodness, growing to a pleurisy,
> Dies in his own too much. That we would do,
> We should do when we would; for this 'would' changes,
> And hath abatements and delays as many

> As there are tongues, are hands, are accidents;
> And then this 'should' is like a spendthrift's sigh
> That hurts by easing. But to the quick of th'ulcer:
> Hamlet comes back; what would you undertake...
>   (4.7.114–24)

The first ten lines of this passage insist that the breathing, rhythms, pitch, and inflections of the actor playing Claudius must all change. It seems in performance as if the thought of Gertrude has drawn Claudius off target, taking possession of his mind without his volition. He had spoken of the Queen at the beginning of the scene but despatched her from his thoughts easily enough; now, however, the structure of his thought is drawn out, the weight of sound lightens, and a new field of imagery is introduced (the same flame image that was to haunt the mind of Othello). Yet Claudius does not mention the Queen directly; and soon his thought quickens once more, as he knows he has to act alone, regardless of his pain, in order to lance the ulcer that he *can* cope with and which Laertes can recognize easily. Response to these changing demands of the text is more than a technical feat employed for the instant: the actor will make this speech credible only by preparing for it long before, by establishing a particular relationship to Gertrude in silence as well as words. This incidental passage is then capable of an impression of instinctive, private thought and of fugitive, delicate, and yet strong feeling. Claudius is forced to torture himself. We can see this in his breathing as he speaks, in the movement and changes of his eyes as he alters the object of his attention, in the relaxation and tension of his body, and in his nervous impulses as his thoughts change and seek to hide irrepressible feelings. He is suffering already and doomed; Hamlet's final actions only complete for Claudius what has started earlier in the play.

Verbal clues to crises in performance may be very brief and easily passed over until explored in the rehearsal room. I remember Sir John Gielgud preparing to play Prospero at the National Theatre in London and seeking the deep assurance and inner suffering required to make "'Tis new to thee" and "In this last tempest" (*The Tempest*, 5.1.184 and 153) register fittingly in their context, using their precise phrasing. As his long role drew toward an end in imperfect reconciliations, Shakespeare's text could bear the great weight of feeling required by the dramatic context only after the actor had discovered, with difficulty, the appropriate means for himself, a delivery that was most delicate and softly spoken and yet reached to the back of the theatre because of the authority, poise, and timing used. Indeed the effect was richer than this, because Gielgud's Prospero seemed also to share with the audience a consciousness of the inadequacy of what was actually spoken; he was playing a part for the sake of those who knew less than he did, and he seemed to take some consoling—or some briefly diverting—pleasure in doing so. These short speeches were so immaculately phrased that the magician and rightful ruler was like a dramatist completing a play, rather than speaking his mind; and yet, at the same time, the father suffered in private and felt a quickening joy.

★   ★   ★

One objection to the kind of study I am recommending is that modern actors are not those Elizabethan and Jacobean actors for whom Shakespeare wrote his plays and that they bring to rehearsals many prejudices and skills which Shakespeare could not have imagined and lack others that he took for granted. But the same argument can be leveled against any reading of the plays. No one person can reconstruct a historically accurate response, even if we could know what that might be.

Of course, any encounter with the text will be flawed and could benefit from a greater understanding of the variety of life and history of thought. But the reading that takes place in a rehearsal room has one great advantage over that of a literary student. Whatever an actor discovers must always be realized in terms of performance, and that includes a great many features of lived experience; it cannot survive as some new argument set forth in words alone. Perhaps Elizabethan actors were cruder or more eloquent, or more formalized and less lifelike, than their modern counterparts, but every actor who steps onto a stage has to bring a whole self into play and must relate what is spoken to what is there, palpably, before the audience. No actor can cheat for very long; incomplete performances, or those which have some elements at odds with others, will be recognized for what they are by audiences and by fellow actors. We need have little doubt that modern actors are responding to qualities inherent in Shakespeare's text; if they did not, they would find acting in his plays a troublesome labor and not a great pleasure.

Another objection to my argument is that rehearsals do not have comparable authority with great performances by the most famous actors from the past. We are told to study the stage history of plays to discover the nature of their theatrical life. But this is to interpose a further historical distortion between ourselves and the text. Accounts of eighteenth-century actors or even of those two or three decades before the present must all be interpreted in light of the production styles of those days and the idiosyncrasies of the star performers. Moreover the earlier performances are no longer there for us to encounter as best we may; all we can do is to read newspaper accounts that were written to make interesting copy rather than to describe performances accurately or comprehensively. We can take special note of what appealed to the crowd as well as to the more judicious critics, but that tells us only about the broader effects and, sometimes, about topical and passing enthusiasms. We can read whatever an actor or biographer has deemed fit to publish about aims and achievements, but very often these books and articles were written by way of apology or self-advertisement. Promptbooks are firmer ground for the student, but stage managers have always been concerned to record the traffic of the stage rather than the nature of performance; their reasons for noting anything are related to maintaining the smooth functioning of a complicated operation, not to the interests of an audience or future students.

The study of theatre history is useful as a corrective and stimulus. We can be blind to some opportunities inherent in a text, and suggestions from the past can alert our attention. But the growing number of books that record the fortunes of plays in the theatre cannot replace the more basic and exploratory work which may be undertaken every time a play is rehearsed by skilled and experienced actors and brought to the pitch of subsequent performance. Every student of Shakespeare, of whatever experience, learning, or talents, needs access to this laboratory and to the testing ground of performance, which is also a place of entertainment. Here is where "speech" as I have defined it earlier will bridge the divide between text and theatrical understanding.

Notes

1. Keir Elam, *Shakespeare's Universe of Discourse: Language-Games in the Comedies* (Cambridge: Cambridge University Press, 1984).
2. Alessandro Serpieri, "Reading the Signs: Towards a Semiotics of Shakespearean Drama," trans. Keir Elam, in *Alternative Shakespeares*, ed. John Drakakis (London: Methuen, 1985), 119–43.
3. Erving Goffman, *Forms of Talk* (Oxford: Basil Blackwell, 1981).

   4. Elam, *Shakespeare's Universe of Discourse*, 280.
   5. John Barton, *Playing Shakespeare* (London: Methuen, 1984), 168.
   6. *Ibid.*, 73.
   7. *Ibid.*, 52.
   8. *Ibid.*, 86–7.
   9. *Ibid.*, 50–1.
  10. All Shakespeare quotations are from Shakespeare, *The Complete Works*, ed. Peter
       Alexander (London: Collins, 1951).

5

Acting in the Plays*

Searching in play texts for clues that would explain how Shakespeare's plays were acted originally, scholars had proposed two opposing answers: an old-fashioned formal style derived from training in rhetoric and oratory and a new one that mirrored life, was called 'natural' and could be mistaken as 'real'. The actor's art was changing at the same time as the playwright's, the two aiding and abetting each other as they drew audiences to the newly built public theatres.

It used to be possible to quote Hamlet's advice to the players, point out that no extravagancies were to be used, and leave the rest to the actor to interpret in the tradition of his art, but today we are told that a completely new technique of acting is needed in order to present Shakespeare's plays in the spirit in which they were written. It is true that not all scholars are agreed on these matters, but even temperate opinion would say that the acting of Shakespeare's contemporaries was "fundamentally formal" and only "shaded by naturalism from time to time."[1] "Formal acting" has not been properly defined but it is generally assumed to be the opposite of "natural," and to make no attempt to give an impression of real life. "Poetry and its decent delivery" are considered "the only real essentials of Elizabethan drama."[2]

The study of Elizabethan acting is comparatively new, and although one book has already been published on the subject,[3] the time is hardly ripe for an authoritative and balanced treatise. But in the meantime, what guidance can scholarship give to actors and producers of Shakespeare's plays? It seems to me that the subject has been approached from an unfortunate angle and that, in consequence,

---

*First published as 'On the Acting of Shakespeare's Plays', *The Quarterly Journal of Speech*, XXXIX, 4 (December, 1953), 477–84.

the evidence has been distorted and misapplied. Briefly, I believe that formalism on the stage was fast dying out in Shakespeare's age, and that a new naturalism was a kindling spirit in his theatre. This naturalism was not what we understand by the word today but, in contrast to formalism, it did aim at an illusion of real life. I want to reverse the statement which I have quoted above, and to say that Elizabethan acting aimed at an illusion of life, although some vestiges of an old formalism remained. If this is the case, our modern actors stand a better chance of interpreting Shakespeare than those who were his contemporaries, for the modern tradition is based on a thoroughgoing naturalism unknown to Elizabethans. If the relics of formalism are properly respected, we can realize the illusion of life with a new delicacy and completeness.

To prove my point, I would have to examine in detail, and in chronological sequence, the whole *corpus* of Elizabethan drama.[4] All I can do here is to counter some of the arguments which might be brought against my statement, and present some evidence which I do not think has been sufficiently discussed.

The earliest advocates of formal acting base their statements on Elizabethan stage conditions; for example, after describing the circled audience and the gallants sitting on the stage, Mr. S. L. Bethell maintains that:

> even with the abundance of make-up, scenery, and properties in use to-day, it would have been impossible for actors so closely beset with audience, to create and sustain an illusion of actual life, especially as they performed in broad daylight.[5]

Obviously these conditions made it difficult to sustain an illusion of real life, but nevertheless it was certainly attempted and achieved. Thomas Heywood in his *An Apology for Actors* (1612) writes:

> turne to our domesticke hystories: what English blood, seeing the person of any bold Englishman presented, and doth not hugge his fame, and hunnye at his valor, pursuing him in his enterprise with his best wishes, and as beeing wrapt in contemplation, offers to him in his hart all prosperous performance, *as if the personator were the man personated?*[6]

John Webster, the probable author of the Character of "An Excellent Actor" (1615), uses almost the same words; "what we see him personate, we thinke truely done before us."[7] John Fletcher was praised for giving opportunity for a similar illusion:

> How didst thou sway the Theatre! make us feele
> The Players wounds were true, and their swords, Steele!
> Nay, stranger yet, how often did I know
> When the Spectators ran to save the blow?
> Frozen with griefe we could not stir away
> Vntill the Epilogue told us 'twas a Play.[8]

Prolonged death speeches must have made the simulation of real life very difficult—*The Knight of the Burning Pestle* ridicules their excesses—but Burbage evidently could achieve it; not only did the audience think he died indeed, but the dramatic illusion extended to the other actors in the scene with him:

> Oft haue I seene him play this part in ieast,
> Soe liuely, that spectators, and the rest
> Of his sad crew, whilst he but seem'd to bleed,
> Amazed, thought euen then hee dyed in deed.[9]

From such descriptions, we must assume that Elizabethan actors aimed at an illusion of real life and that the best of them achieved it.

Even when it is accepted that the Elizabethan actors aimed at an illusion of real life, it is still possible to write down their acting as "formal." So Professor Harbage maintains that

> we are told *what* the actor did (in the estimation of the spectator), but not *how* he did it. Since the conventions of formal acting will be accepted as just while formal acting prevails, testimony like the above is nugatory.[10]

But this argument only "explains" the evidence if, on other grounds, the acting is known to be "formal." Even if this could be shown, it does not imply that our actors today should attempt formalism; the fact remains that an illusion of life was attempted. If our actors are more thorough in this respect, may they not be interpreting the plays in the spirit in which they were written?

The arguments for formal acting which are based on the plays themselves are difficult to answer directly; a detailed, chronological study is required. But one may point out, in general, that much of the evidence is taken from early plays, the famous Towton scene in *III Henry VI* (II.v) being always to the fore.[11] The formal, didactic arrangement of such scenes died out as the Morality plays, on which they seem to be based, disappeared also; it is not representative of the first decade of the seventeenth century. Direct address to the audience is another feature of Elizabethan plays which has been adduced in support of formal acting; such speeches have been thought to shatter "all possibility of dramatic illusion."[12] In this case, it is admitted that Shakespeare's plays do not provide any strikingly clear example,[13] yet even if such were found it would not be an unsurmountable obstacle to the simulation of real life on the stage. There was no gap between the audience and the stage in the Elizabethan theatre, and the actors did not address the audience as if it were in another world. There was a reciprocal relationship; the audience could participate in the drama as easily as the actors could share a joke or enlist sympathy. The very fact that it is difficult to distinguish direct address from soliloquy, and soliloquy from true dialogue, shows that the contact with the audience was quite unembarrassed. They shared the illusion of life.

The use of verse in Elizabethan drama has also been taken for a sign that acting was formal; for instance, of the sonnet embedded in the dialogue of *Romeo and Juliet* (I.v.91ff.) it has been said:

> Shakespeare's purpose can only be achieved if his audience is allowed to respond to the figures, the images, and the metrical pattern of these fourteen lines. There is no need to imitate dialogue realistically.[14]

But once more the development of new styles in writing and acting must be taken into account. When Jonson wrote *Timber*, the style of Marlowe already belonged to another age:

> The true Artificer will not run away from nature, as hee were afraid of her; or depart from life, and the likenesse of Truth; but speake to the capacity of his hearers. And though his language differ from the vulgar somewhat; it shall not fly from all humanity, with the *Tamerlanes*, and *Tamer-Chams* of the late Age.[15]

Once the idea of development is accepted, the question about Elizabethan acting ceases to be "Was it formal or natural?"; it is rather, "Which was the new, dominant style, the fashionable mode in which they would strive to produce even old plays or recalcitrant material?" I believe that the comparison between the style of Jonson's age and that of Marlowe's points in one direction only. It had become possible to speak the verse as if it were meant—as if, at that instant, it sprang from the mind of the speaker. Shakespeare's mature style has the best of two worlds; there is the eloquence, precision, and melody of verse, but there is also the immediacy and movement of actual speech. The dramatist has achieved the ideal which Puttenham sought in the courtly poet; he is now

> a dissembler only in the subtilties of his arte, that is, when he is most artificial, so to disguise and cloake it as it may not appeare, nor seeme to proceede from him by any studie or trade of rules, but to be his naturall.[16]

For such dialogue, a formal, rhetorical delivery would destroy the very quality which the poet had striven to attain. The new dialogue needed a new style of acting, and as the verse became less formal and declamatory, so did the acting. Both aimed at an illusion of life.

The internal evidence of the plays has only been hurriedly considered, for its proper treatment would need a greater scope than this present article provides.[17] I would like to turn, therefore, to one piece of external evidence which has been generally accepted as an indication of formal acting. This is the Elizabethan comparison between the actor and the orator. The *locus classicus* is the Character of "An Excellent Actor":

> Whatsoever is commendable in the grave Orator, is most exquisitly perfect in him; for by a full and significant action of body, he charmes our attention.[18]

A later statement is in Richard Flecknoe's *A Short Discourse of the English Stage* (1664) where it is said that Richard Burbage

> had all the parts of an excellent Orator (animating his words with speaking, and Speech with Action).[19]

The comparison between orator and actor is further testified by the use of the word *action* to describe the bodily movements of both artists. From this comparison several deductions might be made; firstly, the actor used a declamatory voice as distinct from a conversational; secondly, he observed the phrasing, figures, and literary quality of his lines in the manner laid down for the orator; and thirdly, he used "action" to enforce the meaning of his lines rather than to represent the feelings of a character. It has been suggested that John Bulwer's *Chirologia* and *Chironomia*, two books of manual signs for the use of orators, published in 1644, and written by a specialist in the teaching

of the deaf, might represent the "actions" used on the Elizabethan
stage.[20] But the deductions can go further, and the actor is sometimes endowed with the intentions of the orator; it is thought that
he excited the emotions of his audience rather than expressed those
of the character he was representing. Under such conditions a play
would be a number of speeches, or, at best, a ritual, rather than an
image of actual life. It has even been suggested that, in Dr Johnson's
words, an Elizabethan went to the theatre in order to

> hear a certain number of lines recited with just gesture and elegant
> modulation.[21]

Obviously one cannot deny the comparison between actor and orator, but this does not imply that the comparison held at all points;
both artists spoke before the people and used gestures—and there the
comparison might rest. Distinctions between the two were clearly
recognized by Elizabethans. So Abraham Fraunce, speaking of the
orator, says that the gesture should change with the voice,

> yet not parasiticallie as stage plaiers vse, but grauelie and decentlie as
> becommeth men of greater calling.[22]

The distinction may not be flattering to the actor but that there is one
is plain enough. Thomas Wright's *The Passions of the Mind* (1604) makes
another distinction; the orator is said to act "really" to "stirre vp all
sorts of passions according to the exigencie of the matter," whereas the
player acts "fainedly" in the performance of a fiction "onely to delight"
(p.179). These distinctions are quoted by Joseph in his book *Elizabethan
Acting*,[23] but he does not seem to accept their implications.

Rhetoric was taught in Elizabethan schools and universities and
"pronunciation," or delivery, received its due attention. Indeed,
Heywood in his *Apology* shows that acting was used as a means of
training the young orator (Sig's. C3ᵛ-4). If the arts of acting and
oratory were truly similar, here was an excellent "school" for actors.
But the evidence clearly shows that it was not; the scholars learned a
style of acting which was suitable for oratory but condemned on the
public stage. So in *II The Return from Parnassus* (c.1602), Kemp, the
professional actor, criticizes the scholar-players as those who

> neuer speake in their walke, but at the end of the stage, iust as though in
> walking … we should neuer speake but at a stile, a gate, or a ditch, where
> a man can go no further. (IV.iii)

Kemp criticizes them because they did not act as men do in real life. Richard Brome makes a similar distinction against scholar-players in *The Antipodes* (1640):

> Let me not see you act now,
> In your Scholasticke way, you brought to towne wi' yee, ...
> Ile none of these absurdities in my house.
>
>   (II.ii)

The gestures described in Bulwer's books for orators might well be among the scholastic absurdities which Brome inveighs against. In Campion's *A Book of Airs* (1601) the criticism is more precise:

> But there are some, who to appeare the more deepe, and singular in their iudgement, will admit no Musicke but that which is long, intricate, bated with fuge, chaind with sincopation, and where the nature of euerie word is precisely exprest in the Note, like the old exploded action in Comedies, when if they did pronounce *Memeni*, they would point to the hinder part of their heads, if *Video* put their finger in their eye.[24]

Here, the orator's gestures are considered both scholastic ("deepe and singular") and old-fashioned; clearly Campion thought they were not in use in the up-to-date theatres in London.

Perhaps the distinction between actor and orator is most clearly stated in Flecknoe's praise of Burbage which has already been quoted:

> He had all the parts of an excellent Orator...., yet even then, he was an excellent Actor still, never falling in his Part when he had done speaking; but with his looks and gesture, maintaining it still unto the heighth....

Flecknoe says, in effect, that though Burbage had the graces of an orator, *yet even then* he was an excellent actor—in spite of some likeness of his art to that of oratory.

Earlier in the same passage, Flecknoe had claimed that Burbage

> was a delightful Proteus, so wholly transforming himself into his Part, and putting off himself with his Cloathes, as he never (not so much as in the Tyring-house) assum'd himself again until the Play was done.

Such absorption in one's part has nothing to do with oratory; it is closer to the acting techniques of Stanislavsky. It suggests that an Elizabethan actor sunk himself in his part and did not merely declaim his lines with formal effectiveness. A similar impression is given by the Prologue to *Antonio and Mellida* (first performed in 1599) where actors are shown preparing for their parts and speaking in the appropriate "veins." An incidental image in *Coriolanus* implies a similar technique:

> You have put me now to such a part which never
> I shall discharge to the life.   (III.ii.105–6)

In the event, Coriolanus was unable to do as Burbage did and wholly transform himself into his part.

There are many extant descriptions of Elizabethan acting but the value of this evidence is commonly belittled because it is written in the same technical language as the criticism of rhetoric and oratory. So Hamlet's advice to the players is dismissed as "a cliché from classical criticism, equally applicable to all the arts."[25] Or again, it is claimed that

> the poet has put into the mouth of his Prince nothing that conflicts with the directions normally provided by the teachers of rhetorical delivery.[26]

But the fact that the same language was used for acting and oratory does not mean that the same effect was being described. The language of criticism for all the arts was in its infancy and it was perhaps inevitable that acting should be dependent on the technical vocabulary of a more systematic art.

In attempts to interpret descriptions of acting, words and phrases from the criticism of rhetoric and oratory are frequently noted. But their use in another art may give an entirely different interpretation and may be equally pertinent. The phrase *imitation of life* is an example. It is basic to the conception of poetry as an art of imitation, a conception which was not generally understood by Elizabethans— except for Sidney—as referring to the poet's revelation of ideal and universal truth. The usual interpretation is seen in Sir Thomas Elyot's description of comedy as "a picture or as it were a mirrour of man's life"[27] or in Ascham's idea that drama was a "perfite *imitation*, or faire liuelie painted picture of the life of euerie degree of man."[28] The phrase is constantly repeated; Lodge, Jonson, and Heywood all claimed on Cicero's authority that Comedy was "*imitatio vitae, speculum consuetudinis, et imago veritatis.*"[29]

The idea of drama as a picture of life suggests a parallel in the art of painting, and here the meaning of imitation is much clearer.

For instance it is implicit throughout the description of the pictures offered to Christopher Sly in the Induction of *The Taming of the Shrew:*

> —Dost thou love pictures? we will fetch thee straight
> Adonis painted by a running brook,
> And Cytherea all in sedges hid,
> Which seem to move and wanton with her breath,
> Even as the waving sedges play with wind.
> —We'll show thee Io as she was a maid,
> And how she was beguiled and surprised,
> As lively painted as the deed was done.
> —Or Daphne roaming through a thorny wood,
> Scratching her legs, that one shall swear she bleeds;
> And at that sight shall sad Apollo weep,
> So workmanly the blood and tears are drawn.
>   (ii.47–58)

"As lively painted as the deed was done" is the key to the whole of this description, and "life-likeness" or the "imitation of life" were constantly used in the criticism of the visual arts. So Bassanio exclaims when he finds Portia's picture in the leaden casket, "What demi-god Hath come so near creation?" (*The Merchant of Venice* III.ii.115–16), or Paulina claims that her "statue" can show life "lively mock'd" (*The Winter's Tale* V.iii.19). For an example outside Shakespeare, we may take Thomas Nashe's description of the floor of an Italian summer house; it was

> painted with the beautifullest flouers that euer mans eie admired; which so linealy were delineated that he that viewd them a farre off, and had not directly stood poaringly ouer them, would haue sworne they had liued in deede.[30]

The imitation of life was not the whole concern of renaissance artists, but their experiments in perspective and light were at first designed to deceive the external eye; their paintings were meant to look like real life.

When the phrase is used of acting, of performing in the "picture" that was the drama, it seems to carry the same implications of deception and the appearance of reality. So Webster praises the Queen's Men at the Red Bull for the acting of *The White Devil* in 1612 or 1613:

> For the action of the play, twas generally well, and I dare affirme, with the Ioint testimony of some of their owne quality, (for the true imitation

of life, without striuing to make nature a monster) the best that euer became them.

So also, the imitation of life is praised in *The Second Maiden's Tragedy*, performed in 1611:

> thow shalt see my ladie
> plaie her part naturallie, more to the life
> then shees aware on.[31]

Shakespeare implies the same standards in *The Two Gentlemen of Verona:*

> For I did play a lamentable part: ...
> Which I so lively acted with my tears
> That my poor mistress, moved therewithal,
> Wept bitterly.   (IV.iv.171–6.)

The idea of a play as a "lively" picture may be seen in Rowley's verses on *The Duchess of Malfy* (1623):

> I Neuer saw thy Dutchesse, till the day,
> That She was liuely body'd in thy Play.

Perhaps most significantly, the "imitation of life" is implicit in Hamlet's advice to the players: he says that the end of playing is

to hold, as 'twere, the mirror up to nature; to show virtue her own feature, scorn her own image, and the very age and body of the time his form and pressure.   (III.ii.22–5.)

When he criticizes strutting and bellowing, he invokes the same standard:

I have thought some of nature's journeymen had made men and had not made them well, they imitated humanity so abominably.   (II.39–41)

Hamlet is applying the same criterion to acting that Bassanio did to Portia's picture—how near is it to creation?

The conception of acting as an imitation of life agrees with the other evidence I have quoted and suggests that Elizabethan actors aimed at an illusion of real life. It does not explain *all* in the best renaissance painting or the best Elizabethan acting, but it has an important place in the artists' intentions. To describe the resultant art as formal is to deny this intention; *natural* seems a more appropriate word. There is probably some reluctance among scholars to admit that naturalism was a keynote of Elizabethan acting. Some critics would obviously wish the plays to be acted in a formal manner. For instance, it is said that a person in a play may be

> first a symbol, second a human being; … [and the play itself can be] primarily an argument or parable, only secondarily forced, as it best may, to assume some correspondence with the forms and events of human affairs.[32]

This is an extreme case, but there are other hints of a fear that naturalism would make Shakespeare's plays "smaller," that they would lose the meaning and richness that had been found in the study. Formal acting, on the other hand, seems to offer a declamation in which technical accomplishment could be appreciated and the argument or pattern of the drama could stand revealed. But there is more than one kind of naturalism; there is one for plays set in a drawing-room, and another for plays dealing with kings and soldiers, inspired prophets, and accomplished courtiers. A true naturalism would not disguise the high themes of Elizabethan tragedy or the idealism of their comedy.

We have said that Elizabethan dramatists and actors imitated life, but this does not mean that they tried to make their plays exactly the same as real life; they did not labor, in Marston's words, to "relate any thing as an historian but to inlarge every thing as a Poet."[33] Their plays were more exciting and colorful, more full of meaning, than real life; indeed, compared with them, "Nature never set foorth…. so rich [a] Tapistry."[34] Yet we may say that they aimed at an imitation of life and the audience was encouraged to take all this as real while the performance was in progress. Within the charmed circle of the theatre, a new world might be accepted as real, and what they saw personated could be accepted as truly done before them.

George Chapman once wrote a preface to a play of his which had never been performed, and in it he tried to analyze what this play had missed. Unlike some critics, he believed that

> scenical representation is so far from giving just cause of any least diminution, that the personal and exact life it gives to any history, or other such delineation of human actions, adds to them lustre, spirit, and apprehension.[35]

A "personal and exact life" was what Chapman expected the actors to give to his play, and these words may serve to describe the naturalism which I believe to be the new power of Elizabethan acting. If actors in today's theatre wish to present Shakespeare's plays in the spirit in which they were written, they should respect and enjoy the magniloquence and music of the language, enter into the greatness of conception, and play all the time for an illusion of real life. They must constantly expect a miracle—that the verse shall be enfranchised as the natural idiom of human beings and that all of Shakespeare's strange creation shall become real and "lively" on the stage. Because the Elizabethan actor was capable of working for this miracle, Shakespeare, like other of his contemporaries, dared to "repose eternitie in the mouth of a Player."[36]

Notes

1. S. L. Bethell, "Shakespeare's Actors," *R.E.S.*, new series, I (1950), 205.
2. *Ibid.*
3. B. L. Joseph, *Elizabethan Acting* (1951).
4. Previous work on dramatic technique has generally ignored the question of changing or developing methods; e.g., M. C. Bradbrook's pioneering *Themes and Conventions of Elizabethan Tragedy* (1935) explicitly states that "the development of the conventions has been only slightly indicated" because the subject was too large (p. 1).
5. *Shakespeare and the Popular Dramatic Tradition* (1944), p. 31. See also M. C. Bradbrook, *Themes and Conventions of Elizabethan Tragedy* (1935), pp. 20–1.
6. Sig. B4; the italics are mine.
7. John Webster, *Works*, ed. F. L. Lucas (1927), IV, 43.
8. F. Beaumont and J. Fletcher, *Comedies and Tragedies* (1647), Sig. f2v.
9. Quoted from Sir E. K. Chambers, *The Elizabethan Stage* (1923), II, 309.
10. A. Harbage, "Elizabethan Acting," *PMLA*, LIV (1939), 692; the evidence he quotes includes the verses on Burbage quoted above.
11. For instance, see B. L. Joseph, *op. cit.*, pp. 116–22.
12. S. L. Bethell, *op. cit.*, p. 86.
13. *Ibid.*, pp. 84–5.
14. B. L. Joseph, *op. cit.*, p. 129.
15. *Works*, ed. C. H. Herford and P. and E. Simpson,VIII (1947), 587. Jonson's editors date *Timber* between 1623 and 1635, XI (1952), 213, but Professor C. J. Sisson has shown that the work was probably composed as lecture notes while Jonson was acting as deputy for Henry Croke, the Professor of Rhetoric at Gresham College, in 1619, *TLS* (September 21, 1951).
16. *The Art of English Poesie* (1589); G. Gregory Smith, *Elizabethan Critical Essays* (1904), 11, 186–7.
17. Asides, the arrangement of exits, entries, and other stage movement, the use of type costuming and characterization are some of the more obvious details which need chronological analysis.

18. Cf. A. Harbage, *op cit.*, pp. 701–2; B. L. Joseph, *op. cit., passim*; and S. L. Bethell, "Shakespeare's Actors," *op. cit.*, p. 202.
19. Quoted from E. K. Chambers, *op. cit.*, IV, 370. There has been some argument about the validity of this evidence; see A. Harbage, *op. cit.*, p. 695 and S. L. Bethell, "Shakespeare's Actors," *op. cit.*, pp. 200–1.
20. So B. L. Joseph, *op. cit.* Even as an indication of an orator's art the books are suspect, for Bulwer himself confesses that "I never met with any Rhetorician or other, that had picturd out one of these Rhetoricall expressions of the Hands and fingers; or met with any Philologer that could exactly satisfie me in the ancient Rhetoricall postures of *Quintilian*" (*Chironomia*, p. 26; quoted from Joseph, *ibid.*, pp. 45–7).
21. B. L. Joseph, *op. cit.*, p. 141.
22. *The Arcadian Rhetoric* (1588), Sig. 17v.
23. Pp. 54 and 58.
24. To the Reader; *Works*, ed. P. Vivian (1909).
25. A. Harbage, *op. cit.*, p. 690.
26. B. L. Joseph, *op. cit.*, p. 146.
27. *The Governor* (1531), ed. H. H. S. Croft (1880), I, 124.
28. *The Schoolmaster* (1570), *English Works*, ed. W. A. Wright (1904), p. 266.
29. *A Defence of Poetry* (1579), ed. G. Gregory Smith, *Elizabethan Critical Essays* (1904), I, 81; *Every Man Out of His Humour* (1600) III, vi, 206–7; and *An Apology for Actors* (1612), Sig. Flv.
30. *The Unfortunate Traveller* (1594); *Works*, ed. R. B. McKerrow, II (1904), p. 283.
31. Malone Society Reprint (1909), II, 2015–17.
32. Written of *Timon of Athens*; G. Wilson Knight, *The Wheel of Fire* (1930), p. 274.
33. "To the General Reader," *Sophonisba* (1606): *Plays*, ed. H. H. Wood (1938), II, 5.
34. Philip Sidney, *The Defence of Poesie* (1595); *Works*, ed. A. Feuillerat (1923), III, 8.
35. Dedication, *Caesar and Pompey* (1631); *Tragedies*, ed. T. M. Parrott (1910), p. 341.
36. Thomas Nashe, Preface to Robert Greene, *Menaphon* (1589); *Works*, ed. R. B. McKerrow (1905), III, 312.

6

Unspoken Thoughts and Subtextual Meanings*

In rehearsals today actors and directors often speak about 'subtext'. The word was taken from books by Konstantin Stanislavsky, the Russian actor, teacher and theorist, that became widely available in English translations: An Actor Prepares *(1936) and* Building a Character *(1950). For actors, the briefest definition is that 'subtext is what makes us say what we do in a play,' an idea that had proved especially useful for acting and producing plays by Anton Chekhov, Stanislavsky's contemporary and close colleague. Subsequently it was appropriated for acting in films that ordinarily give a more complete and convincing image of actual life than any stage play. Then, more slowly, 'subtext' was drawn into wider use and literary, as well as theatrical, criticism.*

At first, Shakespeare scholars and critics resisted the innovation on the grounds that he was a poet whose meanings and mood were created 'primarily and entirely by the actual words.' I joined the debate in two issues of Tulane Drama Review *(1963–4) and later in* Discovering Shakespeare *(1981), from which the following extract is taken.*

By speaking the lines aloud and attending performances and rehearsals, a student will begin to understand how a text comes alive in speech, action and performance and to recognise the cues which Shakespeare has written into his dialogue to guide an actor and control dramatic effect. Meaning, allusion, reference, repetition, double meanings, syntax, metre, verse-lining, rhetorical structure, exchange of lead, interruption, silence, description of speech or action are

---

*First published as 'Motivation and Subtext', in John Russell Brown, *Discovering Shakespeare* (Macmillan, 1981), pp. 108–12.

among the obvious cues. Others are more hidden, and a reader, like an actor, has to search for them.

Although everyone will pay attention to syntax, it is one of the most undervalued guides to performance. Actors tend to work from phrase to phrase, giving meaning, colour and emphasis according to each word or phrase as it is spoken. Such performances live through the words at the moment of utterance, but they can easily become fragmentary and shallow because the long-term effects of grammatical structure are not utilised.

Both actor and reader should study syntax to discover the unspoken motive for speech: its origin, the point from which true energy springs. Usually this can be found in the main verb, or main predicate, of each sentence, whether that unit is short and simple, or long and complicated. Almost all the details of a speech depend upon this active source even long after it has been spoken.

For example, Desdemona addresses the Senate in *Othello*:

> That I did love the Moor to live with him,
> My downright violence and storm of fortunes
> May trumpet to the world. My heart's subdu'd
> Even to the very quality of my lord.
> I saw Othello's visage in his mind
> And to his honours and his valiant parts
> Did I my soul and fortunes consecrate.
> So that, dear lords, if I be left behind,
> A moth of peace, and he go to the war,
> The rites for why I love him are bereft me
> And I a heavy interim shall support
> By his dear absence. Let me go with him.   (I iii 248–59)

Although her first words are about 'love', these are sustained by the verb 'trumpet' in the third line and dependent upon it; and that idea is also related to 'violence' and 'storm'. So the beginning of her speech is not gentle, reasonable or personal, as the tenderness of its first words might suggest if spoken by themselves, or if the first line were rephrased as a separate sentence. Desdemona starts speaking because she is aware of her own strength, independence, openness and deep, dangerous passion. She is also very much in control, because 'did love' is linked quickly, firmly and even wittily with 'to live'. In contrast, the force of the next sentence lies in 'subdu'd'; a new self-revealing and self-denying motivation, placed very early in the word-order, close to the subject of the sentence, 'My heart'. Desdemona now speaks without hesitation or preparation, and also without over-emphasis because she is able to fill out the new idea in the unforced fourth line, with its pun on 'quality', meaning the soldierly profession that takes Othello away from Venice and also his natural gifts of good nature.

The next sentence changes tense and therefore its basic, underlying attitude. Moreover its verb comes immediately after the singular personal pronoun, 'I saw'. Desdemona now gives evidence directly, although she is speaking of highly sensitive, intimate, moral and social issues. With no sign of conflict or hesitation, she passes on, with a simple 'And', to speak of Othello as a great general and holds back the verb to the very end of the further line. That motivating centre of the sentence is 'consecrate' and it is separated by almost a whole line from its subject, 'I'; it is also emphasised by the preparatory 'Did' at the beginning of the second line. At this stage of her address to the Senate, Desdemona is personally direct, formal, firm, delicate, unhurried and bold: 'I saw ... Did I ... consecrate'. Both her 'soul' and 'fortunes', her hopes of joy in this life and for ever, together with Othello's 'honours' and his brave, strong, physical body are held together by whatever force Desdemona finds in, or gives to, 'consecrate'. That sustaining idea – however dangerously idealised, passionately intense, or childishly confident it may be – controls and colours every other word in the sentence.

At the end of a line and sentence, climactically placed and in charge of divergent thoughts, 'consecrate' is the very heart of Desdemona's appeal. Her next words are simple, but the syntax is quickly complicated. She begins with 'So that ... if I', but carefully interpolates 'dear lords' which is a more assured and direct appeal that breaks through the expression of her own concerns. 'A moth of peace' is a new phrase or idea, and a delicately imaginative one, that interrupts the main line of thought in the 'if' clause. The subject of the new sentence does not come until 'The rites', with its pun on 'rights', as of law and possession. Its verb arrives still later, near the end of the line, with 'are bereft me'. In contrast with her first strong appeal, she is now revealing the fragility and quick, varied impulses of her present condition. A further, more resolute sentence begins with 'And' and is sustained by 'shall support' – again a new tense and therefore a new mental engagement. But this time, the verb is neither at the end nor the beginning; it is followed by a subsidiary phrase, 'By his dear absence', which starts a new verse-line and may be expressed without any contrary colouring from the preceding verb. Perhaps she has come close to tears, with 'bereft' and 'heavy', and now, in a kind of afterthought or release of previously hidden thoughts, his absence fills her mind completely. That would explain the change of syntax, tense and style for the next five words that conclude her speech, 'Let me go with him'. As an independent syntactical unit and as a sequence of almost colourless, open words, this last sentence starts after a brief break in the sense and perhaps a quick breath between sentences. The simple words can speak according to Desdemona's inner sense of her situation as that has developed while she has been speaking. The faces that she looks at may tell her that she has won her appeal, or she may see that she has no true support other than Othello. Or, more simply, she has said all that can be said publicly, and so speaks now with a renewed reserve before her passions repossess her mind in silence. The length of each sentence or complete thought, and the position and nature of the main verb within each sentence, are crucial stage-directions to actor or reader: 'Let me go with him', is unambiguous and free to speak for itself, except as it arises out of the whole foregoing speech and Desdemona's response to those who stand silent around her.

Attention paid to syntax, and in particular to the main verbs of each separate sentence, will show time and again how the sustaining motive or action of a speech flows underground at times, beneath the immediate and obvious sense of single words or subsidiary phrases. Displacement of words from their normal positions, contrasting parentheses, concluding phrases that are not essential for communication of purpose or pursuit of argument, sudden shifts of tense and abrupt changes in the person addressed, are some of the common signs of what actors, since Stanislavski's time, have learned to call 'subtext'. While a person in a play appears to be talking about one subject, the mind may all the time be fostering and developing other thoughts at a different, usually lower or less articulate, level of consciousness. These semiconscious, subconscious or, even, unconscious 'subtextual' reactions can be crucial for the development of the drama and the lifelikeness of speech and performance.

★   ★   ★

The most obvious example of subtext is when disguise requires the speaker to say one thing, whereas the real person beneath the disguise is thinking something quite different. So Iago sounds concerned and honest to Othello, Desdemona or Roderigo, but later he will acknowledge that under the text another thought, 'like a poisonous

mineral', had gnawed his inwards (II i 291). Iago knows well how
contrary thoughts can grow beneath the words that are spoken:

> Dangerous conceits are in their natures poisons
> Which at the first are scarce found to distaste
> But with a little act upon the blood,
> Burn like the mines of sulphur ...   (III iii 330–3)

When, earlier in the same scene in Act III (lines 91–2), Othello says

> Excellent wretch! Perdition catch my soul
> But I do love thee ...

his conscious thoughts may be wholly confident and his words warm
with satisfaction; but at another level of consciousness 'wretch' may
register conflict and 'Perdition' insecurity. Perhaps even Iago does not
know at this time how strongly such reactions are burning at hidden
depths and are pressing Othello's spoken thoughts towards 'when
I love thee not' and a 'chaos' of obliterating horror:

> Excellent wretch! Perdition catch my soul
> But I do love thee and when I love thee not
> Chaos is come again.

Subtextual realities have surfaced into textual suppositions, even
though confidence and enjoyment are still the dominant notes.

So an actor becomes aware of how new elements of speech grow
out of the undermining, unspoken thoughts; and how speech itself
can change consciousness. A reader, too, may catch these flickering
and then developing traces within the text, and so reach further
into the speaker's inner being, its half-formed thoughts and strange
unwilled fantasies.

In Shakespeare's text, a subtextual reality is nearly always present,
although more in later than in earlier plays. When spoken words are
forthright and simple, the motivation to speak them may not be talked
about and not fully explicit in words. The main verb of each sentence
can express the energy of spoken thought, often with remarkable
completeness and clarity, but the [drive] towards that energy may be
at yet another, deeper and silent level of being. It is not expressed in
words, but has been built up through the performance as a whole and
is set in motion by a total reaction to the total situation, moment by
moment. What is said is only part of [an inner drama.]

A reader [or an actor] … can be drawn into the very being of the speakers. For example, when Desdemona, at the beginning of Act III, scene iii, persists in trying to restore Cassio to Othello's favour, she may seem perverse and tiresome, obsessed by a single idea and her own will:

DES.   Be thou assur'd, good Cassio, I will do
         All my abilities in thy behalf.

EM.   Good madam do. I warrant it grieves my husband
         As if the case were his.

DES.   O that's an honest fellow. Do not doubt Cassio
         But I will have my lord and you again
         As friendly as you were.

CAS.   Bounteous madam,
         Whatever shall become of Michael Cassio,
         He's never any thing but your true servant.

DES.   I know't. I thank you. You do love my lord;
         You have known him long and be you well assur'd
         He shall in strangeness stand no farther off
         Than in a politic distance.

CAS.   Ay but lady,
         That policy may either last so long
         Or feed upon such nice and waterish diet
         Or breed itself so out of circumstances,
         That I being absent and my place supplied,
         My general will forget my love and service.

DES.   Do not doubt that. Before Emilia here
         I give thee warrant of thy place. Assure thee
         If I do vow a friendship, I'll perform it
         To the last article. My lord shall never rest.
         I'll watch him tame and talk him out of patience,
         His bed shall seem a school, his board a shrift.
         I'll intermingle everything he does
         With Cassio's suit. Therefore be merry Cassio,
         For thy solicitor shall rather die
         Than give thy cause away.   (III iii 1–28)

In asking the basic question, 'Why does Desdemona use these words, in this manner?', we must remember that in the first scene of Act III Emilia has said that Desdemona has spoken already about this business that morning and Othello has said already that in good time Cassio would be restored to favour. So Desdemona promises here to do what in fact she has achieved already, except for hastening the reconciliation. A reader should consider what has happened to Desdemona: she has recently awoken from her delayed marriage night; the wedding took place in Venice, but the 'fruits' were to 'ensue' at Cyprus (II iii 9). Much of the energy of her speech can derive from an awakened desire to encounter with Othello in any way possible, on what ever occasion. Cassio is someone else who 'loves' her lord, so she must be busy in that 'friendship' too. She wants to be the complete married woman: Emilia's interjection at the beginning of the scene shows one wife sharing the business of another, with a slight edge of rivalry or sense of comparable power; and, in the same way, Desdemona suddenly refers to Emilia again before giving Cassio 'warrant' of his place.

Once the reader remembers that Desdemona's mind is full of the night she has just spent with Othello, and that he is not with her at this moment, her words will reveal new impulses and show that consciously or unconsciously, in her fantasy, Desdemona is enjoying love-play with her husband, eager, quick, combative, strong, pressing for advantage and assurance, warm, generous, self-forgetful, delighting in every prospect of encounter and fulfilment. Many of her words are found in Shakespeare's plays at other moments of sexual arousal: '*assur'd* ... will *do* ... *abilities* ... will *have* ... as *friendly* as you were ... have *known* him long ... well *assur'd* ... in *strangeness stand* no further off ... thy *place* ... *Assure* thee ... a *friendship* ... *perform it* ... the *lost article* ... shall never *rest* ... *watch* him *tame* ... *out of patience* ... His *bed* shall seem a school [i.e. he will there submit to instruction, be under my control] ... *intermingle* ... be *merry* ... *solicitor* ... *die.*' That last word is, perhaps, a conscious climax to the subtextual run of Desdemona's thoughts, for the verb *to die* was used very consciously by poets and writers – and for all we know by ordinary lovers – as a synonym for sexual fulfilment; Shakespeare used it in this way in *All's Well That Ends Well, Antony and Cleopatra, As You Like It, Much Ado About Nothing, Romeo and Juliet* and in many of the sonnets. The subtext of this whole passage is alight with sexual fantasy and a sense of physical encounter that is new for Desdemona; Cassio fails to make her aware of his own sense of the seriousness of his predicament. The subtextual strata of this encounter are unusually persistent in the text; perhaps Shakespeare allowed them to surface strongly in words because a 'boy actor' could not provide a full and life-like physical expression of such reality.

When Othello enters, Desdemona soon returns to the same theme. Almost at once he gives in to her – 'The sooner sweet for you' (line 57) – but Desdemona is impatient for the moment of gift. She delights in recollections of earlier differences that were expressed in merely teasing talk (see lines 71–5), but then vows 'I could do much'. Almost certainly, her thoughts are still on the night she has just spent with Othello. Again he gives in at once – 'I will deny thee nothing' – and so Desdemona's immediate purpose is achieved totally. Yet still she goes on talking: thinking and speaking now of everyday and intimate duties until her imagination runs ahead to further differences between them and far greater giving and taking in pursuit of their love together. Othello gives in to her a third time and now, when he asks her to go, Desdemona is proud to be the loser:

> ... Be as your fancies teach you;
> Whate'er you be, I am obedient.   (III iii 89–90)

Their talk about Cassio has been love-play; in her 'fancies', Desdemona has been reliving the night together and letting her thoughts move backwards and forwards in time. Subtextually she carries off victory, and in performance this shines through the words that render victory to him.

A reader must always be alert to what the text says about performance beyond the strict meaning of its words or the speaker's conscious and explicit intentions. The first step is to seek out the heart of each sentence – each complete verbal activity – and observe how other thoughts forerun, coexist or follow after that. Every complicated sentence has shifts in the speaker's level of consciousness, and these will become clear in speech if the actor recognises and respects the basic syntactical structure. Complicated sentences are common in the plays because Shakespeare knew that human understanding was complicated and wanted to represent its several levels of consciousness. Readers need to become as aware as an actor of this technique, otherwise they will skim off only a surface meaning. In the same way they must watch for puns, double meanings and strange allusions or references, especially those that seem unconscious in the speaker; these, too, betray the mind within: the thought that is not consciously or explicitly expressed in words and yet influences speech and, still more, performance.

★   ★   ★

Besides indications of subtextual impulses and developments, the text may contain implicit stage-directions that carry the speaker into states of mind and states of being that must so transform the manner of speech

that its very matter, or purport, will be changed from what it seems on
a first reading with no thought of performance. This is very clear in the
scene where Othello asks Desdemona for his handkerchief:

OTH.   I have a salt and sorry rheum offends me;
         Lend me thy handkerchief.

DES.   Here my lord.

OTH.   That which I gave you.

DES.   I have it not about me.

OTH.   Not?

DES.   No faith, my lord.

OTH.   That's a fault. That handkerchief
         Did an Egyptian to my mother give.
         She was a charmer and could almost read
         The thoughts of people. She told her, while she kept it
         'Twould make her amiable and subdue my father
         Entirely to her love, but if she lost it
         Or made a gift of it, my father's eye
         Should hold her loathely and his spirits should hunt
         After new fancies. She, dying, gave it me
         And bid me when my fate would have me wive,
         To give it her. I did so. And take heed on't,
         Make it a darling like your precious eye.
         To lose't or give't away were such perdition
         As nothing else could match.

DES.   Is't possible?

OTH.   'Tis true. There's magic in the web of it.
         A sybil that had numb'red in the world
         The sun to course two hundred compasses,
         In her prophetic fury sew'd the work.
         The worms were hallowed that did breed the silk
         And it was dy'd in mummy which the skilful
         Conserv'd of maidens' hearts.   (III iv 48–75)

In the early scenes of the play, Othello has been shown as a soldier and
lover in complete command of himself and others. He is, in reputation

         … the noble Moor whom our full Senate
         Call all in all sufficient …   (IV i 261–2)

He is so much a part of the Venetian world that when Cyprus breaks out into a mutiny, he condemns the rioters from the established position of Christian civilisation:

> Are we turn'd Turk, and to ourselves do that
> Which Heaven hath forbid the Ottomites?
> For Christian shame, put by this barbarous brawl...   (II iii 162–4)

Although Iago calls him an 'erring barbarian' and Brabantio argues that his daughter's marriage is 'against all rules of nature' (I iii 101), Othello's composure has been absolute and a whole army is proud to serve under such a 'full soldier' (II i 36). Now, in this tale of the handkerchief, Othello speaks – very carefully and still in complete command – as if he were a Christian, and not a 'barbarian' motivated by an enchantment which is against the acknowledged 'rules of nature'.

This exchange has numerous pauses at first, the last after 'That's a fault', because the verse-line is incomplete. But the next sentence runs over one line-ending and on to the end of the next verse-line. With this stronger thought and feeling come two words, 'Egyptian' and 'charmer', which introduce pagan and dangerous ideas. What follows at once could be fanciful superstition, but 'perdition' is a dangerous word meaning 'utter ruin' and, in a theological sense, 'damnation'. (As we have seen, it is a word that surfaced strangely in Othello's most intense joy (see p.82); here it is associated with 'darling', 'precious' and 'match'.) Desdemona's 'Is't possible?' is an incredulous and perhaps frightened interjection to which Othello responds with a candid ''Tis true': a phrase which is probably still more frightening for its simplicity. Without pause, he continues to speak of 'magic' and of the 'web' of the handkerchief – this latter a word that Shakespeare associated with fate and dangerous snares. Again the words are shockingly simple; but then, as if caught up in a forgotten world, the syntax is less taut and rhythms lengthen and a decorous, cosmic imagery suffuses his talk of a woman inspired by Apollo and had lived for two hundred years, of silkworms that were purified or held in veneration, and of a dye made out of hearts cut from the bodies of virgin girls.

To say all this, after those few short pauses, means that Othello now operates according to thoughts and feelings – at once tender, grand and terrible – that he has not acknowledged more than fleetingly at any earlier moment in the play. Unlike the angry, passionate cry for violent vengeance that had been his reaction when Iago made him think that Desdemona was unchaste, this passage is calm, assured and intentionally beautiful, and it dwells in the thoughts and feelings, of his earliest years. Othello's words make huge demands upon the actor for innocence, strength, gracefulness and terror. Every word is affected: the pitch of voice, its tone and volume; the kind of breath that vocalises the words; the expression and focus of Othello's eyes and, even, the coldness of his blood. In reading the text, the extreme grace of the lines and their calm rhythms can wholly occupy the mind; but a reader, like an actor, must recognise how innovative, deep and intuitive is the sustaining reality of Othello's inner being.

As the scene proceeds Shakespeare gives unmistakable signs that much has been at stake. An instinctive cry from Desdemona, 'Then would to God that I had never seen it', triggers off an emotional reaction of a simpler kind: 'Ha! Wherefore?' The bare words must strike like lightning, suddenly charged by that deep power which has built up unspoken and inwardly during Othello's account of the handkerchief. Only after a terrible silence is Desdemona able to ask 'Why do you speak so startingly and rash?'. Then she founders, trying to hold on to rational talk from an earlier intimacy. Gripped now by his more violent feelings, Othello cries out, repeatedly, 'The handkerchief!' until he leaves the stage with the almost inarticulate oath, 'Zounds!' (line 98).

★   ★   ★

In scenes of strong feeling, Shakespeare frequently opposed two different reactions, as if one great force needed another, from a different source and often in a contrary direction, to hold it back and give a sense of building pressure until the final climax. In the eighteenth century, actors in the British theatre were especially conscious of these 'transitions' as they called them, creating especially daring theatrical effects to establish them as 'points' of power in Shakespeare's plays. A well known example is Shylock's alternation between hatred for Antonio and grief for the loss of his daughter. Whereas in the scene just studied in *Othello* one reaction succeeds another in textual expression, in *The Merchant of Venice* the two passions exist side-by-side, from one short speech of Shylock's to another in his exchange with Tubal:

> SHY.   … and no satisfaction, no revenge; nor no ill luck stirring but what lights o' my shoulders; no sighs but o' my breathing; no tears but o' my shedding!

TUB.   Yes, other men have ill luck too: Antonio as I heard in Genoa …

SHY.   What, what, what? Ill luck, ill luck?

TUB.   Hath an argosy cast away coming from Tripolis.

SHY.   I thank God, I thank God. Is it true, is it true?   (III i 81–9)

The passions alternate, until Shylock is tortured with memories of his earliest love for his wife Leah and then, at the next moment, takes practical steps to 'have the heart' of Antonio.

In very rapid alternations, this effect could become comical, but Shakespeare usually sets a slower pace. When Othello has actually seen Cassio and Bianca with his handkerchief, his first words are 'How shall I murder him, Iago?' (IV i 166). This is developed, under Iago's prompting, to 'I would have him nine years a-killing'. There may or may not be a silence following, for, like the scene of Shylock's tortured passion, this is in prose and so lacks the frame of metrical regularity. But certainly Othello takes hold of Iago's scorn of 'the foolish woman your wife'. Stubbornly, even against the tide of his revenge, those words sound again in Othello's mind and tap a contrary emotion of pity and love: 'A fine woman, a fair woman, a sweet woman.' From now on he oscillates, while Iago attempts to draw him one way (IV i 176 ff.):

IAGO.   Nay you must forget that.

OTH.   Ay let her rot and perish and be damn'd tonight, for she shall not live. No, my heart is turn'd to stone; I strike it and it hurts my hand. O the world hath not a sweeter creature. She might lie by an emperor's side and command him tasks.

IAGO.   Nay that's not your way.

OTH.   Hang her. I do but say what she is: so delicate with her needle, an admirable musician. O she will sing the savageness out of a bear....

For a time Iago's interruptions have little effect, and Othello merely agrees, mindlessly:

                … Of so high and plenteous wit and invention.

IAGO.   She's the worse for all this.

OTH.   O a thousand, thousand times. And then of so gentle a condition.

IAGO.   Ay, too gentle.

OTH.   Nay, that's certain. But yet the pity of it, Iago. O Iago, the
          pity of it, Iago.

With the simple word 'pity', Othello turns to Iago, as if needing to be
understood. The reply he receives sets the contrary stream of feeling
running, more strongly than ever; and this time Othello's imagination
fastens on the destruction of Desdemona, not of Cassio:

IAGO.   If you be so fond over her iniquity, give her patent to offend,
          for if it touch not you, it comes not near nobody.

OTH.   I will chop her into messes. Cuckold me.

Now that his mind is fixed on the future and his own shame, he no
longer oscillates but concentrates on immediate action.

Such a scene must be imagined step by step, as the words indicate the
inward working of contrary feelings. With the cries, the quick mental
reactions, the reiterations and contradictions, Othello's great body must
shudder almost to destruction. The actor must trust absolutely to the
words of each moment and hope that, after the alternations in imagination and feeling, the end of the scene will have some stability:

OTH.   Get me some poison Iago, this night. I'll not expostulate with
          her, lest her body and beauty unprovide my mind again. This
          night, Iago.

IAGO.   Do it not with poison. Strangle her in her bed, even the bed
          she hath contaminated.

OTH.   Good, good. The justice of it pleases. Very good.

Othello is cruel, but this 'pleases' him because for the moment he is
secure and almost calm: he can avoid more words; his imagination
contains both love and hate, her beauty and his determination, her
body and his. The end of this violent episode is probably very quiet:

IAGO.   And for Cassio, let me be his undertaker. You shall hear more
          by midnight.

OTH.   Excellent good.   (*A trumpet*)
          What trumpet is that same?

In the stillness, Othello hears the voice of Venice and responds as if
nothing is out of the ordinary. In performance, his question can shock

an audience by its simple command. For a while, after Lodovico's entrance, the strength of Othello's feelings are hidden, but when they break out again it is in cruel violence against his wife. He is blind to her suffering and leaves the stage almost at once, crying now against the whole world: 'Goats and monkeys'. After fierce transitions of feeling and their continuance under a temporary appearance of control, those two words break out in savage hatred and wounded, frustrated love. A reader will recognise the teeming sexual revulsion which they express most blatantly, but the violence of the 'transition' and the hammer stroke of the speech should also suggest that this savage speech and action are forcing back a contrary sense of beauty, sweetness and fond love.

Beneath the words on the page the physical and mental reality of the persons of the drama is suggested, not spoken or described. Every speech in the plays has to be searched for indications of a continuing inner life, as it may be created by actors on stage and communicated to their audience. Not only must words be heard as speech, but speech must be received as part of a total, developing and inward imitation of life. This is true as much of the elaborate rhetorical speeches as of the almost inarticulate cries or the silences implied by text and metre. Almost always there are several ways in which a speech may come to life; but, while any one performance will make its own selections, the options become progressively narrowed towards the end of the play. At last the force, weight and authority of inevitable, inward truth may be achieved.

★   ★   ★

The concluding moments of *Othello* provide a remarkable innovation in the words that Shakespeare has written for the protagonist. Previously Othello has acknowledged 'O hardness to dissemble' (III iv 31), but now, with 'Soft you, a word or two before you go', he is able to act out a formal summing-up of his life. Many of Shakespeare's tragic heroes have to perform like actors but few do so like this at the last moment, without preparation or apology. For this moment the surprise can work totally and Othello hide his inner feelings by giving a performance. But he falters at the last moment. As he speaks of

> ...one whose hand,
> Like the base Indian, threw a pearl away
> Richer than all his tribe...   (V ii 349–51)

he breaks down and weeps. Most editors print a long and irregular verse-line at this point, but Othello's words may be understood

best as two incomplete lines. After a moment Othello recovers and
acknowledges his tears as a sign of strange healing powers:

> Richer than all his tribe. Of one whose subdu'd eyes,
> *(He weeps)*
> Albeit unused to the melting mood,
> Drops tears as fast as the Arabian trees
> Their medicinable gum...

He still further impersonates himself and then springs the last surprise
of all, the secret purpose of this whole speech, the action for which
all this dignified performance was only a cover:

> ...   Set you down this
> And say, besides, that in Aleppo once
> Where a malignant and a turban'd Turk
> Beat a Venetian and traduc'd the state,
> I took by th' throat the circumcised dog
> And smote him thus.

He kills himself, and a silence follows before anyone dares to speak.
How that death is achieved is the actor's or the reader's choice – or
rather it is a final clarification of the imaginative inner life that has
been given to the play.

But the stroke of death is not quite the end. Othello has two more
lines to speak, and they are a second innovation in the words of his
part in this final scene. He uses only the simplest means;

> I kiss'd thee ere I kill'd thee. No way but this,
> Killing myself, to die upon a kiss.   (V ii 361–2)

After all the extraordinary words that he has spoken – tremendous
and sensuous imagery, violent oppositions between 'tempests' and
'calms', 'heaven' and 'hell', strong, slow-moving rhythms in the longer
speeches and the compact energy of commands, singing lyricism,
relaxed humour, lightning strikes and open anguish – after the most
demanding words, Othello's last moments are contained in short
phrases and a few words that clash one against each other. The life of
the part, the very blood of the man, streams through the narrow gate
between *kiss* and *kill, I* and *thee*. Othello may utter the words calmly
or with passion: with a physical struggle to reach Desdemona's lips, or
with an embrace that gives renewed strength to his voice and body.

Or he can be incisive and almost unfeeling as he accepts the fate that has already haunted his mind. However the tightly phrased couplet is spoken, the actor must vindicate the words: 'No way but this'. Audience and readers must respond to the inevitability and destruction as fully as they are able. At the end of this tragedy Shakespeare ensures that his protagonist is viewed through a narrow aperture and into the depths of his being.

When we study Shakespeare's texts we must be prepared for great variety. There is no one Shakespearean style: each play has its own; and within each play, the style changes from speaker to speaker and scene to scene. Words and sentence structure are often complex, representing subtle thoughts, conflicting emotions or hidden purposes. Often, speech rises on lyric melody, or veers quickly with sudden force, or stands still with secret and humane humour. On occasion, it is dangerously simple. The way through this fabulous world of words is to follow the *action* of the play, to maintain an imaginary, lively and physical reality for each person of the drama and to watch for hidden reactions until motive is clarified and words and actions have a full and assured power.

7

Using Space*

Wishing to learn more about acting, I joined classes in movement, modern dance and, later, choreography. There I learned how to 'read' physical actions and how movement across a stage influenced the effectiveness of performance as well as its meaning. This encouraged me to envisage Shakespeare's plays in performance on a platform stage, resembling those I had seen in drawings and reconstructions of Elizabethan theatres. The plays' dialogue and some original stage directions were my sole guides in this and helped with problems of interpretation.

Play-texts only record the words to be spoken and a few stage directions, some of doubtful authenticity, and so it may seem that Shakespeare has left little guidance for present-day actors and directors about staging. But, on the contrary, implicit in the dialogue is a network of instructions that, in today's language, can be called the choreography of each play. Shakespeare was very knowledgeable about physical performance. He wrote for a company of actors with whom he had daily dealings over long periods of time. In his formative years he had acted among them on stage in a large repertoire of plays that included his own. As a consequence, when he wrote dialogue he would have seen actors in his mind's eye, and been aware of how they might move and interact with each other. If we read the texts with open eyes, we can trace the imprint of this very close and specialized knowledge, an awareness as lively and careful as his understanding of words and speech.

A stage would also have been present in his mind as he wrote, most often one at the Theatre or the Globe and, later, the rather different

* First published as part of chapter 4, 'Accounting for Space', in John Russell Brown, *Shakespeare Dancing* (Palgrave Macmillan, 2005), pp. 91–101.

one at the Blackfriars. The most important feature these stages had in common was an open space in close contact with an audience standing or sitting on one or more sides and in the same light as the actors. Little else could be relied on because the Chamberlain's and King's Men would also go on tour to less predictable or suitable venues, such as a hall in one of several royal palaces or that of a great house, university, grammar school, or lawyers' inn, or in a guild house, market hall or town hall; occasionally they would perform in a convenient place out of doors. In Shakespeare's mind the stage was pre-eminently a clear space in which actors could move freely and be at all times the object of attention for an audience no more than fifty feet away. The guidance he gave about positioning, movement, and timing had to be adaptable to spaces of different sizes and shapes and was therefore mostly concerned with the relationship of actors to each other and their movements, both in groups and individually. Because of frequent changes of plays in a large repertoire, he would have known that a degree of uncertainty about where to go would always be present and need scope for improvisation. This free and open choreography, but basically ordered none the less by the dialogue, was well suited to the quick-moving freedom of his mind as expressed in the words the actors spoke.

★   ★   ★

In some respects, however, the configuration common to the London theatres has left clear traces in the choreography of the plays. Among a more general flux of motion, made almost continuous by the actors' need to be heard and seen from several sides, two fixed points of entry through the permanent façade of the tiring house at either side of the rear of the stage provided two points of focus, in strong positions for drawing attention. These Shakespeare used to emphasize and define particular moments in a play's action. A third central entrance was used more occasionally to reveal or 'discover' large stage properties or groups of persons by opening curtains. It was also available for entries that were impressively large in scale. When the company was on tour and acted on a stage backed by the screen of a dining or assembly hall, two entries at either side would often be in place ready for use. A larger, central entrance would probably require some temporary structure or hangings. If the company had to act on a freestanding platform, a row of curtains would have been set up at the rear to give the necessary entrances. With little else invariably present, the two points of access at opposite sides to the rear of the acting area were a major resource on all stages. By drawing the audience's eyes away from centre stage, an entry would visually emphasize a person's change of mind, health, or fortune, the passage of time, or a change of locale.

Unexpected entries, especially of persons new to the play, were used to alert an audience to reports of events not represented on stage and to new perceptions of the current situation. They could also have a large visual effect by altering the posture, position, and behaviour of everyone on stage. A well-known example is Marcade's unexpected and unannounced entry during the 'merriment' of Act V, scene ii, of *Love's Labour's Lost* (l. 703) which immediately 'interrupts' the scene, altering its tone, content, and physical alignments, while the dialogue changes from prose to short-phrased, simply-worded verse:

> MARCADE God save you, madam!
>
> PRINCESS   Welcome, Marcade;
>   But that thou interruptest our merriment.
>
> MARCADE I am sorry, madam; for the news I bring
>   Is heavy in my tongue. The King your father –
>
> PRINCESS Dead, for my life!
>
> MARCADE   Even so; my tale is told.
>
> BEROWNE Worthies, away; the scene begins to cloud.
>   (V.ii.703–8)

With Armado the one courageous exception, the actors of the 'show' that is in progress go off stage without a word and the Princess herself is speechless until the King asks 'How fares your Majesty?' She has no words to answer him but turns away to order preparations for leaving Navarre that night. As every word is coloured by her 'new-sad soul' (l. 719), everyone on stage will behave under the same cloud, moving and regrouping as the new business requires. Improvisation, uncertainty, clumsiness, and prolonged silences will be among the extended fall-out of this unexpected entry.

By his late entry, Jaques de Boys springs a surprise to quite different effect at the end of *As You Like It*. No one answers his abrupt request for a hearing but he continues by announcing that he is the second son of old Sir Rowland, a person not seen in the play and whose existence has been mentioned only once in the very first moments of its first scene. In freely flowing words he reports that the usurping tyrant, Duke Frederick, has raised a mighty army to capture and put to death the rightful duke, his brother. This alarming news will be spoken with a contrasting composure because, before anyone can reply, he reports the villain's sudden conversion and subsequent abdication. Those who are listening will not know how to take these amazing changes of fortune and so, as if afraid of not being believed, Jaques pledges his life on the truth of his news. That proves enough for the rightful duke to welcome him and the good fortune he brings to everyone assembled. They all turn attention to celebrations as the Duke orders dancing and rustic revelry: 'With measure heap'd in joy, to th' measures fall' (V.iv.160–73). Spirits have risen as if by magic but now, as partners come together and music plays, the other, 'melancholy' Jaques who has often been an independent figure in the forest, resists the joyful infection. After he has delivered a valedictory speech and refused the Duke's plea to stay, the forward action of the comedy is held back for his lonely departure through the very entrance that has just revealed the new arrival bearing the same name as himself. The Duke then sets all in motion again:

> Proceed, proceed. We will begin these rites,
> As we do trust they'll end, in true delights.

Dancing follows until the festive company leaves the stage, Rosalind being the single exception. She stays behind, or immediately returns to the stage, to speak an Epilogue, both as an actor and as Rosalind.

At the end of both these comedies, the ordering of persons on stage is disturbed when an unexpected entry is made and new dispositions have to follow. Without lengthy rehearsal all the other actors will have to improvise as the persons they play find their own accommodation to what has been reported. Visually the focus will be uncertain until new business is under way and the comedy moves to its conclusion. In *Love's Labour's Lost*, this resolution is tentative and calls for 'honest plain words' (V.ii.741), and, even then, it is not complete: 'Our wooing doth not end like an old play: / Jack hath not Jill' (ll. 862–3). Songs are introduced to complete the comedy with the entire actors' company on stage. This communal event is introduced by Armado, the knight whose performance as Hector in '*The Pageant of the Worthies*' had ended shamefully. His re-entry as leader of the unskilled actors will be the comedy's last surprising entry and his appearance will now be very different. He had left the stage promising to 'right [him]self like a soldier' (V.ii.711–13) but now Jaquenetta, the young and pregnant country wench, will be at his side while songs of the Owl and Cuckoo tell of spring time and winter and of cuckoldry

and love. At the end of *As You Like It*, Jaques prefaces his exit from
the celebrations by pronouncing judgement on each pair of lovers
and the Duke. As for himself, he says that he has much to hear and
learn from the convertite, who has 'thrown into neglect the pompous
court' (V.iv.175–6), that well-established society to which the other
exiles are about to return. In both comedies, words speak of a need
for trust and self-content while, visually, improvised re-arrangements
on stage will show the tentative nature of these resolutions.

★   ★   ★

Besides changing the expectations and grouping of persons already on
stage, the strong focus that entries attract can also alter the parameters
of a play by enlarging the imagined space in which it is taking place.
Macbeth, in this and other ways a spectacular tragedy, has a sequence
of these devices. A '*bleeding* Sergeant', at the start of Act I, scene ii,
meets the king and brings the visual evidence of his own wounds
to augment his account of an off-stage battle. He is on the point of
exhaustion and, as his 'gashes cry for help', he has to be helped from
the stage (I.ii.43–5). By this means, before Macbeth enters the play,
visual evidence evokes the bloodshed of a distant battle, and a painful struggle to speak presents a physical contrast to the security and
ordered business of Scotland's king and his attendants. At the start of
Act I, scene vii, the Folio text has the stage direction, '*Enter a Sewer,
and divers Servants with Dishes and Service [passing] over the stage,*' which
requires movement on stage, accompanied by torches and the music
of hautboys. Choreographically this provides a visual demonstration
of the lavish feast that welcomes the king to Macbeth's castle, the
home in which his murder is being planned. The more elaborate and
unhurried the entry and exit of these un-named servants, the wider
the imaginary perspective in which the audience will view Macbeth
in the very next moment, when he enters alone, speaking of murder
and appalled at the crime he is about to commit.

At the beginning of the following scene the Folio reads '*Enter
Banquo, and Fleance, with a Torch before him.*' The first words are Banquo's,
'How does the night, boy?' which probably implies that Fleance, on
this first entry to the play, walks ahead of his father and carries the
torch: an unexpected and entirely new physical presence. When
Banquo unbuckles his sword to give to Fleance and speaks of his fears
in going to bed, it becomes clear that this 'boy' is his son. Words are
few and simple but the young voice and presence contrast strongly

with those of Banquo and of Macbeth, who enters immediately afterwards: compared with them, Fleance knows almost nothing and can move more freely. The two battle-hardened soldiers were first seen close together as fellow 'captains', and later, the king had held Banquo to his heart as one no less deserv'd' than Macbeth (I.ii.34 and I.iv.29–31), but now, after their encounter with the witches and no longer dressed for battle, they are seen to be watchful of each other, in opposition rather than comradeship. They are also separated by Macbeth's intention to murder the king as a means of gaining the crown and by his lack of such a personal and trusted attendant as Fleance. In the way Macbeth and Banquo physically encounter each other, an audience may see more than either of them acknowledges in words and more than Banquo realizes at this time.

After the murder of Duncan a succession of independent entries and exits express widespread and varied alarm. The drunken Porter, behaving as if he were in hell, starts the action as Lennox and Macduff knock repeatedly at the castle gate. Their clothes, as well as everything they say and do, will show that these men have been riding through the night in a storm of unusual force. Then Macbeth enters alone after a sleepless night during which he has murdered the king. An assumed normality will at least partly hide what is uppermost in his mind – the horror, guilt, and fear which, moments earlier, the audience had seen render him powerless. Watching Macduff leaving to go to Duncan's lodging, Macbeth knows what will be found and dares not speak of it but, to an account of the 'unruly' night, he has to respond or he will awaken suspicion. However earnestly or apprehensively the 'young' Lennox recounts his experience (II.iii.60), the audience's visual focus, during this time of waiting, is bound to return to Macbeth, who says nothing at first: mentally he will seem frozen up, gripped by unspoken, unspeakable terror. Lennox brings a contrasting physical energy and freedom so that Macbeth's four brief words in reply – ''Twas a rough night' (l. 59) – can either wryly and humorously express the obvious, or touch the depth of his true feelings; some actors find that both these responses arise simultaneously. Physical performance and movements on and off stage have ensured that the audience will be watching closely enough to notice the smallest sign of fear or guilt. When Macduff re-enters he is transformed by what he has seen, his cry at once threatening and stunned: 'O horror, horror, horror!' Arrival on stage through the entrance now associated with the king's bedchamber and the subsequent change of everyone's attention, call for the actor's total commitment to what Macduff has seen off stage, so that a genuine horror is heard in his threefold cry and seen in his laboured breathing and shaken bearing. Renewing his energy and at last finding more words, even while knowing them to be inadequate, he sends Macbeth and Lennox to see for themselves while he raises the alarm and calls for a bell to be rung. When Shakespeare was writing the fragmented dialogue for this episode, he must have envisioned all this happening in his mind's eye.

Alone on the stage Macduff must wait for others. As he calls those asleep to join him, his words are repetitive, direct and strong, but varied by ideas and images that arise along with more immediate and practical reactions: natural death, the great doom, graves, and walking spirits. For the moment, one horror-struck, active and morally aware man represents the entire play, its story made palpable in and through him. An audience could not have expected this because, only moments before, Macduff had spoken his first words in the play while his arrival was being up-staged and eclipsed, first by the Porter and then by Macbeth. Later in the action, this person, at this time almost unknown, will escape from Scotland, risking and losing all he holds dear, and then return to seek out Macbeth and kill him. Macduff cannot know this future but an audience might sense it because the actor cannot help being aware of it every time the play is rehearsed and performed. Within this lone figure, that the play's choreography picks out as if with a spotlight, the ending of the play lies coiled at a deep and hidden level of consciousness, ready for release.

The focus now shifts repeatedly as many entries follow. First Lady Macbeth and then Banquo; next, Macbeth and Lennox. Ross also appears, probably at another entrance, and others too in sufficient numbers to carry or lead out Lady Macbeth moments later. Among all these dispersed and urgent movements, every person having risen from their beds only partly dressed or with blankets caught up around them in alarm and fear, an audience will scarcely know where to look. That does not last for long because all eyes on stage will fasten on Macbeth, who comes from the scene of murder and speaks words that both hide his guilt and give a foretaste of the sense of loss and futility that will haunt him at the end of the tragedy:

> Had I but died an hour before this chance,
> I had liv'd a blessed time; for, from this instant,
> There's nothing serious in mortality –
> All is but toys; renown and grace is dead;

> The wine of life is drawn, and the mere lees
> Is left this vault to brag of.
>
> (II.iii.89–94)

Macbeth has found a new way of speaking and his physical bearing will bear signs of what he has seen and done while he was off stage. The act of re-entry will emphasize the change but, with Malcolm and Donalbain coming on stage as he finishes speaking, any exposure of the workings of his mind will be brief. Almost immediately he is faced with the task of explaining why he has killed the two grooms who were guarding Duncan. As he describes the king's mangled corpse and speaks of his love for him, Lady Macbeth faints and that surprise and silent action causes the focus of attention to change yet again. In performance the actor will have to choose whether this faint is real or a pretence. She could be shielding her husband by deflecting attention when she hears him speak of feelings that had earlier threatened his resolve, or her fainting could be an involuntary sign of her own weakness and a foretaste of the 'unnatural troubles' that will draw her to a tormented death (V.i.69–72). Either way, Macbeth stops speaking, perhaps stunned, perhaps relieved of the need to continue: it is Macduff who again takes charge at centre stage, calling for others to help.

As Lady Macbeth is helped to leave, turmoil and uncertainty are brought under control, not by Macbeth or Macduff but by Banquo, who has said nothing so far in this scene, except immediately upon entrance. Now his clear thinking and straight speaking will hold attention, with everyone on stage facing towards him:

> … when we have our naked frailties hid,
> That suffer in exposure, let us meet,
> And question this most bloody piece of work,
> To know it further. Fears and scruples shake us…

Only a few more words are spoken before everyone leaves, excepting the two sons of Duncan. They remain on an otherwise empty stage for rapid and frightened discussion, before hurrying off to different destinations to escape danger.

Besides carrying dramatic action forward, the varied entries and exits, with a continual regrouping of all the persons on stage, have given visual expression to fears and scruples that only Banquo subsequently acknowledges. The effect is to unsettle an audience, not least because Macbeth, having committed the crime, loses the central position on stage while Banquo makes the one call for counter-action and follows that with a declaration of his trust in a more than mortal power. At first, Macbeth merely agrees with him, along with everyone else:

> BANQUO   ... Fears and scruples shake us.
> In the great hand of God I stand, and thence
> Against the undivulg'd pretence I fight
> Of treasonous malice.
>
> MACDUFF   And so do I.
>
> ALL   So all.

Then, at last, Macbeth takes over briefly, concentrating on the need for action:

> MACBETH Let's briefly put on manly readiness
> And meet i' th' hall together.
>
> ALL   Well contented.
>   [*Exeunt*]

The diminishing of Macbeth's contribution to the action is arguably the scene's most revealing feature. It happens gradually, as if by chance and without a verbal decision, but clarified in wordless performance and by a choreography that involves everyone. The call for immediate action, with which Macbeth draws the scene to a close and obliterates other thoughts, will be repeated in a very different form at a yet more crucial moment when, deserted by everyone else, he faces certain death: 'Lay on, Macduff;/And damn'd be him that first cries "Hold, enough!"' (V.viii.33–4). When the audience sees him draw strength from action here it may receive a premonition of the tragic ending; for the actor, this is a preparatory step in a long and deep-set process.

Act II, scene iv, provides an immediate contrast, having little action, careful words, and only three persons on stage. As soon as Ross enters, unannounced, not saying a word but listening to an unnamed person – in the stage direction and speech-prefixes he is simply an 'Old Man' – an audience may sense a mysterious ordering of events. Speaking together of strange portents, man's misdeeds, and the threatening heavens over a 'bloody stage', neither one identifies the location or explains why they have come together. When Macduff joins them, also without explanation, he speaks exclusively to Ross, as if the Old

Man were not present or not trusted to hear what is said. Their talk is about Duncan's murder, Macbeth's slaying of the king's two grooms, and the escape of his two sons, all matters only mentioned vaguely, previously in this scene, as an 'unnatural … deed' (ll. 10–11). Unheralded entries for unspecified reasons, separate discussions, and dialogue at first impersonally allusive and then tersely direct, all mark this meeting as taking place where talk would be dangerous if too open or specific. When Ross and Macduff leave to two different destinations, the Old Man's words suggest that the location may have been a chapel and the underlying intentions of those present moral and political:

> God's benison go with you, and with those
> That would make good of bad, and friends of foes.
>
> (ll.40–1)

Ross has addressed the Old Man as 'good father' and 'father', words commonly used of priests and friars; and his costume and manner might well indicate that this is the sense intended here. If Ross kneels to be blessed before he goes to witness Macbeth's coronation at Scone, their parting will give the audience a momentary view of a more peaceful and trusting way of life.

In this short scene, as elsewhere, choreography is a powerful factor in establishing the wide context of this tragedy. In the Witches' four scenes, including the very first of the play, their movements 'round about' and their repetitive ritualistic actions will physically demonstrate the corporate power of an 'alternative' existence. At first the choreography may hold an audience's attention more strongly and consistently than the weird details of what is spoken. The next Witches' scene, in which Hecate enters the play and addresses them for thirty lines without interruption (Act III, scene v), may seem on first reading to be an exception to this, but visually this too is impressive. The goddess enters alone, without any previous notice, and she may have 'descended' from above because she is 'for th' air' when she leaves (III.v.20). Before saying anything, her mere presence is enough to make the First Witch declare that she looks 'angerly' (l. 1). When she berates the Witches for being 'saucy and overbold', they submit to her harsh judgement. If they now behave as they did in earlier scenes, all three will react physically and appropriately to each clearly marked phase of Hecate's speech: its reproofs and vaunting, and the promise of 'great business' for which they must prepare. Hecate's report of flying to the moon widens the context of the action and, finally, her intention of drawing Macbeth 'to his confusion' will almost certainly be greeted with signs of approval and anticipation. To all this there is no verbal response but from their silent servility we may conclude that the Witches react in the dynamic and outwardly demonstrative style of earlier scenes. They will move both individually and in unison, crouching together in fear or scattering to escape punishment. They may cower, stone-still, and then move quickly to show that they will 'make amends' and start their preparations. They could hear Hecate's promises with excited obeisance and then, finally and climactically, dance together in anticipation of victory. In other plays Shakespeare calls for strong physical responses to the manifestation of supernatural power: in *A Midsummer Night's Dream*, Puck shows eye-catching and swift obedience to Oberon, and in *The Tempest*, Caliban cringes before Prospero, Gonzalo speaks of the 'ecstasy' gripping his spellbound enemies, and Ariel reports on their distraction as his charm 'strongly works 'em'; in the last scene of the play, a spellbound Alonzo returns to the stage *'with a frantic gesture'* (v.i.7–19 and 56 S.D.). If the Witches react to Hecate in the instinctive, corporate, and physically demonstrative manner of their earlier appearances, when all three wound up their charm by chanting and dancing and laid fingers to lips to hail Macbeth and Banquo in chorus, their reactions here will take attention almost as strongly as the words that Hecate speaks – completely so, should she pause to take notice of them.

Scholars have cast doubts on the authenticity of all that relates to Hecate, and certainly Thomas Middleton wrote the songs that are quoted in the Folio text. If someone other than Shakespeare wrote Hecate's long speech, he would have seen the power and significance of the Witches' physical performance elsewhere in the play and could have assumed its continuance here.

Although the Witches do not enter in the last Act, their influence on Macbeth has never been stronger than now. The cutting of green branches to hide the number of opposing forces is the most eye-catching fulfilment of their prophecies but an audience will also see that Macbeth, in thought and action, follows the course that Hecate had promised:

> He shall spurn fate, scorn death, and bear
> His hopes 'bove wisdom, grace, and fear.
> (III.v.30–1)

He considers alternatives but then does as she foretold, as if he cannot do otherwise. His entries and exits make this strikingly clear.

He comes on stage four times within 207 lines, an exceptional frequency for anyone in any of the plays, and each time he enters onto an empty stage, seeking no one and giving no reason why he should come at this time or to this place. Nor is it clear why he leaves or where he is going. Macbeth moves without another thought, as if under compulsion like an automaton. At first he is followed by an unspecified number of 'Attendants' but these drop away, as the Thanes are reported to have done already, and on his last two entrances he is alone. The Doctor who had attended his wife is with him at first but leaves at the end of the first scene, fearing for his own safety, a two-line soliloquy intensifying the focus on him. Seyton has to be called three times before joining Macbeth; he probably brings Macbeth's armour with him but, when asked for it, says that it is 'not needed yet' (V.iii.33). Sent to find the cause of an off-stage cry he returns with news of the queen's death and then is gone without a word to mark his departure; his very name being close to 'Satan', can sound ominous. Choreographically Macbeth's progressive isolation makes visible a closing of options, as if some fate and the consequence of his own actions are bearing down upon him. Inevitably, it seems, he is beyond the reach of anyone's help.

What happens in Macbeth's last moments is uncertain. At the point where he and Macduff join in the final combat something is amiss in the Folio stage direction: '*Exeunt fighting. Alarums.* // *Enter fighting, and Macbeth slain.*' If the killing is on stage as this requires, Macduff will have to leave dragging the dead body after him and re-enter later to display Macbeth's decapitated head as the Folio also requires. Perhaps the last few words of a stage direction are missing and the two should leave the stage a second time with Macbeth wounded but not yet dead. Some present-day productions solve the textual problem by ignoring the direction to '*Enter fighting*' but, if retained in some form, the return will accentuate the seemingly enforced nature of Macbeth's movements on and off stage throughout the last Act, the pace and effort redoubled in a desperate endeavour to fight until the inevitable end. Macduff's arrival bearing the severed head will, in any case, offer a bloody and disfigured object in place of the tragedy's previously resourceful hero. As at the end of *Richard the Second*, where the hero's last entry is in his coffin, Shakespeare has left the audience with a static and physical image that challenges its ability to understand. For both these plays, in the last resort, the players do not 'tell all' (*Hamlet*, III.ii. 136–8). In *Macbeth*, silence becomes an essential element of the tragedy, together with the sight of the bloody head of a murderous tyrant and a victorious army giving allegiance to a new king. Audiences who have been drawn by many sensitive words to think and feel with the workings of the hero's mind are given no words now that will help them to reconcile that sympathy with their horror at Macbeth's inhumanity and the consequences of his crimes. Shakespeare has written the tragedy so that any comprehensive judgement is the audience's responsibility and that task is likely to be unavoidable.

★   ★   ★

Rudolph Arnheim's *The Power of the Center* (1988) starts by demonstrating that the centre of any visual composition strongly attracts attention, a phenomenon that is 'deeply rooted in human nature and ultimately in the very make up of the nervous system we all have in common' (pp. 2–3). Consequently, changes at the centre of what happens on stage are especially significant and can subconsciously influence an audience's response to theatrical performance. In these matters Shakespeare's invention was varied and resourceful, controlling the focus of attention at every turn of a story and, on occasion, calling into question where the centre of power is to be found.

Taking *Hamlet* as example, we find that its three scenes that are located at court and involve almost all the cast are configured in three different ways, the last echoing and significantly varying previously established stage-images (I.ii, III.ii and V.ii). In the first, Claudius, with a mostly silent Gertrude at his side, holds pride of place as the person possessing greatest power, while Hamlet settles himself off-centre and, as the second Quarto has it, *'cum aliis'*. He is briefly drawn into the centre but only commands the stage when everyone else has left and he can speak freely for himself. The second court scene has two centres, one occupied by the players performing the play-within-the-play and the other, as before, by Claudius and Gertrude. Hamlet has refused to join his mother but has again placed himself off-centre where he can watch both '*The Mousetrap*' in performance and the king; he has also placed the silent Horatio to watch Claudius from another position. Only when the double centres have been disturbed and the court has left, does Hamlet again take and hold the centre: now, at last in this scene, the play's forward action depends almost entirely upon him. The third court scene also has two centres. Claudius and Gertrude are once again a powerful focus for attention but, instead of a fictional play, the other centre is the increasingly dangerous duel between Hamlet and Laertes who, with the king's connivance, seeks revenge for his father's death by whatever means he has been able to contrive. The visual balance is broken, as that of the previous court scene had been, but this time repeatedly: by Gertrude's movement towards her son to 'wipe [his] face' (V.ii,286), by her drinking of poison and her painful death, and then, still more strongly, by the 'incensed' fighting (l. 293) that will eventually draw all attention. When the queen and Laertes are both dead, Hamlet moves to the king and, with no one intervening, becomes the centre of the composition as he revenges his father's death. Hamlet holds that position until his own death, by which time Fortinbras and his army have been heard approaching: soon they will provide an alternative focus of attention to Hamlet's dead body.

The repeated presence of Hamlet at the border of the stage-space and yet related to its centre has an emphasis or weight that uses another principle of visual composition, its effect increased because his clothes are entirely black in contrast to those of every other person. As Arnheim puts it, 'the potential energy inherent in an object grows as that object moves away from the center of attraction' (pp.21–2). In the Play Scene, Hamlet's provocative and bawdy talk with Ophelia, entirely contrary to the composure of other spectators, is likely to draw an off-centre attention, as if Shakespeare had wanted to demonstrate this onlooker's heightened sexual responses as the play is about to be enacted and to contrast this with the more passive interest shown by others. As Arnheim notes, an object's resistance to the power of the centre is perceived as additional weight or potential energy:

> One can understand this phenomenon by thinking of the object as attached to the center of attraction by a rubber band. The farther removed it is from the center, the more resistance it has to overcome (p.22).

Once the play has started, Hamlet's interruption of the actors' performance emphasizes his impatience by threatening both the centres of the composition as well as the progress of '*The Mousetrap*': 'Begin murderer; pox, leave thy damnable faces and begin. Come; the croaking raven doth bellow for revenge' (III.ii.247–9). Soon, as the player pours poison in the victim's ear, Hamlet waits no more and, in effect, takes over as the second centre in place of the enacted play. In turn, this disturbance triggers Claudius's total disruption of the other and more static centre:

HAMLET   A poisons him i' th' garden for his estate. His
    name's Gonzago. The story is extant, and written in very

choice Italian. You shall see anon how the murderer gets
the love of Gonzago's wife.

OPHELIA   The King rises.

HAMLET   What, frighted with false fire!

QUEEN   How fares my lord?

POLONIUS   Give o'er the play.

KING   Give me some light. Away!

POLONIUS   Lights, lights, lights!

                                                          (ll. 255–64)

Hamlet has revealed his own very personal and irresistible concern
with the play that Claudius is watching, his account of it culminating in the second marriage of the fictional queen, which mirrors his
mother's remarriage. By having Claudius leave the stage at this point
Shakespeare has ensured that it is not *'The Mousetrap'* that 'catch[es] the
conscience of the King' (II.ii.601) as Hamlet had intended, but rather,
Hamlet himself who takes over from the fictional play as the real-life
son of a murdered king. While the players disperse and take their stage
properties with them, Hamlet remains on stage with Horatio, the other
witness he had placed off-centre. By disturbing the two centres of the
composition, Shakespeare's choreography shows that it is Hamlet's
sexual impulses and filial feelings that drive the action forward. The
tragedy's intellectual themes – its moral, philosophical and political
issues – are presented in many more words than these other compul-
sions but an audience is given powerful visual and kinetic evidence of
them at this time, when they are unnamed and unnameable.

★   ★   ★

Although not always evident to a reader because occurring over a
period of time and without verbal identification, a recurrence of
certain physical activities on stage can give a sense of authority to the
progress of events or a seeming inevitability to their outcome. Even a
single visual repetition can demonstrate the nature of an action in ways
that the persons involved cannot mention or do not recognize. When
repetition brings a significant difference from the previous occurrence,
a play's narrative can be wordlessly clarified or taken a purposeful leap
forward. The repeated entrances and exits for Macbeth, noticed a few
pages back, offer examples of all these effects.

In the comedies, with their multiple story-lines and assorted lovers, the recurrence of certain visual effects is often clearly marked in the dialogue, showing that Shakespeare knew and valued the power of repetition. In Act IV of *Love's Labour's Lost*, the king and two fellow votaries come forward, one after another, to read the verses they have composed to their mistresses and to be overheard and mocked by Berowne, who eventually is revealed as another lover and verse-maker. In *Much Ado*, first Benedick and then Beatrice overhears the talk of others that is intended to trick them into believing that each one is admired and beloved by the other. Near the end of *As You Like It*, Phebe calls on Sylvius to tell Rosalind 'what 'tis to love' and a declaration follows that is repetitive itself and provokes repetitive agreement from all listeners. Rosalind intervenes with, 'Pray you, no more of this; 'tis like the howling of Irish wolves against the moon' (V.ii. 102–4), and immediately starts another series of repetitions with her own promises, which are carefully and mysteriously phrased: these have no verbal responses but all present will react physically in varied and revealing ways. Two scenes later, two other series of pronouncements cover much the same ground, the first shared between a number of speakers, the second spoken by Jaques as a valedictory judgement on the assembled lovers, whose non-verbal responses will contribute at least as much and as variously as any words.

When a number of physical repetitions lead an audience to expect yet further instances, the breaking of that series can attract close attention and mark the innovation unmistakably. In *Othello*, for instance, as early as Act III when Othello vows revenge for what he takes to be Desdemona's unfaithfulness and calls Iago to look as he blows away 'all my fond love', he responds physically as well, his bosom swelling with 'tyrannous hate' (III.iii.446–66). Two scenes later, tortured and murderous passion cause his body to shake until, gasping for breath and broken in speech, he '*falls in a trance*' (IV.i.31–43). When he insults his wife in public and strikes her, his retched out 'Goats and monkeys!' (IV.i.260) is a presage of still more uncontrollable and bestial reactions. Just before the final scene, further repetition of physical violence is promised when Othello speaks of a quick and brutal killing:

> Strumpet, I come.
> Forth of my heart those charms, thine eyes, are blotted;
> Thy bed, lust-stain'd, shall with lust's blood be spotted.
>   (V.i.34–6)

But as preparation for the murder, these words and earlier actions are deceptive because, when he finally comes to Desdemona's bedside, the sequence of violent and frenzied outbursts stops abruptly. As she sleeps in her bed Othello hesitates, marvels at her beauty, bends down and kisses her, and then, against what was anticipated, he starts to weep. When she wakes, he confesses that he has come to kill her and tells her to pray; and when she does pray – 'heaven / Have mercy on me' – he answers by praying with her, 'Amen, with all my heart' (V.ii.34–5). Only when she sees hope that he will not kill her, does this new gentleness vanish, and physical instincts again take over. He utters a sound which is no word at all (l. 39) and she sees a 'bloody passion' in the gnawing of his nether lip and the shaking of his 'very frame' (ll. 40–1, 46–8). With Othello still hesitating to act and both speaking of the stolen handkerchief, their pauses, assertions, and one-word questions and answers indicate an intense struggle to grasp what is happening, as both are emotionally and physically incapable of sustained speech. Only when she seems to weep for Cassio's death, does Othello act with the unrestrained violence that the audience has repeatedly been led to expect, although, even now, it is without the decisive suddenness he had anticipated before entering the bed-chamber. Several lines after 'Down, strumpet!' and 'Nay, an you strive' (ll. 83, 85), Othello silences Desdemona and, as the stage direction says, '*Smothers her*'.

This is the only time that Shakespeare required a woman to be deliberately and gradually killed on stage. The shock and pain must have stunned audiences unprepared for such a scene, even though earlier uncontrollable actions had led them to expect that Othello would kill brutally and compulsively. Why should Othello take the time to smother her when he had intended to act swiftly and stain her bed with blood (see V.i.36)? By the end of the scene it has been revealed that on his person or hidden in the bedroom three weapons have been secreted, any one of which could have done the lethal work quickly. In performance it can seem that Othello is compelled to kill his wife in this slow and deliberate way because he is afraid to 'scar that whiter skin of hers than snow, / And smooth as monumental alabaster' (V.ii.4–5). In other performances, having at last come to the moment for action, his savage violence has been appeased or spent and a sexual necessity draws him to be physically close to her body. The sequence of violently physical reactions ensures that the slow and deliberate killing comes against expectation and that the actor will carry out the murder in whatever way he is led by the progress of the performance, until this moment. Emilia is '*at the door*' and calls before Desdemona is quite dead, yet Othello continues to kill her, until he utters a simple repetition, 'So, so' (l. 92). In each performance the actor will discover whether this is spoken brutally or in satisfaction, relief, or exhaustion.

The repeated attempts to kill Desdemona are appallingly slow to take effect and the impression they make on the audience is heightened by a stumbling inadequacy of speech. When Emilia enters the room, Desdemona revives and speaks again, still very simply but now unambiguously shielding her husband from the consequences of his crime:

DESDEMONA   A guiltless death I die.

EMILIA O, who hath done this deed?

DESDEMONA   Nobody. I myself. Farewell.
        Commend me to my kind lord. O, farewell!

Later, realizing that Iago has duped him and that his wife was innocent, Othello lies down and roars (see l. 200), an action that repeats, in a very different context and manner, his falling on the floor in a helpless trance. Later, after a torrent of words, he lets out a sustained, repetitive, and culminating cry: 'O Desdemona! Dead! Desdemona! Dead! O! O!' (ll. 284–5). Finally, he again speaks at length to give a public account of his entire life and then suddenly, with a weapon no one thought he possessed, he kills himself, and at the last moment, turns to Desdemona:

> I kiss'd thee ere I kill'd thee. No way but this –
> Killing my self, to die upon a kiss.

By these few words and a deliberate physical action Shakespeare was able to combine the bare horror of a self-inflicted death with a renewed assertion of that gentle love and quiet deliberation that, against expectation, had taken hold of his mind and body when he approached his wife to kill her.

Repetition with difference is found everywhere in all forms of art, defining what is presented and developing reception. In music, lyric poetry, painting, or architecture its presence and effectiveness are obvious to any listener, reader, or viewer, but in theatre, spatial and visual repetitions achieve their full power only in performance and a reader of play-texts must take care to avoid missing or undervaluing their choreographic and cumulative effects.

★   ★   ★

Entries and exits, repeated actions and changing spatial relationships from scene to scene are all means of controlling the use of stage-space that leave their marks in a play-text. Other choreographic devices are also visible, the most obvious being changes of costume that introduce new stage business and behaviour. The male disguise of heroines in the comedies alters their physical performance, precedence in encounters, and confidence in movement. When an actor puts on armour or carries a sword his timing, physical awareness, and distance from others are all affected. In Shakespeare's day especially, the clothes for travel were more protective and restricting than those worn indoors, clothes for formal occasions far richer than those for private life or outdoor activities. The significance of dress is illustrated in an episode made familiar by two widely circulated film versions: King Henry the Fifth borrows a cloak to hide his royal insignia when he wishes to behave, outwardly, like an unremarkable man. The all-powerful monarch can then be polite to the boastful Pistol, stand by to watch as two captains quarrel, and listen patiently when contradicted by a small group of footsoldiers. A change from verse to prose accompanies this change in posture, attention, and, to some degree, security, which encourages an audience to see the play's hero in a new light. And here he can be out of focus while others hold attention confidently.

A still more striking and sudden choreographic change occurs in *Henry IV, Part Two* when the actor who was Prince Hal enters in his coronation robes as King Henry the Fifth. Falstaff hails him with 'God save thee, my sweet boy!' but the only reply is addressed to the Lord Chief Justice, asking him to deal with 'that vain man'. When this official fails to staunch his old friend's fervour, the new king halts in his progress and assumes a distanced and dismissive authority:

> FALSTAFF My King! My Jove! I speak to thee, my heart!
>
> KING I know thee not, old man. Fall to thy prayers.
>
> (V.v.47–8)

But the royal personage does not prove to be completely in control of himself: his posture will change as he does remember the past they once shared and his part in it. Only after he has confessed his own short-comings does Henry resume full authority: he moves on, breaking off contact and ordering the Lord Justice to act on his behalf. When this representative of the king returns with Officers shortly afterwards, Falstaff and his company are summarily sent to prison. Falstaff has been given no verbal reply to Henry's repudiation and none is needed because the change in physical behaviour will show visually at how great a mutual cost the transformation has been achieved. While King Henry's words delineate the political and intellectual content of the drama, what Falstaff identifies as the 'heart' of their relationship is expressed through performance and choreography: the actors' speaking of their lines and their contrasted postures, their distance from each other, the timing and size of their movements, the ways in which they look at each other or turn away.

Costumes when especially assumed for making an entrance or carrying out specified actions are a resource that Shakespeare used frequently to control and emphasize physical performance. In *The Tragedy of Coriolanus* the hero changes clothes and behaviour repeatedly. For his first entrance in the play's first scene, he is a young Roman nobleman who meets an elderly friend among a crowd of plebeian citizens and then is found by a number of experienced Generals, Senators, and elected politicians who bring urgent news that demands his response: each of these meetings calls for different behaviour. When he next appears, Rome is at war with invading Volscians and he has become a soldier among soldiers: stage directions require him to enter *'cursing'* (I.iv.29, SD). In the fighting that follows, he enters the gates of Corioli alone and, almost at once, returns to the stage *'bleeding'* (l. 63, SD); he then leaves again for renewed fighting along with reinforcements. After further engagements, at the start of the ninth scene of the first Act he enters with *'his arm in a scarf'* and leaves at its end to wash off the blood that is drying and 'should be look'd to' (ll. 93–4). The action moves back to Rome for Act II and starts by building expectation for the entry of Coriolanus at the centre of a military triumph, his brows, *'crown'd with an oaken garland'*, but then, against expectation, he *'kneels'* to his mother, who at once orders him to stand (l. 162). For Act II, scene ii, he is the reluctant and ill-at-ease soldier at a formal meeting of the Senate, where he is chosen as candidate for Consul. Consequently, he next appears *'in a gown of humility'* in order to petition the plebeians for their votes, as custom insisted; he should also show his wounds, but to that he does not submit.

Now Coriolanus visibly alternates between the politician and the private man. When he is surrounded by *'a rabble of Plebeians'*, he

'*draws his sword*' and challenges them to 'try upon [them]selves' what
they (and the audience) have seen him do on the field of battle
(III.i.223–5). At the start of Act IV, when he is a banished man and
about to leave Rome, a stage direction specifies an entrance '*with the
young Nobility of Rome*' and then, in its fourth scene, located in the
enemy city of Antium, he must enter alone, '*in mean apparel, disguised
and muffled*'. Throughout the rest of the play, Coriolanus is dressed,
as the highest ranking General, in clothes and armour that will have
been supplied by the Volscians. He has become a marked renegade at
a time when a soldier's safety in battle depended on the heraldic colours and distinctive clothing that demonstrated his allegiance. Almost
all the time, however, his presence remains both impressive and dangerous. Cominius; who has been sent to negotiate peace, reports how
he had knelt to his former comrade: 'I tell you he does sit in gold, his
eye / Red as 'twould burn Rome' (V.i.63–4). Coriolanus's behaviour
changes when his mother is about to leave, having come with others
to beg and kneel for peace. Here the Folio text directs '*He holds her
by the hand, silent*' and still more remarkably, as his words subsequently
make clear, he starts to weep: 'it is no little thing', he says, 'to make /
Mine eyes to sweat compassion' (V.iii.195–6). In the last moments
of the tragedy, Aufidius, his Volscian opposite, recalls this moment in
more sensational terms:

> He whin'd and roar'd away your victory,
> That pages blush'd at him, and men of heart
> Look'd wond'ring each at others.
>   (V.vi.98–100)

When Aufidius continues and calls him 'thou boy of tears' (V.vi.101),
this insult enrages him more than being branded a traitor. Repeating
the offensive 'Boy!', Coriolanus provokes the assassination that had
been planned, and which is now carried out ignominiously. In common with other tragic heroes, Coriolanus is last seen as a dead body,
but the manner in which he reaches this end is exceptional, the
conclusion of a long sequence of variously costumed and carefully
choreographed appearances.

★   ★   ★

To understand the wide range of Shakespeare's achievements, a reader
must keep the space of the stage in mind, and the physical reality,

movements, and activities of everyone present. This visible and tangible drama does not always leap off the page but it invariably signifies, alongside the words of dialogue and, sometimes, to a greater or contrary effect. It has the advantage of speaking directly to the senses and so registering in an audience's consciousness without having to be verbally described or understood. The effect of this choreography can be broad or overwhelming when created by a shouting, marching, dancing, or singing crowd, and intimate and specific when one person makes a new entry alone or awakens to a new perception or purpose. Once a reader becomes aware of what is happening on stage, as well as what is being said, Shakespeare's invention and imagination is seen to be as fully engaged in the use of space and directions for the actors' physical performance as it is, more obviously, in his choice and management of words.

Part III

Productions

8

Free Shakespeare*

The more productions of Shakespeare I saw, the more I became restless and unwilling to take all that was offered without question. I did not want to see the plays through another person's eyes and be told what I should think. When reading and thinking about the plays and imagining them in action on a stage, I was continually surprised and challenged but too often when I saw them in performance what was fresh and engaging was dominated by what was traditional, lazy, intrusive or inept. I sought a shared experience that would lead me to a new understanding of the play and awaken sensations and thoughts that caught and held my attention. Frustrated, I tried to share my thoughts in the article reprinted here and subsequently in a short book that is still in print, both entitled Free Shakespeare *(1971 and 1974).*

Shakespeare is unique and those who present his plays in the theatre try to take this into account: usual ways of working may be quite inappropriate.

Matthew Arnold's description of Shakespeare's special qualities has become proverbial:

> Others abide our question. Thou art free.
> We ask and ask: Thou smilest and art still,
> Out-topping knowledge.

In our own words, most of us would agree that we cannot nail down his purposes or be sure that we understand. Returning to a play after a few years, we realise that we have seen only what we had looked for, and that as we have changed so, it seems, has he. But we are also aware of a direct, involving engagement and, like Keats, we will not

---

*First published in *Shakespeare Survey, 24* (1971), 127–35.

sit down to read *King Lear* again without some prologue, at least a moment of adjustment:

> once again the fierce dispute,
> Betwixt Hell torment and impassion'd Clay
> Must I burn through …

Shakespeare seems to draw us into his creation, into fresh discovery and active imagination: we 'burn through' a re-creation of the play in our own minds.

Standing further back from individual plays, we, like Dryden, wonder at the range and power of his mind: 'He was the man who of all Modern, and perhaps Ancient Poets, had the largest and most comprehensive soul.' Coleridge was later to call him 'myriad-minded', in that phrase catching the bafflement that mixes with our admiration. The apparent ease with which Shakespeare wrote is the most attractive and most astonishing of his qualities. Dryden called it 'luck': 'All the Images of Nature were still present to him, and he drew them not laboriously, but luckily…' But while Ben Jonson praised the naturalness of his writing –

> Nature herself was proud of his designs,
> And joy'd to wear the dressing of his lines

– he also knew that the 'joy' depended on craftsmanship, each line being 'well turned and true filed' as in a blacksmith's forge.

Besides these old encomiums, later scholars and critics have added to our appreciation, showing verbal complexity, theatrical variety, social awareness, psychological perception, intellectual grasp and scepticism. No theatre producer could read all that has been written, let alone judge each opinion and find means to reflect them in theatrical productions. The readiest response is to stage Shakespeare according to current theatrical methods and the perception of the moment, and trust Shakespeare to survive. So we should go to the theatre to see new facets of his plays, knowing that in five years' time we shall see still more.

I have long supposed that this was the only sensible course for playgoers or for producers but to spend one's time wholly in the pursuit of 'something new' is to run the risk of being 'too superstitious', as the apostle Paul told the men on the Hill of Mars. If a playgoer or student is able to build up a composite impression of the plays from many partial renderings he has seen, must every student go through the same progression? Must each view be limited by another man's momentary perception? Journalistic criticism of Shakespeare productions reflects the interest which is centred today on the task of deciphering the 'director's intentions' in a production. Trevor Nunn, describing his work, will explain what is 'the whole fascination of the centre part of the play to me', and how that has influenced his directing of it (*Plays and Players*, 1970).

The history of Shakespeare in the theatre shows how each age has, indeed, seen the plays only through the various filters of individual interpretive artists. But in the present century there is a new situation, for now the filter is more likely to be provided by a director than by an actor: we talk of Peter Brook's *Dream*, Peter Hall's *Dream*, or Zeffirelli's *Romeo*. The nature of the intervening filter is changing, for while an actor has to bring himself along with his interpretation and work out his recreation of Shakespeare's character in daily contact with Shakespeare's words and with his own complete personality and being, the director never has to live with what he has created. Good directors do respond widely to the text, will 'live' through the rehearsals using all their experience of life and all their intuitive responses as well as their intellectual grasp of the play and the text. But this is not the same kind of engagement as an actor's, working on a single play with other actors over the course of months or, perhaps, whole years. Moreover, the director has much greater power over the play than any one actor. He can, with his designer, reduce individualised characters to an almost uniform appearance in which the actors, would have to work crudely to make any individual impression: see, for example, the all-red costumes for a Stratford production of *Much Ado* (1968) in which prince and soldier were scarcely distinguishable, or the *Hamlet* (1970) where the whole court was dressed in regulation white, trimmed with fur, and boots. The director can set the play in a period that forces the actors to assume a range of mannerisms which limits their rhythms, tones and responses, and this assumption of a period may well take their attention away from more basic aspects of their task: see, for example, a version of *The Merchant of Venice* (1970) at the National Theatre in London, which was set in Victorian streets and drawing rooms.

Today Shakespeare does not 'abide' the question of audiences. Directors are working all the time to make their own *questions and answers* abundantly clear, by underlining them with the contrivance of set, costume, lighting, sound and the drilling and improvisations of actors: by placing of visual emphasis; by grouping movement,

verbal emphasis, elaborate programmes and public-relations operations. Shakespeare is not free; he is not still. We do not 'ask' because
all the time we are being 'told and told'. Nothing much happens
'luckily', and if it does, it is assimilated into the defined and high-
powered presentation of a particular 'interpretation'. What is forged
in the smithy of the rehearsal-room is nothing 'natural', but a clear,
surprising, challenging, unmissable interpretation of Shakespeare:
'something new'.

★   ★   ★

The 1970 productions at Stratford and *The Merchant of Venice* in
London offered many examples of the director getting the better of
the textual material in order to force the audience to notice his interpretation. Most obvious are the occasions when silent incidents are
interpolated into the plays. In *Richard III*, the director, Terry Hands,
cut the Scrivener scene (III, vi) and kept Richard on stage, silent: he
feels pain in his deformed leg… there is a long silence as he struggles for control… he becomes fretful and childish. The director, has
decided to make the audience consider the grounds of motivation
at this point: the Scrivener, who shows both a man and common
humanity, morality and cynicism, perhaps pathos and certainly irony,
is sacrificed in order to build up a particular view of the central
character. Earlier, as Edward IV leaves the stage after hearing of the
death of Clarence, he speaks a line that might imply self-awareness
or pity, or resolution, or fear, or the mere putting of an unpleasant
thought out of mind – 'Come, Hastings, help me to my closet. Ah,
poor Clarence!' (II, i, 133). At this moment, Terry Hands directed
that the King pushes over a tub from which rolls a heap of skulls. It
had been placed downstage centre, not by necessity of words or of
action implicit in the text, but by the director who is intent on one
unambiguous effect, a reminder of mortality. The trouble is that even
a playgoer accustomed to theatre ways may be more impressed by the
intrusive novelty than by anything else.

In making such simple additions to the plays, directors are often
less resourceful than their texts and fall into clichés. The delayed exit
is one of these. In John Barton's production of *Measure for Measure*,
Isabella does not go out with duke or brother at the close of the play,
but remains for a silent soliloquy, which marks her undeniably as the
odd one out who can say nothing. At the end of *The Merchant of Venice*
both Jessica and Antonio are left on stage after the group *exeunt*, each

reading the letter Portia has just given them; Jessica takes longer than the Merchant to leave, and as she goes, sadly, a voice is heard singing offstage. Jonathan Miller, the director, has insisted that the audience goes away counting the cost of happiness, despite the fact that the text of the play ends with a bawdy joke from Gratiano. Robin Phillips's *Two Gentlemen* ends with a silent tableau as all the characters remain on stage where Shakespeare's text asks for an *exeunt*; at this point the director introduced a further character, a silent, black-visaged Launce who slowly threads his way through the silent figures.

The designer is the strongest ally of the director. When Terry Hands wished to stress the nightmare quality of the end of *Richard III* and extend its influence over previous acts, his designer provided grotesque costumes for the coronation scene (IV, ii), Richard having a large boar's head growing on his shoulder and Ann a vast ruff and a costume so apparently heavy that her arms were supported with crutches as she held the symbols of queenship in her hands. For John Barton's production of *The Tempest*, Prospero was dressed in plain beige, his magic cloak offering no contrast and suggesting no formality; there was no apparent need to ask Miranda to help 'pluck' it off (I, ii, 24). The effect was to get the audience to see Prospero as a man feeling his way through a crisis, not as a powerful magician renouncing power. The banquet and masque were staged with scarcely any pomp or explicit meaning, with scarcely any costumes and the fewest practicable all-male performers. The text speaks of a 'most majestic vision' and of 'revels' (IV, i, 118 and 148), but designer and director had ignored these clues to achieve their clear-cut objective. In the National Theatre *Merchant*, Sir Laurence Olivier appears as Shylock in frock-coat and top hat, so that an unmistakable contrast is made when he dons a Jewish woven robe before calling on Tubal to meet him at 'our synagogue' to prosecute his revenge (III, i, 111): no one in the audience would doubt the religious and racial motivation of that exit, although in the text his words are also full of murder, money and merchandise.

In his handling of actors, the director's aim is often to remove ambiguity and to enlarge those incidents or words that seem most relevant to his own 'view of the play'. How much can be achieved in this way may be seen in Buzz Goodbody's production of *King John*. Here the characters frequently enter like marching toy soldiers, smirk, giggle and repeat phrases in chorus: they pray in unison, with mechanical gestures and toneless voices. Blanche's wedding is proposed with humorous over-emphasis and, at the end, a comic 'phew'. For his death-scene, the King is carried on stage lumped uncleremoniously over a Lord's back. The director wished to stress the repetitions, self-satisfaction and self-interest of politics, and does so with wearying completeness, so that suffering, uncertainty, passion and moral considerations, so often suggested by the text, are crowded out, submerged in what the director is telling us. The Bastard mocks behaviour that is all the time being mocked by the actors.

In *Hamlet*, Trevor Nunn has Alan Howard, as the Prince, kneeling in church, for 'To be, or not to be': and at the end of this he looks round as if not knowing where he is. So the soliloquy becomes an activity that starts as an assumed seriousness and clearly occupies only a part of his conscious mind. In the following scene with Ophelia, she tries to kiss him and there is a long pause before Hamlet exclaims with strength: 'It hath made me mad' (III, i, 147). The director has said that he is examining the 'shifts between real madness and per-formed madness unknown to the person in the middle of it all': and so 'enterprizes of great pitch and moment', relationships with others, suspicion and guilt, philosophical concern with the nature of human existence, all of which can be seen in the text, are allowed no representation; they must not challenge the clear 'line' through the play's action that director has chosen. After the closet-scene with his mother, Hamlet is made to appear almost naked and the King gives him two forceful blows in the crutch: the reasons for this change of dress and sudden brutality are harder to discern. Perhaps Hamlet finds himself by making an obscene gesture of exposure: perhaps he is try-ing to find a new action by shedding his mourning and Claudius is taking the easiest way to stop him for the moment The director has clearly turned Shakespeare's ironic, challenging, uneasy scene into some sort of physical, man-to-man opposition. He is interpreting the scene in the light of his own 'fascination' with the possibilities of the text and has found a physical way of making an unprecedented statement; whatever that statement is meant to say, it overwhelms anything that is actually said or merely implied in the text.

John Barton is particularly fond of enforcing his view of the play by breaking speeches with silences, or by heavy emphasis on a few words or by some eye-arresting gesture accompanying them. Sometimes this underlines what is already plain enough, as in Angelo's reply to Isabella's departing, 'Save your honour!' (II, ii, 161). The text reads, 'From thee; even from thy virtue!', which could be said within the same iambic verse-line. Ian Richardson, however, speaks it with a long pause after 'thee'; this stresses an opposition between the instinc-tive 'thee' and the more demanding 'virtue' of Shakespeare's text.

At the end of *The Tempest*, John Barton found more that he wanted to emphasise in Prospero's farewell to Ariel, than in Shakespeare's conclusion which has Prospero asking the courtiers to 'draw near', implying a general *exeunt*. So the words are transposed, and after a pause as Antonio and Sebastian leave Prospero, the farewell to the spirit is gravely and slowly said as the new conclusion to the play.

In the National Theatre's *Merchant of Venice*, Portia was presented against a background of Victorian comedy, playing in idleness until becoming impatient with her manifestly absurd suitors. Here by-play speaks for the director: Arragon pulls a knotted handkerchief out of his pocket, sees the knot, can't remember what he should remember, and so moves on to the caskets; he drops a lump of sugar, a footman picks it up and swallows it, and the audience laughs again. Jonathan Miller has Portia assume a deep, false male voice when disguised as a lawyer to accentuate the change from frills and curls, and, more originally, has her maintain something of this deeper quality of voice when she faces Shylock across a table and finds herself face-to-face with a man... [and] pleading for the 'quality of mercy'; she is transformed by this experience and so a clear line is given to her characterisation throughout the play. To this end the tricks are played earlier, Bassanio's casket-scene greatly cut, and Portia's yielding speech played rhetorically, rather than responding to the subtle rhythms, delicate hesitations and simplicities of the text.

The choice of a unifying idea for a production, and its expression in settings, costumes, interpolations, by-play, verbal emphasis, manner of performance will always limit the presentation of what Shakespeare has written. It concentrates on one single meaning for almost every ambiguous line. It enlarges one incident and diminishes, or cuts completely, some other incident that carries a contrary emphasis. The productions are not myriad-minded and Shakespeare is not free. If questioned about this procedure, I suspect that most directors would answer that to gain authority and power, a production must be simple and not dissipate its effectiveness, must lead in one way not several and must build up climaxes. They would also explain that Shakespeare is often difficult to understand and that their changes serve to clarify his obscurities.

★   ★   ★

To these usual attitudes, Peter Brook offers some contrasts. In company with Nunn, Barton, Hands and Miller, this director assumes an individual way of working. He refuses to 'take a categorical position' in approaching a production:'I often drive people mad by not making up my mind, but I don't believe it's really a fault. In a work context, the eventual clarity I hope for comes not from any dogmatism, but an encouraged chaos from which the clarity grows'(interview, *Observer*, 30 August, 1970).

The first step towards a production is a series of exercises for the actors, physical, vocal and improvisational, which aim at making the 'actors work more freely together as a group'. The next is to seek a 'collective understanding' of the play, by using specific acting methods to explore the text through voice and body, through experiment in action. Instead of thinking about the meaning of words, the actors are encouraged to see how they can speak them, represent, support or contrast them. They criticise each other's work and wait for something to come right. Peter Brook tells the story of experimental rehearsals for *The Tempest*, when:

> A Japanese actor who, by approaching Ariel through his breathing and through his body, made Ariel something very understandable. A certain force became tangible in something which to the Japanese was easy to understand because in the basis of the Noh theatre, from which he came, there was a certain type of sound, a certain type of cry, a certain type of breath. The idea of that force was truly represented. It could be discussed because it had suddenly happened. There it was amongst us. It was no longer force, an abstract movement, it was *force*, a reality, something which could influence other people (*The Times,* 29 August, 1970).

By asking the actors to respond to the text and to various tasks of the director's invention, different ways of presenting characters and incidents are evolved in random patterns. From these the most 'forceful' are chosen, and so, 'in place of a lack of an intention, an intention appears' (interview, *Plays and Players*, 1970).

Is this 'new' way of directing the means to 'free' Shakespeare, to avoid fixing a production according to a director's 'interpretation' or 'view'? Peter Brook's *A Midsummer Night's Dream* in the 1970 Stratford season was hailed as a revelation by many playgoers: does it provide hope for a specially appropriate production method for Shakespeare?

In the acting some results are obvious. Peter Thomson reported in *Shakespeare Survey*, 24 (1971) that the actors found their work 'fantastic', but it is noticeable that this is because they are working 'with Brook', not with Shakespeare. At least half of their task must have been getting accustomed to the trapezes, coiling wires and stilts, and to the wayward percussive music and sounds that all derive from Brook's decision to work as in a circus, whenever possible. This idiom seems to have been chosen to encourage a 'display of physical virtuosity – an expression of joy'. However, in these skills the actors remained amateurs, and nothing was attempted like the silence that falls in a circus as danger is confronted. The revealing all-white stage seemed suitable for ballet or gymnastics, but only a sporadic attempt was made to move with dancer-like precision or authority. The technical hurdles had been introduced to thrust the actors into unknown territory so that they court discovery, rather than display the effortless skill of artistic achievement. Variety of style seems to have been pursued for much the same reason. Movement varies from solemn simplicity (and often cliché) to novel ingenuity. On occasion the speaking is noticeably slow, especially when the words are about death or virginity, or about the actor and his art, dream and reality. At times, movement and noise obliterate speech, or make so strong a counter claim for the audience's interest that words can scarcely be followed. At other times, the drama seems to be going on inside the minds of motionless and inexpressive performers, and the pace is so slow that either the audience loses interest or is forced to find it for itself in general curiosity.

The production met with such good-will that many of the audience seemed wholly satisfied. When Peter Thomson writes: 'I feel no inclination to defend any of Brook's decisions. I doubt whether the play could have been so well spoken if it had been seriously falsified', he sounds as though he is accepting a piece of novel showmanship entirely on its own terms. He goes on to say: 'More than anything I have ever seen, this production declared its confidence and delight in the art of performance. In doing so, it went, for me, *beyond the meaning of the play* to a joyous celebration of the fact that it was written …' This is not criticism, it is capitulation. But it does suggest that Shakespeare's play might have become open to the audience, with no directorial interference of note, beyond the surface interest of the performance itself.

But if we wish to ask how the production served the play, we must go beyond recording pleasure or distaste. Nor is this difficult, for certainly a single interpretation had been found during the actors' explorations under the director's guidance, and this has been unambiguously presented. Time and again, the audience is forced to take the play in one comparatively simple way. Helena and Theseus hold fixed kneeling positions for soliloquies and so contradict the energy and light rhythmic variety of the writing. The Mechanicals parade on to the stage accompanied by blaring noise that makes them far more broadly comic and assertive than the words alone imply, and quite alter the textual contrast (and similarity) between their speeches and Helena's preceding soliloquy. Certain words are chosen for repetition, usually by a listener, and so are underlined as they are not in the text. Laughter is provided on stage with no direct cue in Shakespeare's words, and while the audience remains silent. Helena's quarrel with Demetrius is made funny by the boy falling on to the floor, the girl crawling on to his back, and he trying to crawl from underneath. Bottom is carried off to Titania's bower accompanied by large phallic gestures and cries of triumph, when the concluding words in that incident suggest delicacy and silence:

> Come, wait upon him; lead him to my bower.
> The moon, methinks, looks with a wat'ry eye;
> And when she weeps, weeps every little flower,
> Lamenting some enforced chastity.
> Tie up my love's tongue, bring him silently.
>
> (III, i, 182–6)

Hippolyta and Titania, Theseus and Oberon, are openly doubled as if the actors' task was to make what likeness exists between the pairs as obvious and inescapable as possible, and to minimise the very considerable differences. Verbally certain phrases are given overwhelming importance by pauses and exaggerated enunciation, which only a directorial decision could permit. One such item picked out for emphasis is 'cold … fruitless … moon' (I, i, 73), so that the incidental phrase becomes a posed invocation, at least an evocation, for which the pace of the action (and of the metre) must be suspended. The actors seeking 'force', 'clarity', 'reality', or 'something which could influence people', are not presenting a free Shakespeare. Above all, they are trying to impress what they, themselves, have found, and Peter Brook has chosen.

Speaking after the rehearsals were complete, Peter Brook was obviously committed to one particular interpretation. While he quotes the text in his own support, it is noticeable how easily he contradicts it, or misrepresents it. Now he is far more concerned with what the experiments have thrown up, not only from the text but also from his own and his actors' experience, predilections and theatrical improvisation. So in an interview, he has said that: 'Theseus and Hippolyta are trying to discover what constitutes the true union of a couple' (*Plays and Players*), but what he should have said is that this issue came to interest the actors who had the task of presenting the two characters. I can find nothing in the text that suggests this concern, and it is quite as likely to derive from the fantasies of the experimenting and questioning actors as from the subtextual possibilities of the play. Speaking of Oberon, Brook put the dramatic point in extreme terms of 'total' love, whatever that means (it is not a Shakespearian phrase): 'a man taking the wife whom he loves totally and having her fucked by the crudest sex machine he can find … Oberon's deliberate cool intention is to degrade Titania as a woman'. The director has here left the text far behind. First, Oberon is a 'creature of another sort', a fairy not a man. Second, he does not choose a 'sex machine' of any sort, but expects Titania to have more general 'hateful fantasies' (II, i, 258) and is prepared for her to 'love *and languish*' for any 'vile thing' (II, ii, 27–34). When Oberon has enchanted Titania, he still does not know what she will 'dote on' (III, ii, 3), and hearing of Bottom's transformation says, specifically, that 'This falls out better than I could devise' (l. 35). Finally, the object of devotion is not an ass, but a man with an ass's head who never says a word suggesting an intention to fuck her, crudely or otherwise. Bottom's first thought is of how to escape, his second of answering Titania's attendants with requisite courtesy. When Titania is seen 'coying' his cheeks and kissing his ears, he is irritated by an itch, feels hungry, and then announces simply – or perhaps ambiguously – that he is tired (IV, i, 1–42). The director, with his actors to help him, has discovered something that is not in the play-text at all, but in the reactions, predispositions, theatrical consciousness and fantasies of their own, and he enforces this upon the audience's attention, with elaborate business, noise, vocal reactions and climactic placing at the end of the first half of the performance.

Most reviewers proclaimed a new way of staging Shakespeare after seeing Brook's production, but what seems newest in his work is a theatrical playing with the text in order to invent business and discover an interpretation that suits his own interests and the actors with whom he is working. This was said to release the potential of the text, but in fact the ' chaos' with which rehearsals began led to a limited, eccentric, single-minded (and rather simple-minded) interpretation. Once more the director has fixed the production so that certain points are made without ambiguity and without any danger that the audience could overlook them.

* * *

Will anyone find a way of presenting Shakespeare freely? Could an audience be allowed to find 'meaning' for themselves, be struck with whatever force or reality that their own imaginations can observe? Could there be a direct audience contact with the stage and with Shakespeare's creation, or do the necessities of theatrical art, the need for preparation and obvious excitement, preclude this open-ended experience? Could theatrical craftsmanship be allied to a production, which seemed as unstrained, as 'easy' and 'natural', as Shakespeare's writing? And as ambiguous, reflective, invitingly difficult, and alive?

To seek for such a way is, I believe, of utmost importance. It would not rediscover the 'essential' Shakespeare or explain anything in the plays for good and all. In no way would it lead to a museum produc- tion, seeking an elusive 'Elizabethan' accuracy of speech or behaviour. But it would bring Shakespearian qualities to the theatre, and allow audiences to respond in ways that are appropriate to Shakespeare's genius. The audience might become seekers – askers of questions, as Arnold would say – whereas, at present, they are invited to accept and share other people's answers.

The first step might be to place the audience in the same unvary- ing light as the actors, so that they can easily withdraw from the play and can look where they please. This would be a fundamental change, and it is, perhaps, no wonder that in an age of experiment this obvious one goes largely unattempted. Smallish theatres, in overall dimensions, and a thrust stage would probably be necessary to allow close contact with the actors and off-set the loss of scenic domi- nance. Composed and highlighted pictures with an obvious centre of interest would be replaced by a group of actors, viewed on all sides, expecting to be 'looked at' rather than displayed.

If a play were set in these conditions, the mere necessity of hold- ing attention would enforce greater vitality and variety in the acting. A far quicker overall pace would be required and varied rhythms, but it is arguable that Shakespeare's iambic pentameters may well be made for such speaking, not for the silences, pauses, exaggerated stresses, slow pulse and explicit sententiousness that are common today. Two-and-a-half hours should be able to accommodate all but the longest plays, and there would be no more productions that wind on to three-and-a-half or four hours, as not infrequently today: this length of time is required only by reason of laboured points, interpolated business, and carefully arranged crowd and scenic effects in which invention stems almost entirely from the director, not from the text.

Overlong group rehearsals should be avoided because they are the director's opportunity to create his own little dramas, and often dull the actors' responses and preclude repeated return with open eyes to the text. Actors could do much of their work alone, or in small groups, and they should not worry about ironing out all differences in approach or interpretation. If actors respond minutely to the varied potential of what they say, and remain open to renewed contact with Shakespeare's text and their own experience, their performances might remain constantly alert and variously suggestive, rather than definitive and limited. Options should be kept open, not decided by the director by the light of his own wit, or by his recognition of what, at the moment of one particular rehearsal, is the strongest of two or more opposing interpretations.

Movement should not be clearly fixed, because this limits an actor to certain rhythms and certain ways of confronting the other characters on stage. The performer should be free to discover new nuances, levels of meaning, contrasts, possibilities of physical action through his own skill, the changing context of the peopled stage, and a growing acquaintance with the text. If the actor remains free to discover, the audience may be encouraged to do the same: they would need to, because a clear line would not run through every incident for them to follow.

Costumes should not be limiting for the actor, nor relied upon to set the tone of a dramatic moment, or create striking contrasts at the cost of others. Both tone and centre of interest would come from the actors, if their physical and verbal performance is sufficiently dynamic. Except for necessary identifications and signs of rank or business, the costumes might well start as uniforms and be modified as rehearsals and performances require.

The dangers of such freedom from a director's limiting conception and guidance for actors, would be confusion, ordinariness, reliance on mere luck, lack of power or variety, and boredom of the audience. To create a work of art is to exercise choice and limitation: the experiment would be to allow the dominating, fixed and limiting influence to be only the easy, natural and complicated words of Shakespeare's text, the presence on stage of the actors and the business called for by the text. The advantages might be great: the audience's creative and necessary collaboration and the actors' continually renewed view of the play and the growth of their imaginative and technical powers.

The alternative to such radical departure from accepted practice would be to find a director who would maintain close contact with the text and seek to avoid limiting the actors' work by a single-minded interpretation. He would be courting failure, but also attempting to release Shakespeare's plays from confinement.

9

Representing Sexuality*

In everyday behaviour and dress, sexuality is now more apparent than in Shakespeare's day but in the plays, language and action express many unconscious or subtextual thoughts about sexual encounters. Close attention to puns and other wordplay, changing rhythms and silences revealed sensations and physical attractions that exercise a strong but tongue-tied influence on the action.

For the first four decades of the seventeenth century, Robert Burton, scholar, priest, dramatist (in Latin), and bachelor, investigated as best he could the varieties of mental and bodily disorders in people who are driven by desire for another person. His account of 'Love Melancholy', capacious and capricious – and sometimes very shrewd – mixes quotations from authorities of different persuasions with statements based on his own observation and reasoning. Both types of evidence are used to support his view that 'This love is the cause of all good concepts, … plays, elegancies … and all the sweetness of our life.' In the words of his own recital of pleasures, love is the reason for making 'all our feasts almost, masques, mummings, … plays, comedies … etc'. 'Danaus, the son of Belus', he goes on, had 'at his daughter's wedding at Argos, instituted the first plays (some say) that ever were heard of'. Theatre, he concluded, had been invented for love's sake and to give pleasure to lovers (*Partition* 2.3.3).

Theatre's association with love and sexual pleasure was taken for granted among most of Burton's contemporaries, whether they approved of the alliance or not. *Romeo and Juliet* was used as a source of effective phrases to be recycled in pursuit of one's own love. The

---

*First published as 'Representing Sexuality in Shakespeare's Plays', *New Theatre Quarterly*, 51, XII (1997), 205–13.

young John Donne was said to be 'a great visitor of ladies; a great frequenter of plays, a great writer of conceited verses', as if writing the early love poems had satisfied the poet in much the same way as female company and repeated visits to the theatres. In performance, actors could appear to be sexually driven and their audiences would respond accordingly. Jonson's Volpone, preparing to seduce Celia, boasts that

> I am, now, as fresh,
> As hot, as high, and in as jovial plight
> As when in that so celebrated scene
> At recitation of our comedy,
> For entertainment of the great Valois,
> I acted young Antinous, and attracted
> The eyes and ears of all the ladies present,
> T' admire each graceful gesture, note, and footing.
> (*Volpone* 3.7.157–64)

In Chapman's *Widow's Tears* (1605), Hylus, when rehearsing to play Hymen, 'ravishes all the young wenches in the palace'; at the subsequent performance, one young woman believes he 'does become it most enflamingly … he is enamor'd too', and another cries out, 'O, would himself descend, and me command' (3.2.19–20, and 83, 88, and 107).

Shakespeare's plays are full of sexually arousing incidents. Sexual passion drives the plot of many of them, notably the comedies, early and late, and *Romeo and Juliet, Othello*, and *Antony and Cleopatra*. In *Measure for Measure*, against his expectation, Angelo gives his 'sensual race the rein' (2.4.160) and so breaks habits of a life-time. At the very centre of this play is 'sharp appetite', 'prompture of the blood', 'a pond as deep as hell'; on its surface 'a momentary trick', 'dark deeds', 'a game of tick-tack' (2.4.161 and 178; 3.1.95 and 115; 3.2.167; 1.1.184–5). This comedy, alone, demonstrates that Shakespeare, expected his actors to show the effects of sexual arousal in their performances.

Even in the histories, the same currents run strongly: the Lady Margaret, soon to be Queen, is 'enthrall'd' to the Earl of Suffolk (*1 Henry VI* 5.3.101); Lady Anne forgets her undying hatred and repulsion in the presence of Richard III; the Princess of France seems to have a 'witchcraft' in her lips that can charm Henry V silent and render him complaisant (*Henry V* 5.2.175). Sexual passion is not central to *Hamlet, Lear*, or *Macbeth*, but none of these will be credible unless the audience senses the force of sexual attraction and appetite that contribute to the course of each play's action. So many plays deal outright with sexual desire and gender difference that anyone wishing to study or stage them needs to ask how Shakespeare dealt with these subjects and the means he expected to be used to enact them.

Silent Sexuality

The presentation of sexual passion has very special difficulties for a dramatist, especially at a time when plays were performed on open stages almost surrounded by a potentially unruly audience, and usually in daylight. Words and the activities of public life were the chief means at an author's disposal in Elizabethan and Jacobean theatres, not a simulation of the more intimate happenings of real life. Speaking a speech was then the appropriate way for an actor to demonstrate his quality.

Yet while sexual encounter was not easy to present in such a theatre, Shakespeare did so in a variety of ways, coping with the difficulties as if he took pleasure in overcoming the obstacles. Perhaps his most noteworthy device, in comparison with the practice of his contemporaries, was to draw attention to the inadequacies of words and so make the audience notice a tongue-tied sexual involvement. 'Silence is the perfectest herald of joy', says the enraptured Claudio in *Much Ado About Nothing* when forced to speak: 'I were but little happy if I could say how much (2.1.275–6).

Silence also grips Orlando when Rosalind approaches him at their first meeting in *As You Like It*: and only after she has left the stage can he speak of the 'passion [that] hangs these weights upon my tongue' (1.2.224–67). Sometimes two lovers are held still, gazing at one another while the words have been given to others: 'at first sight / They have chang'd eyes', says Prospero in one of the silences which mark Ferdinand and Miranda's meeting in *The Tempest* (1.2.440–1). And sometimes a silent exchange involves more than the eyes, as when Goneril, drawn by desire, gives 'strange oeillades and most speaking looks / To noble Edmund' (*Lear*, 4.5.25–6).

The first meeting of Isabella and Angelo in *Measure for Measure* has a sequence of silences which grow in length and strangeness until the sexual content of the scene seems to become almost unbearably stifled. Lucio fills in the gaps with comments on the progress of the encounter, and twice Angelo manages to do so, briefly and with amazement as if in a trance. Although not speaking directly of his overwhelming desires, he also manages to address Isabella, but again so briefly that it seems as if he is struggling to hide his feelings. The awkwardness of the encounter grows until everyone has left the stage, saying very little – and then Angelo acknowledges what has happened, at first using short exclamations and bitter questions. The very inadequacies of speech here suggest the resistless force of his sexual arousal: Angelo hardly knows what he does or what he is. He becomes more coherent in speech only when he tries to dismiss all that has happened as if it were a dream (see, especially, 2.2.173, 179).

Silent encounters are not always so tense. In *Troilus and Cressida*, outward signs of the heroine's sexual arousal are described just before she meets Troilus: 'she fetches her breath', says Pandarus, 'as short as a new-ta'en sparrow' (3.2.32–3). When she comes on stage she says nothing, while in her presence Troilus is also 'bereft of all words' until, after a time, he is able to hold her close to him with a kiss. When, they do start to talk together, it is to acknowledge their stumbling folly: 'the abruption' of what they say and the 'monstruosity' of their love (3.2.39–95).

Later in the play, when she has been taken off to the Greek camp, Cressida tantalizes her hosts with enticing words but, to the watching Ulysses, what she does and what she is are still more provocative:

> There's language in her eye, her cheek, her lip,
> Nay, her foot speaks; her wanton spirits look out
> At every joint and motive of her body.
>
> (4.5.55–7)

In *As You Like It*, sexual desire is said to be sudden and reckless on both sides, like a 'fight of two rams', and its effect brutal and overwhelming, like Julius Caesar conquering Gaul – 'I came, saw, and overcame' (5.2.28–31) – but on this occasion Shakespeare kept the actual encounter offstage and left others to speak of it subsequently.

Prevarication and Passion

Silence given some definition by either description or later acknowledgement did not solve all Shakespeare's problems when he wished to present sexually driven behaviour. He became progressively more skilled at finding the words whereby their speaker could show the processes and growth of desire. Words sometimes suggest sexual passions by what they do *not* say, rather than by what they do.

Prevarications, lies, evasions, hesitations, repetitions, exclamations, clumsy words, and nonsense can all be more revealing than direct and would-be truthful speech. An early example of a verbal reaction that reveals hidden desire while trying to hide it is Julia's repetitive and furious words to Lucetta which lead her to tear a letter sent from Proteus, when all the time she is longing to see and read, and ultimately to kiss, that letter (*Two Gentlemen,* 1.2.33–140).

In the Nunnery Scene, stumbling and lurching prevarications show the frightening effects of Hamlet's inward passion when he is in the sexually attractive presence of Ophelia. For him, she is either unattainable or else hopelessly corrupt, and so speech becomes repetitive, contradictory, and evasive; it strains, buckles, and breaks down into silence. Choice is difficult between the various readings which have found their way from Shakespeare's manuscripts into the original editions:

> OPHELIA How does your honour for this many a day?
> HAMLET I humbly thank you, well.
>   *or* Thank you, well, well, well.
> OPHELIA My lord, I have remembrances of yours
>   That I have longed long to redeliver.
> I pray you now receive them.
>   *or* I pray you now, receive them.
>   *or* I pray you, now receive them.
> HAMLET   No, not I.
>   *or* No, no.
> I never gave you aught.
> OPHELIA My honour'd lord, you know right well you did,…
>   *or* I know right well you did,…   (*Hamlet,* 3.1.92–7)

Such talk, torn into fragments, stumbling and then rushing forwards, driven by the force of deep sexual frustration, does not provide the punctuation and smooth transitions with which editors or compositors feel comfortable – or readers or actors either. Its effect in performance is to make the action appear to take place at a level of consciousness where thoughts cross and feelings collide.

In *Othello*, terrible disjunctions in sexually driven speech render words almost useless even as they are being used. They lead on to an epileptic fit, but not before Othello knows that his passion is beyond rational speech: 'It is not words that shakes me thus – pish! – noses, ears, and lips. / Is't possible? Confess! Handkerchief! O devil!' (4.1.41–3).

Verbal reiteration can show terrible sufferings caused by sexual longings and fears, as in Lady Macbeth's calling her husband to bed in her guilt-ridden sleep-walking or the staggering and driving rush into jealousy of Leontes in the very first act of *The Winter's Tale*. In this play, the progress in representing sexual feeling is towards rather than away from simplicity and silence, as seen at last when Hermione, restored to life, 'hangs about [Leontes'] neck' (5.3.112).

In an opposite and lighter vein, Rosalind recognizes very early on that love can make speech wayward and crazy and then proceeds to exemplify this with all the happy wonder of sudden discovery (*As You Like It*, 4.1.144; 3.2.370–5). Consciousness of sexuality's madness recurs many times in the comedies: the lovers of *A Midsummer Night's Dream* know themselves to be 'wode [mad] within this wood' (2.1.192); in *Twelfth Night*, Sebastian argues that 'I am mad / Or else the lady's mad' (4.3.15–16); in *Much Ado*, Benedick finds he can remember only stupid babbling rhymes to express his feelings (5.2.22–37). Perhaps Petruchio and Katharine both learn the truth of what her sister says: 'being mad herself, she's madly mated' (*Taming of the Shrew*, 3.2.240).

Uses of Bawdy and Personification

When a character is motivated by sexual instincts, a run of *doubles enten-dres* in his or her words will frequently show what is happening and where the mind is going. In *Much Ado About Nothing*, when Benedict and Beatrice spar with each other about warfare or wit, or about their views of themselves and other people, sexual allusion gallops ahead as if both speakers are willing riders of their most libidinous desires even while they are pretending to be at crossed purposes with each other.

When Rosalind talks about love to Orlando, or to Celia or Touch-stone, this bawdiness seems to come unbidden; and so it does between Viola and Feste talking about Orsino, or between Hamlet and almost anyone as he talks about almost anything. In Hamlet desire so mixes with fear that, in Ophelia's presence at the performance of *The Mousetrap*, his obscenities seem a calculated and public affront, or a revulsion so deep that it turns into heedless aggression. Yet bawdiness in Shakespeare's dialogue can also seem benign, an easing of other troubles, as in the 'sweetest morsel of the night' that Doll Tearsheet and Falstaff are about to share or in the teasing wordplay between Katharine of France and Alice, and, later, the warlike Henry himself. Between Florizel and Perdita, both dressed as shepherds at a pastoral feast in *The Winters Tale*, bawdy references slide easily into tenderness and reverence (4.4.127–53).

More directly, words can also bring a heightening of sexual expectation when they are used to call as witnesses the gods, lovers or monsters of Renaissance myth, or to summon memories of fabled dangers or pleasures to evoke an appropriate context. Prospero thus creates for Miranda's betrothal a masque of goddesses who represent female power, harvest riches, and unashamed beauty, and so enacts the 'present fancies' of a loving and apprehensive father for his only child and daughter (*Tempest*, 4.1.122).

Almost all the lovers in Shakespeare's plays seem to have such personifications present and alive in their thoughts and talk about them to show the excitement caused by sexual arousal. In the last act of *The Merchant of Venice*, Jessica and Lorenzo, alone at night and at ease on the beautiful hillside of Belmont, play a quiet and teasing game together, calling on great lovers from mythology to identify the feelings of their love and their instinctive fear, in counterpoint to the fuller harmony of music.

Such mythological references have very little to do with book-learning or pedantry, although scholarly notes in modern editions may give that impression. Sometimes abundant or curious words indicate mental excitement, but mythological names and stories are commonly used by Shakespeare to represent the boundlessness of sexual fantasies and the ever-present sense of sexually attractive bodies which haunt the minds of lovers.

For Perdita, they come almost tumbling out of her memory, as if she is possessed by mythological personages even more than by the delicate sweetness of nature. She responds to these stories as to her own fears and tender feelings:

> O Proserpina,
> For the flower now that, frighted, thou let'st fall
> From Dis's waggon! – daffodils,
> That come before the swallow dares, and take
> The winds of March with beauty; violets, dim
> But sweeter than the lids of Juno's eyes
> Or Cytherea's breath; pale primroses,
> That die unmarried ere they can behold
> Bright Phoebus in his strength – a malady
> Most incident to maids.
>
> (4.4.116–25)

And in *A Midsummer Night's Dream* Helena moves from mythology
to fabled beasts and on to generalized abstractions which bite more
deeply because of the context that has been provided for them:

> Run when you will; the story shall be chang'd:
> Apollo flies, and Daphne holds the chase;
> The dove pursues the griffin, the mild hind
> Makes speed to catch the tiger – bootless speed,
> When cowardice pursues and valour flies.
>
> (2.1.230–4)

For some characters, the supernatural world of holy scripture serves
in much the same way as a carrier of their thoughts. Olivia, intent on
possessing Cesario, calls it up in an instant:

> Well, come again to-morrow. Fare thee well;
> A fiend like thee might bear my soul to hell.
>
> (*Twelfth Night*, 3.4.206–7)

Sexuality and Actuality

Perhaps Shakespeare's most extraordinary use of words to express sexual
desire is the introduction, through metaphor and simile, of references
to the everyday processes of living. These give a tactile actuality to the
strange fantasies of sexual desire, a visual clarity, a shift from unmanage-
able abstractions to direct sensation and the ordinary business of life. By
such means the drama is presented in terms that everyone in the audience will have experienced – not those exclusive to book-learning,
wealthy privilege, or rare opportunity. Examples are everywhere, from
the early *Henry VI* plays to the very latest innovations in Shakespeare's
style and dramatic structure. A suckling child comes to the thoughts of
the Earl of Suffolk when parting from the Queen, his mistress:

> Here could I breathe my soul into the air
> As mild and gentle as the cradle-babe
> Dying with mother's dug between its lips ...
>
> (*2 Henry VI*, 3.2.391–3)

Olivia sees Cesario's lip, and her mind at once races on to think of a
guilty criminal, night-time and noon, roses and spring-time, and only
then comes to the heart of her message:

> O, what a deal of scorn looks beautiful
> In the contempt and anger of his lip!

A murd'rous guilt shows not itself more soon
Than love that would seem hid: love's night is noon.
Cesario, by the roses of the spring,
By maidhood honour, truth, and every thing,
I love thee so ...

(Twelfth Night, 3.1.142–7)

Seeing the youth to whom she is attracted, it is her references to everyday experience that give a 'body' to her speech that an audience is able to feel (*All's Well*, I.i.169–70), and by doing so they make her strange predicament more accessible to an audience in the theatre.

In *Antony and Cleopatra*, the lovers on their first entry speak with exaggeration and airy playfulness which could be taken as signs of mere weakness and triviality, and the Roman soldiers do so interpret them. Yet their mundane references to boundaries of land, beggars, and bills of reckoning (as in a shop or tavern) are all immediately recognizable, and neither grandiose nor exotic as might be expected. These words are not explicitly sexual but they ground the sexual content of this moment in everyday actuality. The reference to a new heaven and earth is to some degree mythic, but will also remind an audience of that new-found world across the Atlantic from which most people present must have seen a trophy brought by ship to London:

CLEOPATRA If it be love indeed, tell me how much.

ANTONY There's beggary in the love that can be reckon'd.

CLEOPATRA I'll set a bourn how far to be belov'd.

ANTONY Then must thou needs find out new heaven, new earth.

(1.1.14–17)

Everyday tactile images are often linked in Shakespeare's plays to the strangest and most unsettling experiences of sexual arousal, as when a lover vows 'to weep seas, live in fire, eat rocks, tame tigers ...' (*Troilus and Cressida* 3.2.76–7).

The Music of Sexual Speech

A further use of words to express sexual realities does not rely on their meanings, references, or allusions, or on their obvious evasions, their lies or incapacities. The very sound or 'music' of utterance speaks directly to the senses of a hearer, and Shakespeare skilfully used this to evoke the moods and rhythms of sexual activity. The effect is both mysterious, because it is never talked about, and compelling, because members of an audience are mostly unaware of this influence upon them and so do little to prevent its operation.

As the sound of performance changes, according to the sound of individual words and the on-going beat of iambic pentameters, so does the pulse of the audience and its attentiveness. In some scenes this music has a strong and heavy beat; in others all is slow and unforced, or uncertain and yet unhurried. In yet others, the variations of syntax, requiring certain pauses and certain extensions of phrasing, together with the metre, requiring certain emphases, build up a complex rhythm over a considerable period of time.

Such effects are not merely verbal and auditory. In the person of the actor, the 'music' of speech may be created by crucial changes of breath and nervous tension. Change of posture may also be necessary. No one can speak without making some bodily actions, and the more demanding the words spoken – in phrasing, metre, texture, reference and so on – the more complicated and impressive are those actions that make speech possible. In effect, the actor's body will take part in a kind of dance which is the physical concomitant of speech, necessarily responsive to it as well as its cause. When sexual activity is a central fact of the drama, performance can become like a combination of dance and opera, so musical does utterance become and so poised and defined its physical enactment.

Without skilled actors and a full audience to demonstrate, this is not an easy matter to prove, so the effect is often missed by readers and critics. Yet the importance of verbal music and its physical enactment as a means of quickening the audience's response can hardly be overestimated. The best proof of this power will always be skilled productions of the plays in a full theatre, but these conditions for research do not come on demand. Lacking this resource, the best alternative would be to read some suitable passage aloud, with an attentive ear and a watchfulness for the physical accompaniments of speech.

To realize the full effect of a speech in performance, any activity called for by the story of the play should also be taken into account. Consider, as an example, the occasion when Cleopatra and her ladies, overcoming earlier fears, are hauling the dying Antony up into the monument in 4.15: the repeated exertion of all their strength and the quick eagerness of Cleopatra's kisses mingle with the effects of speech, its *doubles entendres*, repetitions, emphases, delays, exclamations, its changing sentence structures, the metre's occasionally strong beat and its rests. All this, and the presence of anxieties about death, make up a complex dramatic moment in which the strength of sexual attraction can seem to find its breath as appetite strains for satisfaction.

These strategies in writing for performance have one common characteristic: all rely, to some degree, on the audience making good what is only partially achieved on the stage. Each member is invited to complete the illusion of sexual activity in his or her own mind, and left free to do so according to individual prejudices and predilections. When the drama is re-created, Shakespeare's representation of gender and sexuality is given its immediacy in the audience's active imagination according to each member's innermost feelings and desires. The very incompleteness of his depiction of sexual activity was one of the means whereby this particular subject could be given such a large role in the plays and the reason why it carries conviction in such variety and gives such widespread pleasure.

Modes of Imagination

In the last resort, all good theatre thrives by what happens in the minds of its audience and not by what happens on stage, but this may never be such a crucial factor in success as in its treatment of sexuality. For this subject, talk is never enough and words have comparatively little direct effect. Nor are actors capable of pleasing everyone in these matters, or of attempting to do so night after night and promptly on cue.

For representing sexual encounters, theatre is quite unlike other arts that depict the circumstances of our lives. In painting, sculpture, and especially film and photography, the artist can get his or her chosen effect, as fully as possible, once and for all: but in theatre, one performance is not sufficient. One person in an audience does not see from the same viewpoint as another and nothing can be made fixed and reliable. As if Shakespeare realized all this, sexuality and gender-difference in his writing are consistently suggestive and not definitive.

The task of arousing the private sexual fantasies of his audience and then giving them free play was a challenge Shakespeare undertook repeatedly and with seemingly endless invention. As actor-sharer in the theatre company, as well as dramatist, he must have felt the extraordinary power of this kind of audience response, its spontaneity and recklessness, its occasional intensity and multiple particularity. The actors would act the better for this stimulus so that the performance of an entire play might be given a more compelling life. In an Elizabethan theatre, the portrayal of slow or brooding sexual encounter was not practicable, but a whole world of suggestion was entirely possible, and was Shakespeare's means of awakening the audience's imaginations.

The use of young male actors to play the women's roles is an Elizabethan theatre practice that fits well with this way of writing, because their lack of a woman's sexuality could be supplied, along with much else, by the audience. Too many actresses have triumphed in the female roles for us to believe that this practice limited Shakespeare's imaginative input or that modern productions should follow Elizabethan precedent in this matter, but the texts of these plays are so dependent on suggestion for giving an illusion of sexual encounter that an audience will always be drawn to contribute, even when a female actor supplies more than a young male could ever contrive.

It might even be argued that in their day the 'boy actors' would have been more effective than actresses because their audience was not accustomed to public display of female bodies – as we have become through seeing innumerable advertisements, films, television entertainments, and theatre shows – all of which are frequently explicit sexually, and can depict the most intimate of occasions.

The use of 'boy actors' has been studied in many ways in recent years, so that Stephen Orgel, in his *Impersonations: the Performance of Gender in Shakespeare's England* (1996), can draw together much earlier research on this and related topics: about medical thinking in continental Europe by Stephen Greenblatt; about responses to public performance by Peter Stallybrass; about attitudes of audiences by Lisa Jardine and Jean Howard; about sexual anxieties by Valerie Traub; about the sexual attractiveness of young male bodies and what reactions might have been to this in Shakespeare's day by Eve Sedgwick and Alan Bray.

Orgel adds to this swell of scholarship by careful study of particular women who acted in some ways like men in real life at this time, but he makes his most useful addition to the debate by pointing out that the convention of using 'boy actors' was not a necessity forced on the theatres (see Introduction and p. 35). Women – even James I's own Queen – did act in amateur and provincial performances, while actresses who were permanent members of professional companies in other European countries continued to perform publicly when on tour in England. Scholars have been given a new question to consider: not only, 'How did boy actors serve the plays?' but, 'Why did all professional companies in London continue to rely on them?'

One answer to Stephen Orgel's second question is obvious: that the young male actors pleased their audiences and so the companies continued to use them. As to *why* they were successful, this review of some of Shakespeare's sexually driven scenes suggests that their short-comings when imitating women suited the way in which the plays were written. The audience would complete the suggestions emanating from the stage – and for this, in view of the extremely personal nature of sexuality, the absence of too strong a physical statement had special advantages.

While, some members of the audience might keep the real young man present in their minds as they viewed him imitating a woman, many others would have had no desire or need to do so. Each spectator would complete the image of life that was half-created on the stage for his or her own pleasure, according to individual tastes and instincts. In this respect, the mirror held up to nature presented an image that anyone could enter into and complete, with a sense of wonder and achievement as well as recognition.

It might be objected that such imaginative collusion is too sophisticated a mental activity to have a place in the truly popular Shakespearian theatre which attracted so wide a range of audience in terms of class, wealth, and education. But the fact is that many other equally popular theatres have used all-male casts and a considerable number of them continue to do so at the present time in competition with the mixed casts (and greater accessibility) of film and television.

In India, the Jatra Theatres of Bengal and Orissa, the Kathakali of southern Kerala and Theyam of northern Kerala, and numerous other old forms of theatre have traditions of all-male casts and have always been hugely popular. In Japan, Kabuki was once a popular form and has retained the Onnagata performers even though a great many other features of production have been modernized. In the casts of Beijing Opera, women are now fully established and whole operas have been written for performance by star actresses, but the popularity of the form, especially among younger audiences, has not been increased by this innovation.

An ability to fantasize about sex is not a rare gift and it need not be a sophisticated one: rather, this is a potential in everyone and popular theatre can readily exploit it. By doing so, it gives very reliable pleasures which audiences pay back with enthusiasm and applause.

Arousal Through the Imagination

Shakespeare and many of his contemporaries knew well enough the power of fantasy in the sexual part of anyone's life. Benedick in *Much Ado About Nothing*, having been tricked into thinking Beatrice loves him, has to face her when she is in a very dark mood, saying nothing to indicate any affection or any interest in him of any sort, but the facts of the matter have little to do with what he sees or hears: 'I do spy some marks of love in her', he announces before she has had a chance to speak (2.3. 222–3). When she has spoken, he sees double meanings that express hidden yearning in the least suggestive parts of her brief communication – in words that are, as plainly *un*loving as might well be invented. Orlando, in *As You Like It*, can speak fervently to 'her that is not here, nor doth not hear' (5.1.101); in fact, she *is* there, in disguise, but his words and her reaction to them indicate that his thoughts are not concerned with that bodily presence.

Robert Burton, in the course of his investigations, discovered a lover who would rave about his mistress when she was absent with the same passion and particularity as when she was present, and so become strongly aroused by his imagination alone:

> Her sweet face, eyes, actions, gestures, hands, feet, speech, length, breadth, height, depth, and the rest of her dimensions, are so surveyed, measured, and taken by the astrolabe of fantasy, and that so violently sometimes, with such earnestness and eagerness, such continuance, so strong an imagination, that at length he thinks he sees her indeed, he talks with her, he embraceth her ... Be she present or absent, all is one. (3.1.48)

Elsewhere he wrote of a rich young man who became 'far in love' merely by hearing talk and 'common rumour' about a certain fair woman: he was 'so much incensed, that he would needs have her to be his wife'. Among numerous cases of love induced by fantasy, when 'we see with the eyes of our understanding', Burton quoted Lucian about one who said he never read about a certain woman 'but I am as much affected as if I were present with her'.

All this fits well with modern knowledge, although Shakespeare's contemporaries are unlikely to have understood as fully as we do exactly how such sexual fantasies can be awakened and an audience be tempted to indulge them. We realize that while the new media can manipulate powerful images that directly and blatantly assault the senses, they continue to use suggestion as the major instrument for sexual arousal. While outright and unambiguous sexual statements are common today, a kind of stealth is employed when playing on fears and desires. Images are constructed so that they remain incomplete, understated, or unbalanced, and will thereby create in the mind of a viewer not satisfaction, but rather a wish to complete the impression and so think about the possession of some as yet unobtained object, to fantasize with some hope of enjoyment.

Jon Stratton's *The Desirable Body: Cultural Fetishism and the Erotics of Consumption* (1996) describes some techniques of suggestion which belong to present-day society and economy but work on our minds in much the same ways as those used by Shakespeare for the depiction of sexuality. This recent book would be a more valuable guide about how to read the plays than diatribes by puritan writers who attacked the theatre's practices in Shakespeare's day without enjoying any of its performances, or books of arcane knowledge about the natural world which bears little relationship to what we now know to be the facts.

Because the perennial power of suggestion plays such a large part in the treatment of sex in Shakespeare's plays, two rules may be formulated for readers and for actors and directors. The first is that words cannot always be trusted in this matter and can seldom be pinned down to a single or precise meaning. The second is that the whole truth is seldom presented on the stage: what is placed there is intended to awaken an imaginative response, not to create moments of actuality. Not only are characters given speeches that conceal or evade, but, when sexuality is most important for the drama, a full realization of what is happening has been left to the imaginations of individual members of the audience – it had to be this way, and it was effective and compelling this way.

10

Violence and Sensationalism*

At first, Shakespeare trusted language to represent cruelty and suffering but he then also sought other more direct means. By looking for what happens on stage, I became aware that in King Lear *silent suffering and vicious actions are used alongside sustained verbal expression of pain and tenderness.*

Elizabethan actors briefly chronicled the violence of their times and strove to act up to the sensational texts they performed. The speech from an 'excellent play' which Hamlet says he 'chiefly loved' was Aeneas' tale to Dido, and 'thereabout of it especially where he speaks of Priam's slaughter'. Recounting one of the worst atrocities of the sack of Troy, it re-creates the horror of an eyewitness. Pyrrhus is

> total gules, horridly trick'd
> With blood of fathers, mothers, daughters, sons ...
> And thus o'ersizèd with coagulate gore,
> With eyes like carbuncles, the hellish Pyrrhus
> Old grandsire Priam seeks. (*Hamlet*, II. ii. 451–8)

The armed soldier hesitates before killing the old and defenceless king; but then he goes to 'work'. Christopher Marlowe caught the same moment in his *Dido, Queen of Carthage*, but his Aeneas told how a trembling Priam prayed to Pyrrhus for mercy, and

> Not mov'd at all, but smiling at his tears,
> This butcher, whilst his hands were yet held up,
> Treading upon his breast, struck off his hands. (II. i. 240–2)

---

* First published as 'Violence and Sensationalism in the Plays of Shakespeare and other Dramatists', *Proceedings of the British Academy*, 87 (1995), 101–18.

Soon this Pyrrhus is swinging a 'howling' Hecuba through 'the empty air' and ripping the old man open 'from the navel to the throat at once.' Shakespeare's player continues the story but soon hesitates, begins again, and then comes to a shuddering halt, his face ashen. He weeps and can say no more: Hamlet promises to hear him out later, in private.

Without staging the violent act, theatre can use words to make us weep for Hecuba, requiring us to share the sensations of those who have seen and heard the violence. This histrionic power was an inheritance from ancient tragedy, given wide currency through imitations of Seneca embellished with further images of appalling horror. What can be read today as bad examples of literary over-kill were then played on the stage to 'let blood line by line' (Thomas Nashe, Preface to Robert Greene *Menaphon,* 1589).

But not content with words alone, Elizabethan and Jacobean playwrights went further than classical example. In their plays, defenceless men, women and children were murdered on stage in full sight of the audience. It was said to be 'some mercy when men kill with speed' (John Webster, *The Duchess of Malfi,* IV. i. 110), because death often came deliberately and slowly, the wound 'tented' with 'the steel that made it' (Webster, *The White Devil,* V. vi. 238–9) or a victim's crazed derangement prolonging the suffering. Men and women were tortured by those who seemed to relish what they did. Even a cardinal dying in his bed could hallucinate in terror and 'grin' horridly with the pangs of death. Shakespeare, called 'gentle' by those who knew him, introduced all these violent happenings in his plays and when he did not actually stage the brutality he could force his audience to witness the results of violence. Having presented the rape and mutilation of Lavinia offstage, he soon brought her on again and wrote elegant and ingenious verses so that a by-stander could point out the more sensational and pathetic elements in the spectacle of her suffering:

> Alas, a crimson river of warm blood,
> Like to a bubbling fountain stirr'd with wind,
> Doth rise and fall between thy rosed lips ...   (*Titus,* II. iv. 22–4)

Whereas Marlowe's Aeneas told of the heartless murder of Priam years after the event, Shakespeare's Macbeth, with blood still warm on his hands, speaks of what it was like to slaughter Duncan in his sleep, and he does so for an audience which has just shared the quiet and horrendous moment with Lady Macbeth, at only a little distance from the helpless victim.

It used to be said that the bloodletting so common in Elizabethan and Jacobean tragedies was the reflection of a more primitive age than ours, when men went about the streets fully armed while vagrants and ex-soldiers terrified ordinary persons, when bear-baiting was a popular sport, and punishment, even in homes, schools, or public places, would often be physically brutal and degrading. Now, however, we have come to recognise a day-by-day violence in our own time and, in the entertainments offered in television, film, theatre, and novels, we see that sensationalism is no longer old-fashioned or out of use. Our television screens, our dangerous city streets, the arrests, tortures, bombings, and killings that are reported in our papers no longer allow us to suppose that the violence in earlier plays and earlier lives can be relegated to what is irrelevant about the past. We understand now that a dramatist can feel morally obligated to bring violence on stage and not deflect attention from the most sensational events. Our world engenders violence and a theatre which does not deal with that will not engage with what most troubles us.

Rather than glossing over violence in the plays of Shakespeare or his contemporaries, passing quickly by and looking in another direction, we must pay close attention to their depiction of cruelty, pain, and unspeakable violence. We must recognise that a terrible atrocity has often been placed close to the centre of a play's action, drawing its characters into irreversible changes and affecting the final outcome more than any words. Violence must be taken into account in assessing the plays, as well as deeper niceties of character and finer issues of abstract themes.

The Most Lamentable Roman Tragedy of Titus Andronicus used to be Shakespeare's most unread and unperformed play: 'one of the stupidest and most uninspired plays ever written', according to T. S. Eliot (*Seneca, His Tenne Tragedies* 1927, p. xxvi). But times have changed; *Titus* has now been carefully studied in several editions and, since Peter Brook's production at Stratford-upon-Avon in 1955, it has been revived more frequently. Every critic can see now that in this play are seeds of much that has long been admired in *Richard II, Hamlet, Macbeth*, and, especially, *Othello* and *Lear*. These premonitions involve more than incidental words and images: how scenes are constructed, how silence and laughter are used, how madness can bring clarity of mind as well as pain and obscurity, how journeys off-stage contribute to the action, how alien characters hold their own course, how an ending can be patiently healing as well as catastrophic—all these dramaturgical devices are found driving the action forward in a play teeming with intellectual and emotional life. Could all this have happened if the writing had been seriously flawed by pandering to a public's taste for stupid violence and uninspired sensationalism?

Shakespeare did not abandon the sensationalism of *Titus* or that of the more lurid episodes in the three parts of *Henry VI*. Rather he pursued his interest in violence, and developed his use of it. Naked and undisguised, it is present on stage in later plays, and more especially in those which are commonly regarded to be at the furthest reaches of his imagination, *Macbeth, Othello*, and *King Lear*. Critics do not sufficiently recognise this because present-day readers and audiences often do not recognise or do not see the violence. Readers do not react in horror because they pay too little attention to the stage-directions implicit in the dialogue. Nor do audiences see and react to the violence because directors stage it with busy and intrusive artistry so that it is no longer raw and ugly. Peter Brook's *Titus* represented Lavinia's torture by substituting elegant red ribbons for her blood. The last appalling scenes were rehearsed repeatedly and the text cut progressively until performances were more acceptable and not plagued by the nervous laughter which the crazed brutality had provoked in early previews. Today's directors and designers follow suit and seldom allow a play by Shakespeare to be crude or harrowing. Violent scenes are rehearsed with more care than others until they become more routine, tastefully designed, carefully modulated in tone, balanced in form, fluently ingenious in movement. When blood is spilt, it happens exactly when and where the director decides. Designers make sure that lights are dimmed, or so tricked out with strobe effects that an audience cannot see anything for long and has difficulty in following what is happening. Shakespeare's violence becomes part of a scenic effect which generalises the particular and takes eyes and ears away from the appalling facts and individual responsibility and suffering. Shakespeare's plays should be staged boldly and openly, not with artistically co-ordinated care—an achievement which was unknown and would have been impossible in the theatre of his time. Played for each moment as it occurs on a platform stage without long and deeply considered rehearsals, without carefully controlled lighting, and without subtle and pervasive sound-support, violence in the great tragedies would make an indelible mark. When we read the plays we need to activate our imaginations and ask what the text requires to be done on stage, and then allow time for all that to be carried out in our mind's eye. Then Shakespeare's sensational stage-craft might give unexpected force to both words and action.

★   ★   ★

Shakespeare at the height of his career was still seeking new ways to deal with violence, as if he had not yet probed far enough into its nature and consequences. The most noticeable change over the years was a growing distrust of words to do the work. In the third part of *Henry VI*, when Rutland's tutor is dragged off stage, the 'innocent child' opens his terrified eyes and immediately addresses his assassin:

> So looks the pent-up lion o'er the wretch
> That trembles under his devouring paws;
> And so he walks, insulting o'er his prey,
> And so he comes, to rend his limbs asunder ...   (I. iii. 12–15)

The boy goes on to beg for his life, for time to pray, for a reason for his death. He reminds his killer that he has a son who might be slain. Then after the death-blow, he quotes Ovid's *Heroides* ironically, as his tutor might have taught him. So violence is made apparent by words, one step at a time, but in *Macbeth*, written years later, the young son of Macduff is silent when a messenger enters telling his mother to flee 'with your little ones' (IV. ii. 68). When the murderers enter, he seconds his mother's defiance recklessly—'Thou liest, thou shag-eared villain!'—and then, as a killer turns on him with 'What, you egg?/Young fry of treachery!', all is over and the boy cries out, 'He has kill'd me, mother./Run away, I pray you.' That is all; according to the folio stage-direction the mother exits crying 'Murder!' and prob-ably carries with her at least one more of her 'little ones'. Inchoate cries shatter the tension and a child lies dead. After the mother has run out, the last visual focus will be on the small corpse, until some-one, saying nothing, drags it away. Years earlier, in *Henry VI*, the last focus had been controlled by the exultant words of Clifford directing attention to his blood-covered sword.

Desdemona is given words to speak when Shakespeare for the first and only time directs that a woman should be slowly killed on stage. The shock and pain must have stunned audiences unprepared for such a scene, even though they had been led to expect that Othello would kill her. As early as Act III he had vowed revenge (III. iii. 451–66) and, before he fell down in a fit, he had revealed his tortured and murderous feelings. When he insulted and struck her in public, his retched-out 'Goats and monkeys!' (IV. i. 260) had foretold barbarity.

Just before the final scene, a quick and brutal killing is foretold in the frenzied hatred of his short soliloquy:

> Minion, your dear lies dead,
> And your unblest fate hies. Strumpet, I come.
> Forth of my heart those charms, thine eyes, are blotted;
> Thy bed, lust-stain'd, shall with lust's blood be spotted.
>
> (V. i. 33–6)

But as a trailer for the murder, all this is deceptive: Othello does not act in brutal frenzy but is charmed silent by Desdemona's beauty. He gives her time to pray and, having overcome her disbelief, he prays for her: 'Amen, with all my heart' (V. ii. 37). Then he utters some sound which is no word at all (l. 39). She reads a fatal message in his eyes and in the shaking of his 'very frame' (ll. 40–1, 46–8) but, unlike Rutland, she speaks uncomprehendingly. He still hesitates to act while pauses and repetitions indicate that they both have great difficulty in talking of what is about to happen. Only when she seems to weep for Cassio's death, does Othello act violently, but still without the decisive suddenness the audience has been led to expect. With 'Down, strumpet!' and 'Nay, an you strive—' (ll. 83, 85), a physical struggle begins and it is several lines later before he succeeds in silencing her and, as the stage-direction says, '*Smothers her*'. Why smother her? Indeed why struggle at all, when it is clear by the end of the scene that on his person or hidden in the bedroom there are three weapons that could all have finished the lethal work as soon as resistance was encountered? Emilia is '*at the door*' and calls, but still Desdemona is not dead; he continues to kill her until his short words, 'So, so' (l. 92). The actor must choose whether these are brutal or relieved, for at this point in the painfully protracted murder, Shakespeare has left the physical fact of death as the only undeniable piece of evidence about what has happened. The slowness of this killing is appalling, as are the inadequacies of speech.

After she has been left for dead, Shakespeare has Desdemona revive and speak temperately to shield her husband from his guilt. Yet one of the rare comments of a playgoer that have been recorded from Shakespeare's day tells us that this play was remembered for a physical fact, not for its moral issues or racial tensions, and not for its poetry:

> Desdemona, killed by her husband, in her death moved us especially, when, as she lay in her bed, her face only implored the pity of the audience   (*Times Literary Supplement*, 20 July, 1933).

Othello too, as he realises what he has done, expresses himself in terrible physical action: he lies down and roars (see 1. 201), and then, after all the torrents of words, he lets out a sustained and culminating wail: 'O Desdemona! Dead! Desdemona! Dead! O! O!' (l. 284). Later he does have a long death-speech, summing up his life for those who wait to take him prisoner to Venice, and it is justly famous for its commanding dignity; but as he compares himself to a 'base' Judean or Indian, and to a 'malignant' Turk, he also, against all habit and training, loses physical control and weeps. Finally, his true feelings are expressed unmistakably in action. In Shakespeare's source, the 'Ensign' and 'Moor' had pulled down one of the house's rafters and crushed Desdemona beneath it; Othello also exerts all his strength but, taking himself as a dog by the throat, destroys himself instantly. The text indicates that his action overwhelms everything that has been said. After an appalled silence, indicated by the incomplete verse-line, 359, Lodovico and Gratiano mark the change unmistakably: 'O bloody period!—All that is spoke is marr'd'. Othello then kisses, or strives to kiss, Desdemona's corpse; and adds a very few simple, bitter, and loving words. Then, for those present on stage, he and she have become an 'object [which so] poisons sight,' that it must be hid (ll. 367–8). If readers do not give themselves enough time to imagine what happens as well as what is said, or if the long delay and brutal action are not harshly and boldly represented on stage, Shakespeare's presentation of violence will be under-rated and his text itself misrepresented.

Shakespeare's earlier tragic lovers kill themselves using many words. Romeo is able to reflect on his own reactions:

> How oft when men are at the point of death
> Have they been merry! Which their keepers call
> A lightning before death. O, how may I
> Call this a lightning? …   (V. iii. 88 ff.)

Juliet supports her own decisive actions with far fewer words, but they are incisive and highly strung with conspicuous wordplay. It is almost as if Shakespeare did not wish the physical and emotional reality of teenage suicide to be experienced directly by the audience. Subsequently the families enter and express their grief in many words, as if Shakespeare wanted to compensate for having poeticised the violence.

Incoherent and physical reaction to violence is almost the rule in *King Lear*. The suffering of Gloucester is prolonged, unremitting, and often silent. His interrogation and blinding are carried out by Regan and Cornwall with a precise verbal marking of physical brutality which is reminiscent of the much earlier *Titus Andronicus*: 'Upon these eyes of thine, I'll set my foot' and 'Out vile jelly! / Where is thy lustre now?' (III. vii. 67, 82–3). They provoke Gloucester's defiance and condemnation, but when he is finally thrust out of doors the blinded man is silent. Finding Edgar to guide him to Dover, he does not recognise his son's voice and so stumbles forward uncertainly, even when supported and shown the way; he is at anyone's mercy, and when he meets Lear, whom he recognises by his voice, he cannot communicate with him. Eventually, after crying out 'Alack, alack the day!' (IV. vi. 182), he briefly begs to be killed by Oswald. When this crisis is over he does speak at greater length, envying the king for being mad:

> … how stiff is my vile sense,
> That I stand up, and have ingenious feeling
> Of my huge sorrows! Better I were distract;
> So should my thoughts be sever'd from my griefs,
> And woes by wrong imaginations lose
> The knowledge of themselves.   (IV. vi. 279–84)

When drums foretell battle he submits without words to being led away, and we can only guess at his feelings and 'imaginations'. When first brought before Regan and Cornwall, Gloucester had seen himself as 'tied to the stake' like a bear which has to 'stand the course' of being baited by fierce dogs trained for the job (III. vii. 53, 57): now, in the last battle, he is like one of the blind bears who were kept as more special attractions, to be tied to a stake and then whipped. (See Joseph Strutt, *The Sports and Pastimes of the People of England*, ed. J. C. Cox (1903), p. 206.) Gloucester remains motionless of his own free will by the tree or shrub to which he has been led. Edgar tells him to 'pray that the right may thrive'. (V. ii. 1–2) and then leaves. Now all that happens is '*Alarm and retreat within*', and even that will be in sound only if the noise of battle is heard from off stage as the Folio text directs. As the action of the entire play hangs in the balance, all that the audience is shown is a worn-out old man, who can see nothing and do nothing, and does not even understand who has brought him to where he is. Does Gloucester react at all as the sound of battle rises and dies away? We do not know, because Shakespeare has withheld all further words and stage-directions. All we are shown is the long-suffering body and sightless eyes.

This reliance on physical action was extraordinary and risky, as three considerations show. First, we know that the whipping of a blind bear in Paris Garden, not far from the Globe Theatre, was

> performed by five or six men standing circularly with whips, which they exercise upon him without any mercy, as he cannot escape because of his chain; he defends himself with all his force and skill, throwing down all that come within his reach and are not active enough to get out of it, and tearing the whips out of their hands, and breaking them.

No one approaches to whip Gloucester and this blind victim provides no entertainment. So what does this audience think, or do?

Second, consider productions of *King Lear* in present-day theatres where the hunched figure of Gloucester sits in a carefully chosen place, carefully cross-lit. Lights dim progressively, and a vast backcloth may redden to represent the off-stage battle; or perhaps carefully drilled soldiers with implements of war cross and recross in front of Gloucester; and all this time, appropriate music and semi-realistic sound will work on our minds with changing rhythm, pitch, and volume. The audience will sit in the dark, their eyes and ears controlled completely by the play's director working with a team of highly trained technicians. Then consider in contrast a performance at the Globe Theatre where the light on stage could not be changed or the sounds of battle orchestrated for maximum effect and meaning, and where all was what it happened to be as the play was revived for that one day only. The audience members, in the same light as the stage, were free to withdraw attention, move around (many were standing), and talk among themselves. The actor playing Gloucester had nothing to help him attract attention and not a word to say, as he sat alone with his eyes shut; he could have had only the vaguest idea of how long it would be before Edgar returned. The elaborate speeches of *Titus Andronicus*, holding the sufferer still and controlling the audience's thoughts, and the pyrotechnics of Pyrrhus's speech in *Hamlet*, are both missing. So too are the searching words of Romeo or Juliet, which simultaneously presented and veiled the horror of teenage suicide. Gloucester gains or loses attention because he is there, victim of violence and of his son's inability to speak to him of his presence and his love. The audience would have paid attention to Gloucester or not as they chose, and would have understood for themselves, or not. One might come to feel very alone, sitting in an audience which did not see what you saw or did not care; then suffering would seem to exist in a disregarding world. If one sat in an audience equally moved by what was silent on stage, then you might wonder if some words had been forgotten or if no words were the only possible response. Shakespeare has presented the consequences of violence so that the audience has to shoulder responsibility for its own reactions.

Third, we should remember how mutilated old men are shown on television or film. Briefly they fill the screen in arresting and horrific images, and then disappear before attention can flag, leaving no trace behind; and that effect is created, not as part of the continuous performance of a play, but as something cunningly arranged, for that moment, by make-up artist, costume designer and fitter, the people in charge of set, lights, and sound, and, most significantly, by cameramen and editor. The result is no more than a few seconds of overwhelming horror or pathos, instead of being one part of a sustained performance by an actor who in some real ways has been living in the role. In the theatre, an actor represents the lived experience of violence, rather than achieving, with other people's help or hindrance, a moment or two of sensational effect.

★　★　★

The death of Gloucester is off-stage, but a little later Edgar tells how he revealed himself to his father:

> I ask'd his blessing, and from first to last
> Told him my pilgrimage. But his flaw'd heart—
> Alack, too weak the conflict to support!—
> 'Twixt two extremes of passion, joy and grief,
> Burst smilingly.   (V. iii. 195–200)

The words are unsensational; rhythms hesitant and delicate; yet the line of thought is sustained until a new idea is introduced on 'pilgrimage'. This word relates the whole story of Gloucester and his son to traditional ideas about the course of human life. The word has not been heard before in the play, but in this context when the audience's mind is free from any on-going action, the single word might be able to shift perspective and draw events together. It could suggest that Gloucester had no longer resisted 'further' travel (see his words at V. ii. 8) or that Edgar is putting the best face on the 'fault' of not revealing himself to his father earlier; or it could encourage an audience to think for itself and be ready to believe that what it has witnessed has had some purpose or some purging effect. The

single, unsensational word is not prescriptive, but it could act as a
mental lever to lift the story of Gloucester into a different context
and encourage revaluation.

This reference to a pilgrimage draws on a part of the inheritance
of Elizabethan tragedy which was at least as important as the classical tradition mediated through Seneca. Reading the scriptures aloud,
delivering sermons, and performing plays were all ways of re-enacting
the story of the Old and New Testaments and as such provided example to dramatists who wished to reflect the violence of the times.
Until the last few decades of the sixteenth century, various kinds of
death, torture, and suffering were presented on stage in the highly
popular mystery plays. Their audiences saw people like themselves
acting the violent killing of Abel by Cain, the scourging of Christ and
his crucifixion, and the multiple martyrdoms of saints. In the Massacre
of the Innocents, Herod's knights slaughter one new-born baby after
another, deliberately and with slow pleasure or mockery. Blood flows
and the mothers cry, roar, curse, lament, fight back, and call for vengeance, like the victims of atrocities in Elizabethan secular dramas:

> Alas, my bab, myn innocent,   my fleshly get! For sorow
> That God me derly sent,   of bales who may me borow?
> Thy body is all to-rent!   I cry, both euen and morow,
> Veniance for thi blod thus spent: 'out!' I cry, and 'horow!'

As they fall on the ground, the old trots are told to get up, 'Or by
Cokys dere bonys / I make you go wyghtly!' Scenes of such violence were acceptable when presented as part of the whole story
of God's dealing with mankind. They were provided with various
verbal signposts—such as the anachronistic reference to God's bones
in this quotation—and with symbolic actions and stage-properties.
Angels, devils, prophets, saints, and God himself were brought on
stage, or above or below the stage, to watch, comment, or interact.
Any violence might therefore become acceptable by being seen in
a wider and more considered perspective than that provided by its
immediate context.

Elizabethan dramatists profited from this example. In Marlowe's
Faustus, the Good and Bad Angels are only part of the intellectual
setting for the horror of Faustus' entry to hell; besides calling on the
horses of the night to run slowly, he also sees the stars that reigned
at his 'nativity' and 'Christ's blood' streaming in the firmament. In
Edward II, before the king is forced to resign his crown and is then

tortured and hideously murdered, Marlowe brings on 'a mower', seen
at first as

> A gloomy fellow in a mead below;
> 'A gave a long look after us my lord … (IV. vi. 29–30)

So Time is calling for Edward, as he does for Everyman. For the
murderer of the last scene, Marlowe, invented Lightborn: Edward
never hears this name, but the audience has had it marked clearly for
them, so that mankind's first innocence may be lodged somewhere
in their minds during the final tense and then elaborately brutal
confrontation.

The Ferryman in the anonymous *Arden of Faversham* (*c.* 1591–2),
who appears out of a 'mystical' and 'smoky' mist, speaks with the
authority of a Charon, offering prophecies, and prompts an audience
to see the moment over against the challenge of death and punishment for sin. 'He looks as if his house were afire, or some of his
friends dead', he says of a man with a deceiving wife, speaking to
Arden who is in just that situation. Again, 'I hope to see him one day
hanged upon a hill', he says of Black Will (xi. 13–4 and xii. 38) who
is due for such a fate. Yet, like the rest of the play, the Ferry episode
is set in everyday surroundings and not at the entrance to Hades on
the shores of the Styx.

John Webster used strong symbolic markers as his tragedies draw to
a close, some pagan or folk in origin, some Christian. Just before the
end of *The White Devil* (1612), Bracciano's Ghost appears with a '*pot
of lily-flowers with a skull in't*' and he throws earth on Flamineo and
shows him the skull. Lilies were—as Ben Jonson had it—'special hiro-
glyphics of loveliness', (*Masque of Beauty,* 1608, marginalia f) but to
that are added the symbolic earth and skull. Flamineo knows that the
appearance is 'fatal' for him. In *The Duchess of Malfi* (*c.* 1614), Bosola
brings on stage '*coffin, cords and a bell*' and calls himself 'the common
bellman', sent to condemned persons before they are hanged; the
whole parade is like a masque, intended to bring the Duchess 'By
degrees to mortification' (IV. ii. 173–7). But the strongest symbolic
marker in this play is created when Webster, altering his sources, has
the Duchess escape to the shrine of Our Lady of Loretto. Two pil-
grims are marvelling at the 'goodly shrine', as in Caravaggio's painting of the Virgin's appearance at Loretto carrying the infant Christ
(1603–5). Reputed to be Mary's own home transported miraculously
from Galilee, the famous and extremely wealthy shrine was dominated

by a great statue of the Virgin with a nobleman in armour kneeling before her. So Webster has the fugitive Duchess and her family kneel to pay a 'vow of pilgrimage' to the Virgin whose functions were to be an example of domestic virtue and to intercede for men and women, being the closest of them all to the godhead. The Duchess is soon surprised at her devotions and banished from the state of Ancona, but this solemn and elaborate show of reverence will make a large and lasting impression in performance; there has been nothing like it in the play so far, and later echoes will help to keep it in the audience's mind. After the Duchess has knelt again, this time to be strangled, she is given some of the properties of the Virgin. When she revives from death and her eyes open, Bosola says 'heaven in it seems to ope … to take me up to mercy' (IV. ii. 342–59)—'Mercy' being what the Virgin begs on mankind's behalf at the throne of God. It was widely believed that when the Devil demanded Mankind from God, the Virgin Mary interceded and obtained Mercy for him; see, for example, *All's Well that Ends Well*, III. iv. 25–9. Later the Duchess seems to appear in a vision to Bosola and strengthens his 'penitence' (V. ii. 345–9). With a 'face folded in sorrow' as if at an empty tomb, she appears also to her husband, while an echo 'like his wife's voice' tells him to 'fly his fate' (V. iii. 44–5, 26, 35). Protestants in England considered the cult and miracles of the Virgin to be vain superstitions but Webster used them to define the nature of his play's violent action in contexts where his characters themselves were unable to do so.

Shakespeare introduced markers to chart the course of violent action. Obvious examples are the Clown in *Titus Andronicus* who carries two pigeons as gifts to settle a brawl, the Pursuivant and Priest who encounter Hastings on his way to the Tower in *Richard III* and so remind him of the affairs of the world and those of heaven, the death-like Apothecary at Mantua in *Romeo and Juliet*, the Gravedigger in *Hamlet* who had started digging graves the day young Hamlet was born, and the 'good' King of England, reported to be just off stage in *Macbeth*, whose hand has been given such 'sanctity' by heaven that it cures 'wretched souls' (IV. iii. 140–59). In each case the audience is alerted during the course of the tragedy so that whatever happens in its violent conclusion may be seen over against the traditional view of life and death.

The strategy of this device is clear enough, its effect much less so. At this distance in time it is hard to put oneself on the same footing as members of Shakespeare's audience. Yet it would seem that an acceptance of the widest context for violence might have been part of the reason why attitudes to public executions were so very different from those of today. In London, before a large or small gathering, the public executioner would hold the severed head aloft and cry out 'Behold the head of a traitor', and that seems to have justified the barbarity of the occasion. It is hard for us to credit that the horrific stories in *Foxe's Book of Martyrs* should have been considered such good reading that copies were made publicly available in churches and colleges, and at court; or that Sir Francis Drake should take a copy around the world with him for recreation and kept himself from being bored by colouring the pictures. (See William Haller, *Foxe's Book of Martyrs* (1963), pp. 220–3.) Repeatedly the extreme tortures described are said to be suffered for the Protestant faith of England, and that seems to have made the unbearable tortures acceptable and profitable reading.

Shakespeare's conventional markers accompanying a play on its way to a sensational climax do not insist on a religious or doctrinaire interpretation. They activate the audience's minds to think of the consequences of what is happening but do not supply a firm moral framework or comprehensive judgement on a play's action. In *King Lear* even the persons who act as markers are not clear-cut or distinguished from the other characters, as the English King and Gravedigger had been. The stages of Lear's journey toward a last torture on the 'rack of this tough world' (V. iii. 313–5) are marked by encounters with persons in his story who have been transformed so that they represent a series of recognisable challenges whereby mankind's resources are progressively displayed and tested.

The King had sought out the Fool when he returned from hunting but when the storm rages the Fool proceeds to lose confidence and becomes absorbed in his own loneliness. He shivers with cold and Lear sends him to take cover as if he represented 'houseless poverty' (III. iv. 26): in him, Lear and the audience have witnessed 'what wretches feel' (l. 34). The next person he meets is Edgar transformed to Poor Tom, the mad Bedlam beggar obsessed with fiends. The audience sees Lear take the false madman for real, especially when he is most violent. Edgar does not answer when Poor Tom is asked the cause of thunder, but when asked what his study is he replies as Tom at once: 'How to prevent the fiend, and to kill vermin', and it is at this point that Lear takes him aside to talk 'in private' (III. iv. 154–61). When Tom says '*I smell* the *blood* of a British man' (ll. 179–80), Lear and he leave the stage together: defiance, killing, and darkness unite King and madman in a common cause. The Bedlam hospital took special precautions against inmates attacking visitors; as Thomas Dekker explained, they could be

> … like hungry lions
> Fierce as wild-bulls, untameable as flies,
> And these have oftentimes from strangers' sides
> Snatched rapiers suddenly …
> (I, *The Honest Whore* (1604), V. ii. 162–5).

Unlike the audience, Lear believes he is in the presence of a dangerous madman, pursued by fiends and obsessed with violence, and this is now the company he seeks. When next seen he is intent on destroying his daughters, in a most terrifying way:

> To have a thousand with red burning spits
> Come hizzing in upon 'em—   (III. vi. 15–16)

Here the Quarto and Folio texts vary, but both show that, from this moment on, Lear is determined to arraign or anatomise his cruel daughters, and stay close to Mad Tom. Gloucester acts as the next marker—a blind man ready to recognise authority—and Lear's mind lurches forward again to see the exercise of power in a new or even revolutionary way: morality as a cruel joke, and the world as 'a great stage of fools'.

None of these three encounters is necessary to Lear's story; they are in the play solely because Shakespeare has invented and willed their presence. By their means violence and pain are shown in a meaningful progression, through physical to mental torture, through suffering in one's self to suffering together with a misused, violent, and unjust world. The course of Lear's suffering may seem so purposefully ordered that a Jacobean audience might have accepted it without flinching, even without being offered any religious consolation or explanation; and any audience might be encouraged to recognise what is at stake.

The culminating atrocity of this tragedy, Cordelia's assassination and Lear's immediate revenge upon the assassin, takes place off stage. But just as amazing is the old king's continued physical energy when he enters carrying his daughter's corpse, crying out in suffering, longing, and anger, and searching for a sign that Cordelia lives. Lear, like all of Shakespeare's later tragic heroes, attempts to assert himself by means beyond the use of words. Saying 'never' repeatedly to express his sense of loss and despair involves him in a physical struggle which leaves him in need of a deeper breath, so that he asks for a button to be undone. Today we would say that Lear struggles against the restriction of breath associated with a heart attack; it would seem that Shakespeare was recreating the actual circumstances he had witnessed in a death from a series of strokes.

He thanks the servant and emphasises, with short-phrased, repetitive questions and injunctions, his need to see, or to think he sees, that Cordelia lives, and his need for others to see and believe it too. Does he think that she indeed revives? We cannot know, because he falls silent. What we do know is that he continues to give signs of life until Edgar says 'He is gone indeed', four lines later. The end of this tragedy is not summed up in the last words of its protagonist; it is defined by Lear's physical struggle to assert his will to live and to hope, in a body that can bear no more. The words which others speak ensure that the audience watches intently as the actor draws on his own hidden resources to sustain the role to its wordless end. Here, lies the performative centre of the play's last moments. Then as Albany orders 'Bear them from hence' (I. 318), a procession will form and move off slowly, keeping in view the bodies of the King and his daughters after all words are spoken.

Lear has to experience the consequences of violence, his own as much as that inflicted on him; there is no palliative available except endurance and a sharing of the experience. When Lear says 'Thank you, sir' to whoever undoes the button, it may be a sign that he has changed so that now he 'takes care' of other nameless people (see III. iv. 32–3). But who could be sure of that? Perhaps this servant is a last 'marker' on Lear's journey, introduced to show, as if accidentally, a change in the hitherto thankless king. The only time he has thanked anyone before is when Kent, as Caius, trips up and berates Oswald in Act I, scene iv. What is certain is that nothing less than the actor wholly concentrated and open in performance at the end of an exhausting role is able to bring continuous credibility and force to Lear's broken speeches and so carry him beyond words until he 'is gone indeed'. Showing the utmost reach of Lear's consciousness, Shakespeare seems to withdraw from the contest, leaving actor and audience responsible for any meaning that might be extracted or constructed from what has happened. He has brought the audience so close to the consequences of violence, that only the actor's power to complete and find the accumulated truth of his role, stands for the play's conclusion.

This sustained and finally close focus on the person who suffers has consequences for many who try to understand what Shakespeare has written. For dramatists writing today, it demonstrates a way of exploring the nature of violence and its consequences which should make them pause before using more modern devices drawn from film and television. These accentuate momentary sensation rather than process and discovery; and provide visual images so compelling that an audience must either submit to them uncritically or withdraw attention, as if it were not happening.

The performative nature of the conclusion of Shakespeare's later tragedies should encourage theatre directors and designers to seek ways of staging them that will not destroy the close-focused particularity, immediacy, inexplicability, unpredictability, and deep involvement provoked by his stagecraft. An artful and commanding impressiveness is not an acceptable substitute.

The critic and scholar have a harder task, for no amount of quotation from the words of a text is sufficient to explain the image of violence and suffering which the plays provide. Nothing short of the whole progress of the action, through familiar markers, can give some sense of what is at stake at the end of a tragedy. The issues declared in the play's dialogue are comparatively easy to grasp, but to understand how Shakespeare held the mirror up to the violence of his times, and so to the violence of ours, it is necessary to pay attention to what is done as well as what is spoken. This implies that criticism should not only refer to the words of a text, but also to an experience of the play in sustained performance.

The demands on an actor are perhaps greatest of all. If you have ever been present as an old and bereaved father dies of two successive heart-attacks and at this last moment tries to assert to his friends his will to live, his love, and his hope for the future, then you will know the kind of reality which Shakespeare has asked the actor to perform at the close of this prodigious play. Instead of holding attention with impressive rhetoric and affecting images, the actor must appear to struggle physically to speak of the simplest but crucially important matters so that those who listen cannot know precisely whether Lear dies in hope or in despair. Both must have taken possession of his mind during the last eddyings of consciousness. Gone are the plumed troops of words and the pretended horrors of bloodletting, and in their place the summation of a life and a performance before which an audience must be hushed and attentive. As a dead march concludes the play, any comfort the audience draws from its painful events must be derived from its own thoughts; from those on stage is heard only:

> The weight of this sad time we must obey;
> Speak what we feel, not what we ought to say.
> The oldest hath borne most: we that are young
> Shall never see so much nor live so long.

Has any dramatist left more to a single actor than Shakespeare does as King Lear dies? Has any dramatist left more to an audience? In the last moments of this tragedy, having earlier posed many questions and named many doubts, Shakespeare gives little guidance on how to react to what is played on stage. What does it all mean, what can be understood? What does it *do* for an audience? After showing the violence in sensational ways, Shakespeare offers an opportunity for silent thought and compassion.

Part IV
Directors

11

Franco Zeffirelli's *Romeo and Juliet**

Directors use Shakespeare's dialogue to suit their own purposes and it can become a question as to whether an audience sees the original play or a new adaptation of it. After extensive rehearsals and workshop experiments, a mixture of both is usually staged and a careful account of performance is needed to evaluate the director's shaping influence.

An editorial in *Theatre Notebook* spoke of 'revelation', *The Observer* of 'revelation, even perhaps a revolution', and *Theatre World* of excitement, 'unity of presentation', and a 'reality which lifted one inescapably back to medieval Italy'. These are examples of the enthusiastic reception which kept Franco Zeffirelli's production of *Romeo and Juliet* in the repertory of a London-based or touring company of the Old Vic from 4 October 1960, into 1962, bringing them a greater success than they had enjoyed for more than a decade. Yet on the morning after its first-night, the critic of *The Times* spoke coldly of the performances, and in *The Sunday Times* Harold Hobson described a failure: to his disenchanted view, Romeo was 'well-spoken' but 'pasty-faced and sulky', Juliet flapped 'her arms about like a demented marionette'. After its season in London these conflicting reactions seem less remarkable: it was a production of unique and consistent achievement which exchanged a number of conventional virtues for others which are not often found in our presentations of Shakespeare. And it was effected with such intelligence, sympathy and authority

---

*First published as 'S. Franco Zeffirelli's *Romeo and Juliet*', *Shakespeare Survey*, 15 (1962), 147–55.

that we can now take stock and ask how important these unusual
virtues are for this play and, perhaps, for others.

★   ★   ★

The break with custom was clearest in Zeffirelli's visual presentation
of Romeo. Audiences have come to expect a dark handsomeness,
reminiscent of Sir Laurence Olivier in a production of 1935. A white
shirt was usually open at the neck; a dark wig accentuated a tall, noble
brow; eyes were made-up to appear large and deep. The pose chosen for
official photographs usually suggested a lonely, haughty and brooding
mind. With some additional swagger from the cloak Motley designed
for him, Richard Johnson's Romeo at Stratford-upon-Avon in 1958
was in this tradition. Another recognizable but less common strain is
the poetic: this is graceful, fluent, light. Michel Bernardy's Romeo
for Saint-Denis's Strasbourg company in 1955 exemplified it, looking
like some 'herald Mercury'. Both these traditions Zeffirelli broke. John
Stride, his Romeo, wore no velvet; he had no wig, no cloak, no orna-
ment; his shirt did not open at the neck. One of his costumes, devised
by Peter Hall (the designer, not the director), seemed to be made of
tweed, and none of them imposed grandiloquent postures; they were
comfortable, hard-wearing, familiar clothes in greys and greyish-blues.
In them, this Romeo could sit, squat, run or stroll; he could run his
hand through his hair and look insignificant among a crowd. He was
so little the gilded youth that it seemed odd that he should have a personal servant. Clearly, this director had paid less attention than usual
to the opening words of the Prologue: 'Two households, both alike in
dignity'; but in recompense he had avoided the meaningless gloss of
'fancy-dress' which many other Romeos assume with their splendid
clothes. John Stride seemed to be English rather than Italianate, lively
rather than sensuous; and he looked more convincingly in his teens
than other actors of the part who have, in fact, been equally young.
   To varying degrees all the young people in the play, except Paris,
shared these qualities. Perhaps the Capulets were more richly dressed
than the Montagues, but all the youth of Verona were at ease. Running
and sauntering, they were immediately recognizable as unaffected
teenagers; they ate apples and threw them, splashed each other with
water, mocked, laughed, shouted; they became serious, sulked, were
puzzled; they misunderstood confidently and expressed affection
freely. Much of this behaviour had been seen before in Peter Hall's
productions of *A Midsummer Night's Dream* and *The Two Gentlemen*

at Stratford-upon-Avon, but besides dispensing with the magnificent clothes of Hall's Lysander or Silvia, Zeffirelli did not condescend towards his young lovers and did not underestimate them. He gave prominence to a sense of wonder, gentleness, strong affection, clear emotion and, sometimes, fine sentiment, as well as high spirits and casual behaviour. His characters were exciting and affecting as well behaved and less responsive heroines and heroes could never be.

After the first visual surprise there were others. Despite the prodigality of the director's invention, the stage-business seemed to spring from the words spoken, often lending them, in return, immediacy, zest or delicacy. So the unpompous behaviour could catch the audience's interest for the characters and for the old story. In the balcony scene after Juliet (Judi Dench) had been called away, there was a still silence on her return before she dared speak again or Romeo dared to come out of hiding: this was given meaning by Romeo's preceding soliloquy:

> I am afeard,
> Being in night, all this is but a dream,
> Too flattering-sweet to be substantial. (II, ii, 139–41)

And by illustrating their mutual sense of awe and fear, their response to the seemingly precarious nature of their new-found reality, which at this time needs each other's presence to be substantiated, the still silence gave added force to the memory of Romeo's words. It also helped to prepare the audience for the direction and urgency of Juliet's following speech:

> If that thy bent of love be honourable,
> Thy purpose marriage, send me word tomorrow…

Words and stage-business together drew the audience into the dramatic illusion. Such should be the aim of all directors of plays, but Zeffirelli was unusual among his contemporaries in unifying Shakespeare's words and an inventive, youthful and apparently spontaneous action. Again, as the lovers leave the stage with the Friar to be married, Romeo walked backwards so that he continued to face Juliet who was supported on the Friar's arm: Romeo was 'bewitched by the charm of looks' (II, Prol., 6) rapt in

> … the imagined happiness that both
> Receive in either by this dear encounter. (II, vi, 28–9)

So the stage-business took its cue from the words spoken and centred Romeo's interest, without respect to absurdity or other concerns, on his delight in love. As they met adversity and danger, phrases like 'Stand not amazed' (III, i, 139), ''Tis torture' (III, iii, 29), 'Blubbering and weeping' (III, iii, 87) were all directly and convincingly related to the action, and consequently they were far more compelling than is customary in productions which deliberately seek a sumptuous setting and exotic mood.

The street 'brawls' were realized in the same way. The fight between Mercutio and Tybalt had a mixture of daring and mockery which reflected the exaggeration of the text:

> Consort! what, dost thou make us minstrels? an thou make minstrels of us, look to hear nothing but discords: here's my fiddlestick; here's that shall make you dance. 'Zounds, consort!   (III, i, 51–5)

Since few people in a modern audience can judge its fine points, the conventional duel usually appears either elegant and correct, or dangerous, or sometimes impassioned; it rarely reflects the tone of this passage. Yet Zeffirelli made the fight high-spirited, like the words. Mercutio, gaining possession of both swords, used one as a whetstone for the other before handing Tybalt's back—stopping to wipe its handle with mocking ostentation. With such preparation, Romeo could respond to Mercutio's sour jests after he is wounded as casually as the text demands—'Courage, man; the hurt cannot be much'—without appearing callow; the dying man's protestations could be taken as the holding up of an elaborate jest. Enacting the mood of the text in this way did not devalue the scene: the bragging turned to earnest all the more effectively with the suddenly involved and simple words of Romeo, 'I thought all for the best' (l. 109).

Visually, Zeffirelli's presentation of the young characters was remarkable, but not very original: he had gone further and was more consistent in a development already common—in less subtle and responsible hands, it is all too common. The greatest innovation of his production lay in unifying words and stage-business, in making the actors' speech as lively and fluent as their physical action. The result was that the dialogue did not appear the effect of study and care, but the natural idiom of the characters in the particular situations. It was a long time since Shakespeare's text had been so enfranchised. Juliet's 'I have forgot why I did call thee back' is often answered with rhetorical neatness, or passionate emphasis, or fanciful humour, in

Romeo's 'Let me stand here till thou remember it' (II, ii, 171–2), but in this production the reply was frank and happy, appropriate to the quick sensations of the situation and suggesting a mutual response; the literary finesse of the text was not used to draw attention to itself but to give form and pressure to the dramatic moment. Or again, the interchange between the Friar and Romeo:

> *Fri.*... wast thou with Rosaline?
>
> *Rom.* With Rosaline, my ghostly father? no;
> I have forgot that name, and that name's woe.   (II, iii, 44–6)

was transformed by making Romeo blurt out 'I have forgot that name' as a sudden realization, a thought which had, at that instant, come to him for the first time: it was still an antithesis to the Friar's expectation, as a literary analysis of the speech would show, but its sudden clarity was represented and accentuated by the manner in which it was spoken.

Some critics complained that this treatment of the dialogue destroyed the 'poetry' of the play. But it would probably be truer to say that the poetry was rendered in an unfamiliar way. Zeffirelli has directed many operas, and turning to a Shakespeare production he ensured that many speeches were tuned with musical exactness. Changes of tempo, pitch and volume were used to strong dramatic effect. For example, when Romeo called 'Peace, peace!' at the climax of the Queen Mab speech, Mercutio's 'True' followed quickly and flatly, and then, changing the key, 'I talk of dreams ...' was low and quiet, rapt in mood. This director knows more about musical speech than most of those working in our theatres today. There were, however, some notable lapses: Mercutio's speech and Juliet's potion soliloquy lost their cumulative effects because they were broken by too much stage-business (Juliet writhed about in a red spot-light); the moments of incantatory stillness, which can have, in T. S. Eliot's words, a 'winged validity' beyond their immediate dramatic impulse, were surrendered for livelier effects; and the actors seldom delighted in the 'concord of sweet sounds'. But Zeffirelli's animated style of speech was appropriate to much of the dialogue of the young characters in the play: in its new dramatic life the 'poetry' showed its bravery, *élan*, gentleness. By making it sound like the natural idiom of the lovers and their companions, the director was restoring many of the original tones, and original freshness. In *Much Ado About Nothing*, Benedick says that Claudio was 'wont to speak plain and to the purpose, like an honest

man and a soldier', but being turned lover he is 'turned orthography;
his words are a very fantastical banquet, just so many strange dishes'
(II, iii, 19–23). Romeo is such a lover: meeting with Mercutio after
the balcony scene his verbal wit runs 'the wild-goose chase' and
he is told: 'now art thou what thou art, by art as well as by nature'
(II, iv, 94–5). The 'art' of much of the poetry in this play was surely
intended to sound like a delighted and energetic response to immediate sensations, and in regaining this impression the actors responded
in an appropriate way to the conscious artifice of their text. Their
speaking reflected many of its moods, mixing humour with concern
(as in Juliet's 'Swear not by the moon'), mockery with envy, passion
with fear and hesitation. The metrical basis of the speech was sometimes insecure, but its colour and movement were often wonderfully
present. Individual actors and actresses have achieved this dramatic
life in Shakespearian roles—Laurence Olivier and Dorothy Tutin in
recent times gifted and unfailing among them—but here the same
quality was sustained through whole scenes. The director had treated
wit, rhetoric and 'poetry' as an integral part of his production.

★   ★   ★

His success was chiefly with the young characters in the earlier part
of the play. The first signs of merely routine handling were in the figures of authority. The Prince was given customary emphasis by two
attendants with halberds, a voluminous gown and, by the standards
of this production, rich accoutrements. On his first entry he stood
right up-centre, and his words were accompanied by a muffled, roll-
ing drum off-stage. But he lacked dramatic life comparable with
that of the figures around him: the stage devices had added only an
undefined impressiveness. This might be judged appropriate for his
early appearance, but on his return after the death of Tybalt, when he
stood down-stage centre, he still seemed out of touch with the other
characters, for these hitherto agile and fluently organized figures
immediately became fixed in postures at either side. In the last scene
where the Prince finds himself implicated in the general sorrow and
guilt ('for winking at your discords'), he stood unmoving, high above
the heads of everyone else on the stage, and necessarily spoke in the
earlier lifeless and formal manner. The director did attempt a more
animated Friar, but here the business he invented seemed inapposite
and occasionally impertinent: in the middle of his first speech a bell
sounded off-stage and he stopped to kneel and cross himself, and

when Juliet met Romeo at his cell he stepped between them to effect a comic collision involving all three figures—a kind of humour wholly different from that quieter kind written into the lines he speaks—and this stage-trick was repeated before the end of the short scene. In the last act, at the tomb, the Friar had such little relevance to the dramatic situation that he did not re-enter after he had left Juliet alone with Romeo's body: his speeches and all reference to him were cut.

While Zeffirelli had created an animating style for the story of the young lovers, he had not found a means of comparable life-likeness to represent the authoritative figures which Shakespeare has made the centre of important scenes..... Even when it was Romeo and Juliet who assumed new dignity and authority in confronting catastrophe, this director seemed unsure of touch. Juliet's 'Is there no pity sitting in the clouds...?' (III, v, 198) was said hurriedly, sitting on the floor, as if she needed no strength of mind to frame and speak this question.... Juliet's concluding line in this scene, with its authoritative and calm phrasing, 'If all else fail, myself have power to die', was said lightly on the point of running from the stage. Similarly, Romeo's stature in the final scene was belittled by failing to show his authority and compassion before the dead bodies of the other young men, as Shakespeare's text ensures: his description of Paris as 'One writ with me in sour misfortune's book' and:

> Tybalt, liest thou there in thy bloody sheet?
> O, what more favour can I do to thee,
> Than with that hand that cut thy youth in twain
> To sunder his that was thine enemy?
> Forgive me, cousin!

were both cut from the text and no such effect was attempted.

Important moments of grief also seemed underplayed. The distraction, frustration and fear of the young lovers were well represented with nervous intensity; the fault here was that the cries and groans and other physical reactions were sometimes at odds with the technical demands of long speeches with elaborate syntax and rhetoric. It was the more general and more considered grief that seemed hollow. The mourning for Juliet when she is discovered as if dead was staged formally like the authoritative scenes, and anonymous servants were introduced mechanically, two at a time, to extend the tableau and so attempt to effect an impression of climax. This indeed is one old-fashioned way of responding to the formal nature of the verse [and] elsewhere it might serve; but in this production it was in glaring contrast with the minutely and freshly motivated stage-business of adjacent scenes. The dramatic illusion previously established was lost in this presentation of general sorrow and was replaced with something that bore little or no resemblance to it. Romeo's address to the Apothecary showed the failure to represent a more considered grief. This is a speech of peculiar difficulty, for it must manifest complex reactions. In a vigorous handling, Zeffirelli concentrated on its agitation, so that his Romeo repeatedly struck and browbeat the 'caitiff wretch'. Here the difficulty was that this manner could not present consideration and compassion, responses that are implicit in:

> The world is not thy friend nor the world's law;
> The world affords no law to make thee rich;...
> There is thy gold, worse poison to men's souls,
> Doing more murders in this loathsome world,
> Than these poor compounds that thou mayst not sell...
> Farewell: buy food, and get thyself in flesh.   (V, i, 72–84)

And the long and detailed description of the apothecary's shop and wares issued strangely from the mind of this Romeo, given over to turbulence and spite. The scene should surely be directed in a way that can show how grief *and* resolution have entered deeply into Romeo's soul, making him precise, understanding, compassionate, sharp, subtle and even cynical: it is a complex moment that cannot be presented by a simple pursuit of energetic expression.

The still moments of general or deliberate grief were, like the figures of authority, unsatisfactory. The concluding scene indicated how far Zeffirelli, despite his sympathetic handling of almost all of the earlier acts, failed to respond to Shakespeare's text in these matters. He cut a hundred and twenty consecutive lines, those from the last of Juliet's to the Prince's 'Where be these enemies?...'. The outcry of the people, the 'ambiguities', the concern to find the 'head' and 'true descent' of the calamity, the general [sense of failure] in which the Prince at last finds himself implicated along with the others, the call for 'patience', the demand for 'rigour of severest law', were all sacrificed. The main reason for this was not shortage of time, for the scene was then extended by much interpolated silent business: anonymous servants embraced in pairs, symmetrically placed as a statuesque expression of general grief; [in unison,] without being ordered to do so, they moved the bodies of Romeo and Juliet to the catafalque; in a slow procession, accompanied by singing off-stage, the supposedly reconciled families departed with composed neatness at opposite sides of the tomb, without a look at the dead bodies and without recognition of each other; Benvolio and the Nurse were then reintroduced to take silent farewells of the bodies; and, finally, to swelling music, the lights faded with impressive slowness until the curtain fell. The ending had been refashioned as a solemn, exotically illuminated dumb-show. In comparison with the animated interplay of words and action that had preceded it, this spectacle seemed empty and meaningless. The conclusion of a production that had gripped and moved its audience was pretentious, sentimental and vague. Again it must be admitted that the discrepancy was not unexpected ... Directors working in the English theatre seldom respond to Shakespeare's presentation of authority and responsibility or of understanding and compassionate grief. This is surely a loss. The Prince's acknowledgement of complicity is Shakespeare's own addition to the story as he found it in Arthur Brooke's narrative poem, *The Tragical History of Romeus and Juliet.* Moreover we know that he was deeply concerned with the ways in which responsibility is learnt in adversity: the theme recurs at important crises in plays throughout his career. It is found when Richard the Second is imprisoned, when Henry the Fifth prays before Agincourt, and, later, when Lear, Pericles, Cymbeline, Leontes and Prospero become suppliants. Such a climax in *Romeo and Juliet* depends on the preceding hundred and twenty lines which Zeffirelli cut. And these lines have important dramatic interest on their own account. Compared with Arthur Brooke, who gave Juliet two long speeches immediately before her death, and with Otway, Cibber and Garrick, who revised the play in the seventeenth and eighteenth centuries and invented final speeches for the heroine, Shakespeare has hurried her last moments; he allowed her only the briefest possible utterances and brought the busy watchmen on stage immediately afterwards. Shakespeare gave time, words and action at this important culmination of the tragedy to the crowded stage as one after another of the characters kneel as 'parties of suspicion' and as the two families stand silently listening. The Friar's long speech is so tightly written that it is difficult for a director to do anything but keep it almost intact or cut it out entirely; its very texture shows that it cannot represent a slackening of interest by the dramatist but rather a determination to show the manifold ways in which small, over-confident human decisions had worked together with some kind of density, a 'greater power than we can contradict'. Shakespeare's complicated and highly-worked last movement of the tragedy suggests that, however powerful destiny may seem, man and a Prince among men react to catastrophe with a sifting of responsibility and a demand for justice:

> Go hence, to have more talk of these sad things;
> Some shall be pardon'd, and some punished.

Zeffirelli's change to dignified dumb-shows of grief could not endow these words with the socially responsible, seemingly endless particularity of Shakespeare's full text. To present *Romeo and Juliet* satisfactorily [the performance must sustain] the dramatic life of the entire last scene and those earlier moments of authority, responsibility and compassionate, understanding grief, which prepare for this conclusion.

★   ★   ★

In part the shortcomings of this production may have been due to a lack of sympathy because several of the less successful passages are known to be capable of lively presentation. In part it was probably due to a weakness in the metrical control of speech, for most of these moments involve sustained utterance or counter-pointed phrases. It may also be bound up with the timing of the production as a whole.

At the very end the director used a slow pace in order to make the invented conclusion impressive, but this was after he had hurried some speeches which demand time to give the impression of consideration and after he had cut much from the second half of the play: III, iv and IV, iv were cut completely, the beginning of IV, ii, the musicians from IV, v, the first twenty-three lines of the important scene of Romeo in Mantua. It looks as if the earlier Acts had been given too easy a rein. Discounting two intervals, the performance lasted two hours and fifty minutes: the first part, up to the end of II, ii, took an hour; the second part, up to the end of III i, took forty minutes; and this left but an hour and ten minutes for most of Act III and the whole of Acts IV and V. It may well be that Zeffirelli purposely tried to speed up Acts III, IV and V, sensing that the tempo had become too slack.

The beginning was slow in order to establish characters and atmosphere. For example, Romeo's first entrance was long and silent accompanied by shouting and laughter off-stage; it showed his solitary, self-absorbed nature at the cost of narrative pressure. To introduce Mercutio with Benvolio in II, iv, time was taken to show them lounging in the street and encountering two casual passers-by who then left the stage before the first of Shakespeare's words had been spoken. After the Prince had pronounced judgement for the death of Tybalt, the stage emptied very slowly until only the Chorus was left and then he closed the scene by slowly walking the full depth of the deserted stage and, again slowly, lifting his hands in a gesture of despair. Some of the long pauses were made in order to strengthen the lively speech and action, but the style of acting was not the chief cause of slowness: that was rather the scenic realism. Twice a curtain rose to show the stage covered with smoke giving a hazy impression and to singing or calling and a whole crowd of stage-dressing super-numeraries. Two sets of curtains were used within the proscenium so that the scenery could be changed on every possible occasion, even if to disclose merely 'another part of the streets' or 'another room in Capulet's house'. Some of the changes marked the change of mood implicit in the text: the most effective was to Juliet's bedroom with pale blue walls and a tall bed furnished with the same blue and white, making these colours dominant for the first time and giving a sense of space, femininity and domestic peace. But all too many scene-changes were trivial in effect, one being only more or less commodious than the other or cumbersomely providing a large and by no means essential property, such as the desk for Friar Lawrence placed before an all but meaningless back-drop.

The audience and critics generally admired the settings which were designed by Zeffirelli himself—although their mechanism and scenic realism were often old-fashioned in contrast to the style of act-ing. But on reflection we may question their usefulness and tact. With a simpler, but not necessarily less evocative setting, the new, alert style of action and speaking might have made an even greater impact and the 'realism' centre more in the human behaviour on which the story and the tragedy depends. By the same means, the tempo could have been more brisk which would have strengthened the motif of 'sud-den haste' which is found in Shakespeare's text repeatedly, and with insistence:

> It is too rash, too unadvised, too sudden: Too like the lightning... on a
> sudden one hath wounded me, That's by me wounded... Tybalt, that an
> hour Hath been my kinsman... let Romeo hence in haste... Hie to your

chamber... Hie you, make haste... hie hence, be gone, away! ... Come, stir, stir, stir! ... Uncomfortable time, why camest thou now ...? ... O mischief, thou art swift... Stay not to question ... then I'll be brief.

Such phrases are found in almost every scene after the first few and are not without significance. The pace, or momentum, of events can help to represent the 'star-crossed' elements of the love story and so enable Romeo and Juliet to appear to be fighting with growing urgency against an increasingly complex concatenation of misfortunes, against a narrative logic that seems to emanate from 'inauspicious stars' beyond man's control. The speedier overall tempo which a simpler setting would have permitted could have aided this element of the tragedy.

And, to return to the earlier and even more important point, a simpler setting with a brisker pace would have allowed the director to give the breathing time which is necessary in Acts III, IV and V for presenting the theme of responsibility and the deeper understanding which men learn through this catastrophe. The young characters of this production were so compellingly alive that the loss of the full play is the more unfortunate. It would be a pity if Zeffirelli's unity of speech and action, his enfranchisement of the elaborate dialogue as the natural idiom of the characters of the play, were to be associated in the public's mind with a tragedy which seemed to have lost its momentum and lifelike qualities half-way through performance.

12

Three Kinds of Shakespeare*

Acting style, stage settings and stage business, as well as verbal emphasis and characterisation, are powerful ways in which a director can control a play in performance. Noting the means that are favoured in a production will reveal the director's contribution and is a measure of the play's possible effects on an audience.

At the National Theatre, in 1964, those fortunate or persistent enough to obtain a ticket saw a starred performance by Sir Laurence Olivier, an Othello whose words could startle and whose actions were inventive and sensuous. His last speech can serve as an image for the whole production. Othello, naked beneath a simple white gown, closed only at the waist, kneels on a low bed placed down-stage centre with tall hangings around it disappearing into the 'flies' behind the top of the proscenium arch. He clasps Desdemona's dead body to his chest, as if she knelt with him, and he raps out a loud: 'Soft you!' After the following pause his voice is surprisingly quiet, almost soft: 'a word or two before you go'. And then without break, continuing the impulses that had changed his voice, Othello kisses Desdemona on the neck, sensuously engrossed. Then the speech follows with recollected formality: 'I have done the state some service...'.

For the production of seven history-plays in a series at the Royal Shakespeare Theatre, Stratford-upon-Avon, in 1964 (the three parts of *Henry VI* freely adapted to form two plays only), a representative image might be a scene change. There is music and a slow, purposeful filing off-stage, nicely judged to illustrate the political factions and the concerns of the characters. The lights change and two large, dark,

*First published as 'Three Kinds of Shakespeare', *Shakespeare Survey*, 18 (1965), 147–55.

triangular-based structures turn before a dark, trellised back-ground. And the stage is now a battlefield, with instruments of war, care-worn soldiers, and the slow yet alert tempo of battle. Other notable features could be chosen to represent the Stratford productions, especially the acting of Peggy Ashcroft and Hugh Griffith, but the deliberate scene-changes are demonstrative of the originality and distinction of this season as a whole.

At the 1964 Edinburgh Festival, Joan Littlewood's production of *Henry IV, Part I* by the Theatre Workshop Company (with re-arrangements and cuts and some interpolations from *Part II*) can be represented by the conclusion of its first half. Hal is backing away on the bridge stage that was constructed across the Assembly Hall of the Church of Scotland. Poins remains in the centre. He wears a trim, black velour bowler hat, a single ear-ring, high heeled, blue suede boots, and dark ski-pants. He bends forward as he listens to Hal's words (addressed to Peto in both Quarto and Folio texts): 'We must all to the wars, and thy place shall be honourable.... Be with me betimes in the morning; and so good morrow, Poins.' The delivery of the words is not remarkable and in the centre of the picture is the listener, not the speaker. Poins is smiling; puzzled; embarrassed, perhaps; ingratiating; there is a servility in his jaunty appearance, an insecurity in his knowing manner.

One element common to these three images is a determined realism, of sensuous embodiment in Olivier's Othello, of the side-effects of power politics in the Stratford Histories, of psychological observation in Joan Littlewood's *Henry IV*. This element is realistic in the sense that it is meant to awaken in the audience a recognition of actual events. And the realism is determined because it is continu-ously attempted in contrast to unrealistic elements: the undoubted showiness of the star actor; the simplification of the motives of men involved in power politics; the witty vitality of the highway, tavern and rustic scenes in the Workshop production.

Eccentricity is another feature of the three productions. But Shakespeare is so large that any enactment tends to seem odd; even those rare productions, that seem on first viewing to fill a play to its very limits, will be thought in ten years' time to have missed whole areas of Shakespeare's invented world. And with eccentricity these 1964 productions had a further object in common: a strenu-ous search for a 'way to do Shakespeare'. For more than sixty years English directors have been engaged on this quest, but their efforts have recently been intensified and multiplied. (Financial help from the State for two competitive theatres may be a cause of this, or new influences from contemporary dramatists and from theatre directors of other countries, or, perhaps, the thought that a distinctive brand of Shakespeare, a production with a clear image, would gain more attention from the general public.) Today theatre directors are convinced of the need to make Shakespeare 'come alive'. They search, experiment, debate, justify and try to learn.

★ ★ ★

The stage-settings at Stratford represent only one part of that theatre's obvious and advertised experimentation. The isolating effect of John Bury's cross-stage platform for *Measure for Measure* in 1962 or the dwarfing effect of his spacious flats, steps and ramp for *Julius Caesar* in 1963, have given way to a more variable design. Sometimes a vast background without local emphasis is seen behind a completely empty, level stage, marked with rectangles in a perspective that enhances the impression of space. At other times, one or two large pieces of scenery, with steps, recesses, doors or windows to choice, come in from either side, giving intimate and localized settings. Trees, greenery, thrones, prison-bars also vary the setting, but large steps or rostra are seldom introduced so that movement can always be free and often wide-ranging. For battles, group entries or spectacular opportunities (like the lists at Coventry in *Richard II* or the embarkation of Henry V at Southampton) the stage is filled with nimble and well-drilled supernumeraries giving, by action, costume, properties and make-up, an extraordinarily complete attempt at verisimilitude. This mixture of the vast and localized, with a reliance on actors to 'dress' the stage, is a useful solution to the problems of providing a decor for Shakespeare; it is capable of sustaining the audience's interest through most of the seven plays. At present it is used too indulgently, in that too many items are introduced to support the actors—especially torches, carts and animals; and scene changes or fairly simple entries often take up thirty to sixty seconds before the play can proceed. The scenery accounts in part for the slow tempo of the Stratford productions.

In colour the set has small variations of a basic brown, black and grey, and simple sharp contrasts for costumes and properties. The variations are shrewdly used and associated with differing textures (not unlike a fashionable mode of interior decoration): wood, various metals, gloss, matt and stippled surfaces, coarse fabrics and

smooth, leather and silk. By apparently economical (though probably
expensive) means the stage can vary as widely in tone as in form.
Particularly memorable was the austere use of black and white for
the Archbishop Scroop scenes and the black, dull tones for Henry
IV's bed-chamber. The French court was distinguished from the
English by the usual means of colour contrast, but in this neutral set
the details of peacock blue and gold were more than usually effective.
The only conspicuous omission in the range of effects was wealth
and assured regality; Henry IV's words:

> the perfum'd chambers of the great,
> Under the canopies of costly state ...

bore no relation to what the audience had seen.

The directors of the plays—Peter Hall, John Barton and Clifford
Williams, working in collaboration—would not be likely to judge
this omission to be important. For another of the experiments of the
Stratford season was a continuous emphasis of violence and of the
shallowness of politicians' pretensions. The plays became a high-class
cartoon, a relentless horror comic. An elevated tone was sustained
by restrained colour in the setting, slow tempo and deliberate utterance. And, with this, horror and violence were presented by liberal
splashes of blood, and by inventive business that elaborated every
opportunity for the exhibition of cruelty and pain that the text suggested, and more that were foisted on to the text. Joan of Arc cut
her own wrist like a Tamburlaine with a very large sword; Young
Clifford's head was cut off on stage and carried around upon a spear;
Clarence was drowned in the malmsey-butt at the back of the stage,
rather than 'within' as the words of the text direct. Going beyond the
requirements of the stage-directions and dialogue, action was realized as horribly as possible: Richard II struck the dying Gaunt with
a whip repeatedly; when he smashed the looking glass in he did so
with his bare fist and so inflicted pain upon himself; in prison he was
tethered by a huge, noisy chain that had to be flung aside to allow
movement and which he used as a weapon that threatened to pull
himself down in the last struggle with his warders—the sound and
apparent weight of that chain may well have been the dominating
impression given by the prison scene. Fights were arranged with
persistent ingenuity, important ones with disparity of weapons to
heighten interest, as Hotspur with a two-handed sword against Hal
with sword and buckler, or Douglas using a spiked mace against a

sword. Deaths were thoroughly painful; sack was thrown around and splashed liberally; Hotspur and Lady Percy rolled on the floor in their love-fights; Henry IV was given a foul-tasting potion to drink after its ingredients had been ground in a mortar by a monk-like doctor clothed in black. Repetition lessened the effect of these devices, but they were placed importantly at dramatic crises: *Henry IV, Part I* did not end with the king's deceitful and dramatically ironic exhortation:

> And since this business so fair is done,
> Let us not leave till all our own be won

but with Vernon in death agonies, swinging in a noose; he was then cut down and Worcester climbed to take his place. This experiment had a slight connection with current talk of a 'theatre of cruelty' and the Royal Shakespeare Theatre's experimental programme of that name shown to the public in the L.A.M.D.A. studio in 1963; but it lacked the severity of Peter Brook's innovating production of *Titus Andronicus* or the emotional depth and rigour required by Artaud in his newly translated *The Theatre and its Double*. Its most obvious effect was a grand-guignol grip on the audience (especially in the first four or five plays that each member had seen); its most assured effect the verisimilitude given to certain horrific episodes in the text of *Henry VI*, the earliest in date of composition. The most interesting achievements were the mob-violence that accompanied Bolingbroke's judgment on Bushy and Green, building that into a scene of general social unrest rather than a farther revelation of the emergent ruler, and, more surely within the scope of the text, the very ample provision of exhibits for Falstaff's discourse on a dead man as a counterfeit. Thus the directors' exaggeration of violence served to accentuate one vein in the text of these plays that has often been obscured by a picturesque indulgence in pageantry and royal panoply.

The shallow, cartoon-like presentation of the major political characters was another continuous feature of these productions, and it, too, was most satisfactory in the plays written earliest. Sharp verbal juxtapositions were pointed for comic effect without concern for the loss of dignity. Burgundy's

> I am vanquished; these haughty words of hers
> Have batt'red me like roaring cannon-shot
> And made me almost yield upon my knees.
> (*1 H VI*, III, iii, 78–80)

so relished the rapidity of his change of sides that the audience was encouraged to laugh. So too, the multiple throwing down of gages before Aumerle in *Richard II*, IV, i, quickly deflated the pretensions of the newly loyal nobles. Wars and rivalries became what Shakespeare once called them: a 'comic sport'. Edward IV wooed the widow so slowly that his lechery was foolish as well as his government; and later when Warwick surprises him, '*bringing the King out in his gown, sitting in a chair*' (IV, iii, S.D.), the directors had him dragged out on a mattress where he was lying with a whore and sent both off-stage as nearly naked and foolish as possible—a rhetorically impressive scene was made to seem like a notorious comic strip. Equally, Henry VI's ineffective attempts at friendship and love were comically played. David Warner in this role, and in the first half of his *Richard II*, used nervous smiles and a loose-limbed awkwardness to suggest anxious timidity. Richard's commands were under-played so that even these gave an impression of weakness:

> Think what you will, we seize into our hands
> His plate, his goods, his money, and his lauds

was said with neither assurance nor effort. Later, when York remarks on his eye 'bright as is the eagle's', Richard's 'We are amaz'd' was very quiet and flat.

For the central political characters of the later plays, Hotspur, Hal, Henry IV and Henry V, and for the virtuoso role of Richard III, the lack of psychological subtlety deprived the productions of long-valued qualities. Ian Holm's Richard was childish in his humour; he sat alone after the scene with the two religious men—here soldiers comically disguised—and kicked his heels. At the end, he was more concerned with his own importance than with his fear, stressing, for example, the second personal pronoun in: 'I fear ... *I* fear'. His character did make a changing impression as the play proceeded, but in one direction only; towards violent fury, expressed in vocal power and tremendously taxing fights. At the end a monster died: he had struck Catesby a blow when he offered help, but his voice began to fail so that 'A horse! a horse!' was weak as well as terrible and mad; and his death pangs were prolonged close to the audience at the centre of a vast empty stage. Here was little intimation of a tragedy, little scope for any reaction to Richard besides aversion.

Hotspur was comic and coarse, so that Lady Percy's praise of his 'chivalry' seemed wholly fantastic (and out of keeping with her own hoydenish behaviour in the first part of the play); and Henry IV's envy of his character, wishing Hal were like him, seemed absurdly misplaced. Henry IV was nettled and sour, with little indication of his ability to rule and his strength of spirit. Hal was coldly played, as if the actor's main task were to prepare the audience for his 'rejection' of Falstaff. When this point was reached it was easily reached, so that the new king's speech was neat and wholly controlled. The major impression of the last scene of this play was left for Falstaff and his fellows to make in the succeeding episode. Henry V was unexpected in another way. He was so obviously thoughtful, careful and, occasionally, sharp, that he never attempted to enter the outline depicted by the Chorus of 'cheerful semblance and sweet majesty ...' or 'A largess universal, like the sun'. The Chorus was allowed to orate and make flourishes about a quite different play, as if the directors thought that all he said had to be ironically wrong.

Although simplification of character was not the most noticed feature of the Stratford productions, it was probably the most regrettable because it obscured deeply observed and imaginative elements of Shakespeare's art. The directors indulged and supplemented the horrific and the curiously picturesque; they neglected the humane, the psychologically true, the emotional and affective. The rivalries of the Wars of the Roses were presented clearly and relentlessly as kid's stuff.

A further objective of the whole season—an attempt at a uniform vocal style that respects the poetic qualities of the text—was potentially a safeguard against this sort of simplification. Peter Hall can justly claim in the pamphlet, *Crucial Years* (1963): 'There is no question that the verse-speaking of this Company has improved. It has started to be noticed ...' Gone are almost all the glossy tones and meaningless pomposities that could be heard twenty, ten or only five years ago. The speaking often echoes 'ordinary speech', and can be both alert and pedestrian. David Warner and Ian Holm have these qualities abundantly, and almost all the company seem to strive to follow them. But, as Peter Hall is aware, this is a noticeable beginning rather than a maturing of the company's style that could lead them into Shakespeare's imaginative world. The early achievements have brought unhelpful side-effects. First, there is a lack of sustained line or rhythm, and a would-be impressive slowness. Long speeches are broken with pauses and far too frequently short speeches are prepared for with silent business, or followed by further similar invention. The aim, here, is not psychological subtlety or depth of feeling but effectiveness and psychological actuality for each simplified moment; the broken and slow delivery at Stratford is an aspect of the company's determined realism. And, unfortunately, it combats the excitement of Shakespeare's writing, its ability to draw the audience like a kite in the wind.

Besides rhythm, music and forward pressure, rhetorical energy is also lost, and effective emphasis and climax. The new style is, in fact, uneconomical. And it is self-important in that the actors seem to think the audience will always wait for them. Hamlet's was good general advice for acting Shakespeare's plays: 'speak the speech ... trippingly on the tongue'. An actor must, of course, rehearse in slow tempo and study the phrases of his part one by one, but in perform-ance he should not expect the audience to share this trouble. Within a strongly paced production the necessary moments of slow speaking will grow in power, and the whole design gain in eloquence. So, too, the production will gain the subtle influence of a continuous metri-cal control.

The second side-effect of the new vocal style is a sacrifice of affec-tiveness to effectiveness. The actors seem to lack temperament and size, as if they tried to be clever at the cost of developing an impres-sion of great feeling. Of course, this is apt for the directors' denigrating attitude to the characters of the plays but two performances that out-shone all others were reminders of the limitations elsewhere in the productions of both acting and direction.

These interpretations—acclaimed by rapt and heightened atten-tion and by press-notices—were achievements of temperament and bold psychological conception. Hugh Griffith, as Falstaff, occasion-ally took his time too much in common with others and resorted to repetitive hand movements to sustain interest, but using an individual and comparatively florid delivery he played up his role. Although the production demanded a Falstaff ripe for rejection, a 'sink of iniquity', he added a visionary's temperament, the surprise, wealth and endur-ance of an imaginative life. 'The rogue fled from me like quicksilver' (*Part II*, ii, iv, 217) was not simply an empty boast, irresponsible and slick, but a ruminative and beloved indulgence, played as if Falstaff for the moment believed in a long-past valour. When he acted Henry IV to Hal's Falstaff in the play-within-the-play, Falstaff became Harry's benevolent father indeed—in his imagination—and peacefully touched the prince's head and face on the concluding: 'And tell me now, thou naughty varlet, tell me, where hast thou been this month?' (*Part I*, ii, iv, 416–17). Occasionally the general style of the production hampered his performance; the sherris-sack soliloquy was held back from its natural rhythm by realistic business with a tun of wine and a drinking cup, and the Orchard Scene (v, iii, of *Part II*) was interrupted by a dim-witted three-man band fussing around on stage. But this Falstaff had size and a consistent and inventive complexity: at the end of *Part II*, when the new king has left the stage, Hugh Griffith showed the struggle for an imaginary and imaginative survival; and there was a last breakdown as he allowed Pistol to help him to his feet, so accenting the silent exit that Shakespeare has given him.

Peggy Ashcroft's Margaret, in the two parts of the re-arranged *Henry VI* and in *Richard III*, started with an intrusive lisp. (At times it seemed as if this was intended to be a 'funny' foreign accent.) But in the Paper Crown Scene (*Part III*, i, iv) her portrayal of weakness in cruelty and helplessness in victory, brought depth of understanding and a sustained beauty of phrase to the rhetoric; other barbarous episodes seemed trivial and merely shocking in contrast. The cruel humour of the lines was played close to hysteria: 'I prithee grieve to make me merry' (line 86) was an almost necessary request to excuse Margaret's impulse towards helpless laughter, a physical and emotional relief and a breakdown of control. Margaret was constantly changing her stance and position as if instinctively; her taunts were controlled and insistent so that only her body, moving repeatedly, could show the inward instability. As York replied in pain and passion, Margaret was silent, after one last, and now forced, laugh. When she stabbed him it was with a quick movement, and then she wept. And then the tears stopped with a wild, painful cry. In this scene the violent was emphasized as much as anywhere, but there was also rhetorical and musical control and a daring, emotional performance.

In *Richard III*, Margaret's long scene with the mourning Queen Elizabeth and Duchess of York (iv, iv) lacked the consistency of style for its shared (and concerted) rhetoric. But Peggy Ashcroft's first scene, entering alone to Edward's divided court as an old, vindictive woman, was compelling. She spoke from compulsion ('I can no longer hold me patient') and caught the strange verbal exaggerations of her speeches, accentuated them, and added the physical deformities of extreme age and spite. She was crazed and helpless. No one could effectively speak to her except Richard, and he resorted to shock and surprise. She talked to herself as well as to her victims, and to the heavens: she *actually* asked, 'Can curses pierce the clouds and enter heaven?' and with 'Why then, give way' she clapped her hands for attention. She entered, too, into the cruelty she described: 'Look when he fawns, he bites', she warned Buckingham, and then acted the biting and gave a mad laugh. The scene was held back only by the inability to show on the stage a commensurate response: 'My hair doth stand on end to hear her curses', says Buckingham, but this in his performance seemed untrue after the sharp reality, deep feeling and persuasive rhetoric of this Margaret.

★   ★   ★

A director's shaping hand has great influence over a production; but psychological truth, emotional, ambitious acting, and Shakespeare's rhetoric and poetry can be more powerful. In Joan Littlewood's witty and intelligent *Henry IV* much of what she had devised to demonstrate her reading of the play seemed slight tricks beside some superbly right and sustained performances that she encouraged among the comparatively minor characters. She saw the king and nobles as cold politicians, uniform in dress and clipped and unemotional in speech. Only Hotspur, played by Julian Glover..., was allowed to make flourishes and he, lacking any answering voice, seemed to beat the air. The director permitted no uncertain effect here. A neurotic reading of the letter scene (II, iii) where added emphasis and quickening tempo turned assurance into an expression of fear—'a good plot, good friends, and full of expectation; an excellent plot, very good friends'—indicated that Hotspur's grandiloquence was *meant* to sound empty. A single, huge cannon, awkwardly pushed into position behind Henry IV for the battle of Shrewsbury, showed that the king was *meant* to lack stature on his own account. So half the play dwindled at the director's command; through manner of speech and action, costume, stage-movement, this half became a demonstration of inadequacy.

It was hardly surprising that newspaper critics, uncompensated with the picturesque and horror-seeking realism of the current Stratford production, castigated Miss Littlewood. But they rightly excepted from censure the actors of some minor characters to whom she had given more rewarding roles. In the highway, tavern and rustic scenes (including the recruiting episode from *Part II*) there was music and abundant activity to make them generally entertaining and here the characterization was more ambitious. Victor Spinetti, the most accomplished actor in the company, was Poins, and there were inventive and strong performances from Murray Melvin as Gadshill and Shadow, and Brian Murphy as Bardolph. Costumes throughout the production were modern, with hints of the 'historical' in cloaks, hats and accessories, and this appearance was matched with modern ways of speech and behaviour. While the politicians suffered by these devices—they were given the fixed poses and grey-and-black colour of newspaper photographs—other characters gained: there was no verse to combat the modern inflexions, and lines and incidents normally guyed in performance were acted so that they gave new recognition to meaning and truthfulness. The wide range of Poins's responses to Hal was revealed. Gadshill's boast that he has nothing to do with 'landrakers, ... six-penny strikers, ... purple-hu'd malt-worms' shed all its footnote fustiness to become the compensating gloss of a slight-bodied rogue, a cheap, street-corner exquisite. His 'Tut', his negative constructions, his eagerness ('She will, she will'), reliance on a group-image ('We steal ... we have ... we walk'), and scorn of others, concern with others, together with posh airs, and scornful dismissals, all ceased to be unusable lumber from Elizabethan London, and became amusing and revealing dramatic lines: 'Go to; "homo" is a common name to all men. Bid the Ostler bring my gelding out of the stable. Farewell, you muddy knave' (*Part I*, II, i, 96–7). At Stratford, Francis was a gormless lout, kicked around for broad comic effect, but in the Theatre Workshop production, played by Jeremy Spenser, his scene with Hal revealed honesty, loyalty, ambition, ignorance—a small, conventional and intense imagination; and all this was given by a production taking much less acting-time than at Stratford. Richard Gurnock as Feeble, the woman's tailor, was mincingly polite, nervously pulling down his jerkin and smiling with each speech. Not only was this character more 'recognizable' and funnier than at Stratford but the scene as a whole was more lively and complete; instead of trying to make Feeble's philosophy sound impressive by an answering pause after 'we owe God a death', Joan Littlewood turned Bardolf's 'Well said; th'art a good fellow' into a quick, smirking response to make everything easy again, after this rather too smug and tactless facing of facts. Feeble's good nature was as firmly established, but his philosophizing was not produced as if it were philosophy; he was the sort of man who might quote Patience Strong in the barrack-room. 'Faith!, I'll bear no base mind' expressed inexperience as well as bravery, self-concern as well as honesty; it was of a piece with the whole characterization.

Falstaff, without the traditional whiskers and ruddiness, was an unsentimental picture of a public-bar soldier. His bulk, high-living and capacity for friendship were as much a part of his fantasy as his valour. But here the dialogue Shakespeare has provided leapt ahead of the characterization; the verbal energy and colour of the text bore little relationship to the physical image or the tone and rhythm of speech. The search for a contemporary portrayal of Falstaff is not finished; a realism depending on the accurate observation of human behaviour and a general vitality and invention did not fill out this role.

★   ★   ★

The production of *Othello* at the National Theatre, directed by John Dexter, aimed at grandeur; except for its sombre colours and wide groupings, it was reminiscent of a Stratford production five or ten years previously. But it also gave an impression of uncertainty; on recollection, it might seem that the current trend towards realistic stage-movement had been responsible for some awkward entries and exits, but in performance they often looked like clumsiness. So time was wasted in repeated backward turns for Emilia after giving Iago the handkerchief and the drunken scene was staged in a corner of a largely empty stage so that the actors had to work too hard to give an impression of conviviality.

Characterization also seemed uncertain. Or perhaps some roles were deliberately scaled down in confident expectation that Laurence Olivier's Othello could best succeed as a solo performance. Ian Finley as Iago so neglected the verbal dexterity required by the technical difficulties of his speeches that he was often hard to hear from centre-stalls. This looked like miscalculation until it became clear he was not suggesting the danger, evil or, even, energy under his 'honest' appearance; perhaps he wished to seem wholly ruthless and blunt. Maggie Smith as Desdemona may have intended to be cold and doll-like, responding to danger and loss by tension and then simplicity. Either of these interpretations would have been more successful within their own terms by added scale or intensity.

The interpretation of Othello was not as remarkable as the artistry which presented it. Here was a sensuous man of primitive culture breaking through social propriety and making a great misjudgment. (A conception reminiscent of Alfieri's summing-up of Eddie in Arthur Miller's *View from the Bridge*: 'even as I know how wrong he was, and his death useless, I tremble, for I confess that something perversely pure calls to me from his memory—not purely good, but himself purely....And so I mourn him—I admit it—with, a certain ... alarm.') In token of a movement back to primitive responses, this

Othello tore from his breast the crucifix he had worn and sometimes fondled.

In execution the most original element was Olivier's persistent sensuousness: a full-lipped make-up, cat-like walk, soft and low-pitched passages, caressing movements. In his first scene he entered carrying and smelling a red (twentieth-century) rose. This emphasis continued to the end: in Shakespeare's text Lodovico says:

> Look on the tragic loading of this bed.
> This is thy work.—The object poisons sight; …

and immediately commands 'Let it be hid'; but here the implicit stage-direction was not followed; rather there was a very slow fade with lights focused on the two dead bodies, Othello's chest naked. Olivier gave a sustained impression of physical power even in relaxation, as if Othello practised weight-lifting weekly in a gymnasium.

His verbal delivery was equally accomplished and more ambitious. At first his speech had remarkable ease, allowing a low, self-amused and quick laugh on 'Upon this hint I spake'. But in 'Farewell the tranquil mind …' which was given immediately before the single interval, two hours after the play began, Olivier revealed a tremendously increased range of voice. He spoke the repeated 'Farewells' with lengthened and varied vowels, and gave an illustrative expressiveness to the succeeding evocations of 'big wars … shrill trump … rude throats … dread clamours'. Olivier strongly marked a rhythm that grew more insistent throughout the sustained passage so that vocal virtuosity was combined with a compelling performance. At this point, too, his postures became more studied or artificial, often held for several lines and occasionally restraining Iago in an unmoving grip. With 'ne'er ebb to humble love', there was a long silence after 'humble' while Othello forced himself to say the word 'love' that had stuck in his throat; this silence was full with the impression of physical struggle and when at last the word came it was, convincingly, quiet. This device was similar to the many pauses in the Stratford productions, but Olivier used time more sparingly, worked hard to deserve each split second and, by controlling the tempo and shape of each speech and episode, counteracted an occasional slowness with a display of both temperament and art.

The central performance of the National Theatre's *Othello* was a demonstration of the huge opportunities Shakespeare has provided for an actor who is at once realistic and histrionic. While several small performances at Edinburgh brought a more immediate recognition of psychological truth, and the Stratford Falstaff and Margaret had more imaginative reach and emotional depth, Olivier's performance was supremely inventive, sustained and astonishing. As so often in the past, an actor rather than a director had created his own kind of Shakespeare.

Part V

Audiences

13

Playgoing and Participation*

I knew very well from productions I had directed that an audience's reception of a production affects everyone helping to create it and alters the effect of performance. Clearly a study of the plays in performance should try to take into account the composition, experience and response of audiences.

When a play becomes part of a theatrical event, anything that happens on stage will have meaning, give pleasure, or cause uncertainty according to how the audience receives it. In one way, this makes judging its effect easier because we can all be members of an audience and use our own experiences to elucidate what happens on any one occasion, but our experiences will differ and we have little means of holding on to passing impressions. In trying to understand a play's effect on an audience, the best way to start is to stand back and observe other people's behaviour as well as our own, and to start at the beginning.

How we come to the theatre and take our places in the auditorium and how we relate to the actors on stage provide the basis for every other experience, and these factors differ greatly from one theatre to another and from one age to another. For us, theatre-going to see a play by Shakespeare is an experience very unlike anything he might have envisaged and so our understanding of the theatrical event has to be qualified by theatre history and by present-day theatre practices that satisfy audiences with very different repertoires.

Playgoing in Shakespeare's day was a lengthy, complicated, and unpredictable business, having to be fitted in after a long day's work or other diversions, or before an evening meal. To get to the Globe,

---

*First published in John Russell Brown, *Shakespeare and the Theatrical Event* (Palgrave Macmillan, 2002), pp. 7–29.

you probably had to walk through the tangle of narrow city streets and then cross the single bridge over the Thames or pay a waterman to ferry you across – the latter option not always an easy trip with a quick-flowing tide. Or you might travel on horseback, finding a boy to take care of your mount during the show; if very wealthy, you could use a coach and its attendants. Performance started at two o'clock in the afternoon but, for a popular attraction or on a holiday, you would be well advised to arrive much earlier to secure a good seat or be sure of admission to standing room in the yard. At the Boar's Head, we know that doors were shut to the inn's regular customers at eleven in the morning when the business of theatre began to take over for the afternoon's performance.

In winter, at the height of the theatrical season, a play would end at half-past four or five, in twilight or, perhaps, darkness, and then you would have to make your way home through unlit streets. In Spain at the end of the seventeenth century, performance time in the open-air courtyard theatres was brought forward in winter by up to two hours so that playgoers could be home before dark, even though their theatres, being much nearer to the Equator, enjoyed longer winter daylight. In London, going to see a play could take five or six hours of your time and a good deal of effort and ingenuity as well. If you stayed on for a jig – a comic diversion after the main attraction – you would need still more time. Refreshments were necessary in such conditions and so drinks and snacks were on sale during performances.

Not everyone could be kept happy all the time, and those who had expended a good deal of energy to stand and see what they hoped to enjoy could well become restless and sometimes disorderly if they were disappointed. Scuffles and general lawlessness were not uncommon and pickpockets thrived in the crowds. Only in comparatively recent years has theatre-going become peaceable, comfortable, and convenient; well into the eighteenth century, two armed grenadiers were posted at either side of the stage as a reminder that the audience had to be kept under some measure of control. A notorious example of theatre rioting occurred in New York in 1849 when William Charles Macready was assaulted on stage with eggs, apples, potatoes, wood, and at least one bottle of drink; the performance of *Macbeth* had to stop and the actor escorted to his lodgings as the rioting spread to the streets and numerous people were killed. Although these Astor Place riots were fired by nationalistic as well as theatrical rivalries, the fact that a theatre audience could be aroused to such an effect marks how far playgoing in comparatively recent times was more volatile than in our own.

At the end of the nineteenth century, a visit to the theatre could still be a lengthy and uncertain business. Seats were unreserved and, for a popular attraction, queues would form before doors opened in late afternoon. To secure a good seat for the first night of Henry Irving's *Hamlet* in 1874, you would have to arrive some hours early or send someone else to stand in line for you. When the audience had settled into its places, a farce was performed before the play itself could begin and then the production took its own time. You would not leave the theatre until five and a half hours later, well after midnight, and then you had to get home; the streets were better lit and policed by this time but, since the city was now more widespread, the journey might well take longer. To be sure of seeing this performance of *Hamlet*, you had to set aside some six or seven hours of one day and at least one of the next.

Today, in a more prearranged world, playgoing is much easier. Access is comparatively easy, either by public transport or by using convenient and subsidized carparks. Promotion and sales have benefited from modern technology so that we always know what is showing and what seats are available. We can phone or e-mail to reserve a seat and pay by credit card. In some countries, we can buy a subscription for a whole theatre season and take whatever is on offer, month by month, assured of the same excellent seat on every occasion. If we decide to go at the last minute and fail to get a ticket on arrival at the theatre, we can always go off to some other play or enjoy some other entertainment that is available: a film, concert, or sports event; or we could go home to watch television or videos. Once in the theatre, we expect to sit comfortably in undisturbed darkness while the actors play to our respectful attention; we are likely to be hushed by other playgoers if we start to talk or make the slightest disturbance, such as rustling sweetpapers. Our day-by-day lives will be very little disturbed because theatre occupies only a few predictable hours.

At best, our theatre-going is a minority enthusiasm, not a popular and communal event. Educational initiatives, tourism, and state subsidies have turned it into an accredited leisure activity and journalists tell us what to expect. Perhaps the greatest change has come with the arrival of television, video cassettes, and film libraries that offer new ways of viewing Shakespeare in performance. Our experience of these is dominated by visual images that have been chosen for us by the director, cameraman and editor. Our responses are continuously guided by frequent change of location and focus, highly controlled use of colour and light, sudden cuts from one point of view to another, and an all-pervasive soundtrack. Moreover the actors' performances never vary in the slightest detail from one viewing to the next. With the arrival of inexpensive videos, most of us can see performances at home and at our own convenience: we can be on our own or in chosen company, and we are in charge of the occasion; a favourite scene can be repeated as often as we wish and we can stop the show to make notes and skip what begins to bore us. None of this is possible in a theatre and none of the versions seen on a screen, whether large or small, provides an equivalent experience. Seeing Shakespeare on video is like feeding ourselves on convenience foods, the plays packaged and reliable, easily consumed but falling short in nourishment when compared with a specially prepared product. We should hesitate before assuming that we understand what reception Shakespeare expected for his plays.

Changes that time has brought are just as striking once a performance has begun. Seldom today can it be said of an audience that

> Within one square a thousand heads are laid
> So close, that all of heads, the room seems made.
> (Thomas Middleton and Thomas Dekker, *The Roaring Girl* (1612), I.ii).

We do not suppose that the theatre building might 'crack' with the vigorous response of a 'full-stuff'd audience', as John Marston imagined in *What You Will* (1601), III.ii, or that it might actually 'shake when shrill claps' greet the performers, as Michael Drayton claimed in his poem, 'The Sacrifice to Apollo' (1606). We are seldom part of an audience so continuously active that the theatre resounds with 'shouts and claps at ev'ry little pause' and we will not have experienced the 'rare silence' that, according to Thomas Dekker, sometimes took possession of such an unbridled crowd (*If it be not Good* (1612) Prologue).

Also gone is the assumption that the audience belongs to the same world as the actors, separated according to their roles of watchers or performers but sharing the same light under the same sky. That is not possible when a stage faces the audience and is not surrounded by it, and when productions are augmented by sound and lighting effects that have been developed for large-scale and fantastic musicals. Some of the audience in an Elizabethan theatre would have sat in galleries immediately adjacent to the acting area and favoured members were accommodated on the stage itself. Reports tell of audience members talking to the actors during a performance or leaving their places to take part in the action. When a person in the play was threatened in a fight, spectators might run onto the stage in order to 'save the blow' (Verses prefixed to the Beaumont and Fletcher, Folio, 1647). The loss of immediate contact between actors and playgoers is probably the most fundamental difference between our theatres and those of Shakespeare's day.

We can build Elizabethan-type theatres, with thrust stages and encircling galleries, and use Elizabethan-type settings that provide an unchanging and structured background for the whole perform-ance, but audiences will still be entirely modern and will usually be kept in what is now considered to be its place, in the dark and in allotted seats. Safety regulations are partly responsible for resistance to Elizabethan tradition in these respects, insisting on fixed seating, clear gangways of regulation size, illuminated exit signs, and no more than a maximum number of spectators. A darkened auditorium is the preferred choice of theatre producers and directors because it enhances the effect of stage lighting and strengthens the visual impact of performances. It is also liked by audiences because it enhances their privacy and encourages quiet behaviour: going to a theatre has become a serious business that requires an unrestricted view of the stage and the peace of mind to respond as each individual wishes. Occasions do occur when an entire audience is moved to respond vigorously but very different expectations are signalled everywhere in the carpeted and capacious foyers, the stalls selling playtexts, souvenirs and programmes setting out the artists' biographies, photographs of the production, and informative and critical essays. Elizabethan play-going was riskier than ours because an audience would not know what to expect and liked it that way. Account books of the Rose theatre at the turn of the sixteenth century show that plays were very seldom repeated within a week and that an average of 17 new plays were performed each year by that company. In 1633 Thomas Heywood said that he had 'had either an entire hand, or at the least main finger' in 220 plays (Epistle to Thomas Heywood, *The English Traveller*, 1633): that gives him an average of more than five plays a year in a career of 40 years. Elizabethan audiences seem to have had an insatiable appetite for new plays whereas we wait for reviews or word of mouth about a production before paying to see it, even when we have enjoyed earlier work by the same author and the same actors and director.

In the nineteen-nineties, a brand new Globe theatre on Bankside in London brought physical conditions much closer to those of original performances, but safety considerations have dictated that some 30 ushers are employed to watch over the audience, especially those members who are standing in the pit around the stage. Admission tickets can be booked in advance and audiences are well briefed on how to behave in the replica theatre. Vocal response to performances tends to have a self-conscious air, as if spectators were in some privileged and good-humoured charade, playing their parts as 'groundlings' with stereotypical behaviour. Despite the best intentions, any 'reconstruction' of Elizabethan audiences is bound to be incomplete, because it is impossible to change minds and habitual responses, but at the new Globe, resistance to older procedures is also evident in the work of producers, directors, and actors. The management has not attempted to produce a large Elizabethan repertoire with one company of actors presenting a different play every day, with 20 or 30 in a single season and a good number of them entirely new. Its actors perform in a very few parts in the same plays day after day and, because of the passage of time, the words they speak have lost most of their previous relationship to everyday speech.

Going to the original Globe put an audience in touch with the present moment and, through the created illusions of the drama, gave a unique view of the world in which everyone lived. In those days men and women knew only their own small circles since they were without newspapers or a cheap and regular postal service and, of course, without radio or television. It might well be that only at a theatre could they gain a fuller perspective on their lives, encounter other opinions, and see the consequences of actions not entirely dissimilar from their own. Sermons, official publications and proclamations, occasional single-page broadsheets, ballads, and word of mouth were the only other means of mass communication, all less engaging and most of them giving only a single viewpoint. Books were still comparatively expensive and literacy far from universal. Theatre, in contrast, was accessible to almost everyone and always up to the minute; no wonder it was carefully censored by the authoritarian state. Actors were, as Shakespeare's Hamlet said:

> the abstract and brief chronicles of the time; after your death you were better have a bad epitaph than their ill report while you live.
>
> (*Hamlet*, II.ii.517–20)

In an often closed and divided world, one of the attractions of theatre was that its 'players cannot keep counsel; they'll tell all' (ibid., III.ii.136–41).

The experience that playgoers enjoyed was more varied, as well as more communicative, than their usual lives, because they would find themselves among a crowd more mixed in status and wealth than any other company with which they were familiar. Some public occasions, like a royal visit, the return of a victorious general, or some acts of religious worship, would also draw a wide range of people but they would expect to be segregated according to class. By seeing a play, Shakespeare's contemporaries shared an entertainment with almost every kind of person in town, except those who disapproved of theatre on moral or political grounds. For a new play, it was said that a theatre could so 'swarm' with spectators that 'gentles mix'd with grooms', against the decorum in force elsewhere (*Pimlico, or Run Red-Cap* (1609), sig. C1r). The Merchant Tailors' Company of the City of London decided to ban the use of its hall for the performance of plays on the grounds that:

> at our common plays ... every lewd person thinketh himself (for his penny) worthy of the chief and most commodious place without respect of any other, either for age or estimation in the common weal; which bringeth the youth to such an impudent familiarity with their betters that often times great contempt of masters, parents, and magistrates followeth thereof (*Early History of the ... Merchant Taylors* (1888), p. 235).

Today we visit a theatre with people very like ourselves. Everyone tends to be in the same salary group, the price differential between the most expensive and the cheapest seats having shrunk during the last few decades. Some theatres have a single ticket price, others sell a high proportion of seats to season-ticket holders or to registered and paid-up patrons who are thereby assured of sitting among other regulars every time they go to the theatre. By closing the galleries in our older theatres, with their wooden benches and restricted view of the stage, managements have lost a previously significant and often vocal part of the audience, packed close together and positively enjoying its freedom from supposedly superior company. Audiences have become less diverse and more predictable.

Actors in Contact with their Audience

Remembering that Hamlet respected the censure of a single 'judicious' auditor more than the reactions of a 'whole theatre of others' (*Hamlet*, III.ii.28), we might suppose that Shakespeare was not concerned with the 'fool multitude that choose by show' (*Merchant of*

Venice, II.ix.26). But his individual characters do not speak for him; if they did, he would have held many strange and contradictory beliefs. Given the behaviour of Elizabethan audiences, we can see that a prince might care little for a crowded theatre while an author would have a quite different opinion. Shakespeare could not be guided by any single person's view of his plays, not even the monarch's before whom they were likely to be played, because unless a wide public endorses performances by its attendance and attention, the theatre loses money and the actors lose confidence. Even in these days of well-behaved playgoers, a theatre company has no more demoralizing experience than playing to an empty or indifferent house; everyone in the theatre senses the rejection, like a smell permeating the entire building. While Hamlet castigated audiences as incapable of anything but 'inexplicable dumb shows and noise' (III.ii.12), Shakespeare, for his own peace of mind and that of the players, could not neglect those customers. His task was to please the public and, at the same time, write the plays he wanted to write.

To experience the kind of demands that audiences made upon Shakespeare and so understand his need to respond to them, we can go to see those companies that perform today in streets and public places. They will not be using Shakespeare's texts and are likely to be small in size and poorly equipped, but they work in conditions much closer to those of Elizabethan theatres than those enjoyed by more established companies. Their actors can draw mixed and active audiences and engage with them on their own terms. Much in their performances is improvised, introducing new words and new business when they see the need, and sometimes offering new twists in the story-line or new interpretations of character as they see opportunity. Welfare State company, for example, developed a strong public following for its open-air performances so that its actors speak of audiences from long and varied experience:

> You're waiting for the energy of your audience… If you're one end of a square it's quite hard to relate to the other end, but if you're in a circle, you can run round the edges and you're all together … [then] the audience puts in 50% of the energy…
>
> On the street, the performer must take power and charge the space, so that no matter how many trucks drive past, or jets fly over, the audience's attention is seized. That does not necessarily mean belting it out to drown the surrounding din … It can mean a performance so totally still, controlled and concentrated, that no one can walk away from it.

Eye contact is vital – sharing with the audience. It is a vibrant communication. They can, after all, reach out and touch you if they want to … You are there – it is not the telly – it is really happening live before them. It may go wrong, it may be marvellous. The tensions are real, and that bond is what the performer works with, and must be awake to (Tony Coult and Baz Kershaw (eds), *Engineers of the Imagination: The Welfare State Handbook* (1983), pp. 28–9, 34–6).

The structure and content of their plays, the effect of words and actions, and the use of the stage are spoken of here in the same breath as contact with an audience and that audience's reactions. These elements are all inextricably mixed in such theatres, as they are likely to have been in Shakespeare's.

John McGrath has described the work of the 7:84 Theatre Company which he founded and directed in the nineteen-seventies and eighties. Performing in Working Men's Clubs in the North of England where audiences were free to move around, drink, talk, and respond in any way they chose, this company developed its own kind of theatre. McGrath, who wrote the plays, as well as directing and acting, was forthright about audiences:

If a writer in theatre does not love his or her audience, he or she will die. It can be a critical love, an aggressive love, but if it turns to indifference, cynicism, hate, or simply exploitation, then the theatre-maker will turn into a solipsist or a psychopath.

He judged any play in relation to its appropriate audience: it could 'completely change its meaning, given the wrong theatre, or wrong publicity, or even the wrong ticket prices' (*A Good Night Out: Popular Theatre – Audience, Class, and Form* (1981), pp. 116 and 6–7).

Theatres whose audiences are in close contact with the stage and encouraged to respond freely, will have their own rules for performance. They might start with the advice of Bim Mason who founded the Mummer and Dada Theatre Company in 1985 and proceeded to conduct many experiments to find ways of drawing and holding an audience. For a 'stationary show', as opposed to mobile performances, he believed that:

the most important aspect of performance [is] timing. Timing cannot be fixed as in a musical score, it has to be gauged according to the mood of the audience. If they are with you then the act can be slowed down and played for all it is worth and more, by improvisation, inventing and extending the movements. If they are getting bored or restless, then pace will need to be quickened, but not rushed, otherwise control is lost and it looks desperate...

Expectation and tension can be built into each section of the show but must also be built into the whole structure. A show with a narrative can set up situations that set the public wondering how they will be resolved... Surprise is a key element to any show. It keeps the audience alert and maintains expectation because after one surprise who knows what others might be concealed...?

To a good performer most interruptions are not a problem, on the contrary they are a gift. Because they present a situation that could not have been rehearsed, the audience is fascinated to see what will happen and how well it is handled.... Audiences will give warm sympathetic support if it is well handled. Aggression always looks bad but so does indecisive weakness...

Since society has become so fractured into sub-cultures, it is necessary to use stories and archetypes that transcend divisions of age, sex and class (*Street Theatre and Other Outdoor Performance* (1992), pp. 98, 99, 101, 117).

The work of all such theatres is very specific to the location and time of performance, current political and moral issues, and the talents of the performers. In so far as Shakespeare worked for a similar audience–stage relationship, he is likely to have followed much the same rules, modified according to time and place, and the participants in each theatrical event.

These ways of performing are not those of the highly regarded theatres that stage Shakespeare today, but they are common elsewhere: in the highly efficient Jatra theatres of Bengal, Orissa, and Bangladesh, for example, or the long-running Marathi productions in and around Mumbai, and in many small-scale touring companies throughout Asia. Around the world popular theatres thrive by contact between actors and audiences: it brings a sense of shared achievement at the close of a play and ensures that a theatrical event is a truly public and social occasion, often becoming an irreplaceable feature in the year's calendar or a necessary ingredient of communal celebrations.

A recurrent and basic feature of Shakespeare's playtexts is the use of asides, a frequent sign that they were written to be played in open contact with an audience. Modern editions usually mark the most obvious of these with '*Aside*' or '*They speak aside*,' but the device was so common in Elizabethan performances, so constantly to be expected, that authors, scribes, and printers seldom bothered with these stage-directions. Editors add them today for readers and actors who are not familiar with performances that are open to an audience and might miss the comparatively few occasions where speaking aside is necessary for making sense. If contemporary actors start looking for further opportunities to speak directly to their audience, they will find them everywhere in Shakespeare's plays. Many lines in the longer soliloquies can be acted in this way, the audience becoming another self or *confidante* for the speaker to address, or persons who are sharing in the situation that is being confronted. An alternation between self-communion and communication, with appropriate changes in projection or phrasing of the words, encourages a mental and emotional dynamic that contributes to that energy in performance by which the actors of Welfare State hold the attention of their audiences. Sensitively timed according to the mood of the moment, direct address can also spring surprises, sharpen focus or raise questions. By the manner in which an address to the audience is phrased, a speaker can share a sense of desperation, confidence, or ease, or a search for some new initiative or understanding.

If the actor of Hamlet frequently changes to whom he speaks in soliloquy, he is likely to keep attention and be better able to develop his own interpretation of the role. The first time he is alone, 'But two months dead!' can be directed to the audience, sharing an outright anger or disbelief; or he might speak the phrase to himself either tenderly or in bitter recollection, not addressing the audience until 'Nay, not so much, not two', as if he now wants to be sure that he understands rightly what had happened. This qualification can be spoken in one phrase or in two or, even, three, all addressed to the audience, or only the first or last, the weight of each word changing with each choice the actor makes. Similarly, the following lines can be spoken either to himself, in self-reproach for forgetfulness, or to the audience, in anger or disbelief. When he speaks of the wind touching the skin of his mother's face, he can become more remote, caught up in his own memories and sensations:

> Nay, not so much, not two.
> So excellent a king that was to this
> Hyperion to a satyr; so loving to my mother,
> That he might not beteem the winds of heaven
> Visit her face too roughly.

Feelings can now break out of conscious control with 'Heaven and earth!', spoken neither to himself nor to the audience. Then two very different impulses lie behind the question and exclamations that follow, either one dominant: specific memories of his mother and father together in intimacy and a larger vision of the natural course of life pulled awry and destroyed by 'woman':

> Heaven and earth!
> Must I remember? Why, she would hang on him
> As if increase of appetite had grown
> By what it fed on; and yet, within a month –
> Let me not think on't. Frailty, thy name is woman! –
> A little month, or ere those shoes were old …
> (*Hamlet*, I.ii.137ff.)

When memories are uppermost in his mind, Hamlet is likely to speak to himself; when his sense of betrayal and disaster is stronger, he may speak out to the audience as if demanding its belief and support. 'Let me not think on't' can suggest that a sexual obsession has taken hold of him, after which, in contrast, 'Frailty, thy name is woman' is likely to be a sudden accusation, perhaps directed out to the audience and spoken violently, as if he is accusing the women who are watching the play. Or it can be spoken to himself, in the bitterness of experience and with a precise and profound sense of loss. Then Hamlet changes again, remembering his mother on the day of her new marriage, even to the shoes that she wore.

Somehow the actor must manage and shape the great range of feeling and consciousness that this speech implies and expresses. No regular exposition or sustained argument can order its delivery: syntax and phrasing, as well as words, require many changes of consciousness. Repetition calls for certain key issues to register forcefully with varying emphasis: 'two months … not two … within a month … a little month' and, a little later, 'must I remember? … Let me not think on't'. Delivery that is sensitive to Hamlet's conscious and half-conscious thoughts, both driven and held back by overwhelming feelings, can make an audience uneasy by many different appeals for its attention: sometimes told what to think, sometimes left to itself to be amazed at the force of feeling or puzzled by Hamlet's uncertainties. When an actor is in contact with his audience on an open stage and gives a strong dynamic to this soliloquy by changing the direction in which it is spoken, his hearers may feel the emotional pressures within Hamlet's mind; they may even share the sensations that he experiences.

Longer speeches addressed to a whole court, army, family, or other assembly can be spoken to include a theatre audience so that it tends to merge with the onstage audience. By acknowledging the presence of this wider public, an actor can gain both a sounding board and a visible, if not vocal, response. Audience members can be drawn together or divisions marked among them, for instance between the young and old, privileged and disadvantaged, conservative and radical, according to the issues involved. They can be wooed by both sides in an argument; in *Julius Caesar*, III.ii, the two very different funeral orations that follow each other are an obvious example of this: by addressing both to the theatre audience, these political rivals can each make his own pitch and directly invoke a positive response. A particularly close focus of attention will be achieved by addressing only one person in the crowd of spectators, personalizing an appeal or giving point to a joke.

Everywhere in Shakespeare's dialogue, actors can find opportunities for direct address to their audience. The Fools do so most of the time, commenting on other persons and their attitudes, sharing jokes or undermining assumptions or presumption. Some characters who more directly drive the action of the play forward have a similar freedom: Richard the Third, Iago, and Edmund; Beatrice, Rosalind, and Falstaff; Brutus and Cassius. Affected by an apparent openness, in which words seem to be spoken only for them to hear, an audience will be drawn to these persons and may identify with them, even when what they are saying or doing seems improbable, reprehensible, or downright wrong. By these means direct address plays a prominent part in Shakespeare's handling of story and argument, as well as in the relationship between audiences and individual actors and the persons they present.

Some actors in major parts have been given comparatively few opportunities to address the audience, but these are carefully placed and occur at vital points in the narrative. For example, in the first scene of *King Lear*, when the king addresses the entire court, the actor can choose whether he includes the theatre audience in his formal pronouncements. Later scenes have more obvious opportunities to address the audience, as if it were an actual witness of his misfortune:

> Does any here know me? This is not Lear.
> Does Lear walk thus? speak thus? Where are his eyes?
> Either his notion weakens, or his discernings

> Are lethargied. – Ha! waking? 'Tis not so. –
> Who is it that can tell me who I am?
>   (I.iv.225–9)

Some 50 lines on, when Lear calls on Nature to hear his sustained curse, the king's isolation will be more apparent if he now turns away, not only from Albany and Goneril, but also from the audience to whom he had previously addressed his words.

All this time, while other persons in the play have had numerous opportunities to address the audience in soliloquy or asides, Edmund and the Fool particularly, Shakespeare has not given Lear a single soliloquy with which to establish contact, only some passing and optional opportunities for direct address. In his next scene, however, Lear does come closer to a sustained soliloquy during his encounter with Regan and Goneril:

> Those wicked creatures yet do look well-favour'd
> When others are more wicked; not being the worst
> Stands in some rank of praise.

Soon after this, he may soliloquize with greater passion:

>   You think I'll weep.
> No, I'll not weep.   *Storm and tempest.*
> I have full cause of weeping; but this heart
> Shall break into a hundred thousand flaws
> Or ere I'll weep.
>   (II.iv.255–7, 281–5)

Contact with an audience remains intermittent. Alone with the Fool on the heath, Lear addresses the storm, then himself, and only then, perhaps, the audience: 'No, I will be the pattern of all patience; / I will say nothing' (III.ii.37–8). Soon he speaks to specific persons whom he imagines to be somewhere within call: the 'perjur'd', the 'simular man of virtue / That art incestuous', the 'caitiff' who would practise on a man's life (III.ii.51–9). Having addressed 'poor naked wretches, wheresoe'er you are', he may turn to the audience to confess: 'O, I have ta'en / Too little care of this!' (III.iv.28–33). As madness takes progressive hold and he meets with the blind Gloucester, opportunities to speak to the audience grow more frequent and less reserved: 'They told me I was everything; 'tis a lie – I am not ague-proof'.

Speaking of Gloucester, he calls all who hear him to witness: 'see how the subject quakes'. He seems to see persons he knows and asks the theatre audience to see them too: 'Behold yond simp'ring dame ... See how yond justice rails upon yond simple thief ... Thou rascal beadle ... Why dost thou lash that whore?' (IV.vi.103–61).

In the last scene of all, when Lear speaks rarely, many of his words can be addressed to the theatre audience as if to a wider court of appeal. By this means, direct access is given to his sense of what is happening, his conflicting feelings, and the continuing exertion of his will:

> This feather stirs; she lives. If it be so,
> It is a chance which does redeem all sorrows
> That ever I have felt...
> I might have sav'd her; now she's gone for ever...
> Do you see this? Look on her. Look, her lips.
> Look there, look there!
> (V.iii.265–7, 270, 310–11)

As Lear draws close to death, those on stage know that 'vain is it / That we present us to him' and that, finally, they must obey the 'weight of this sad time' (V.iii. 293–4, 323). If direct address involves them in this death, a theatre audience may also feel powerless, neither moving nor making a sound in response. Careful manipulation of the contact between actor and spectators has progressively encouraged a sensitive perception of the hero's suffering and powers of endurance.

The manner of Lear's death can be seen as a development of Shakespeare's continuous experiment with the engagement of an audience in the theatrical event. His very last moments exist in two different versions, that in the Quarto of 1608 and a longer version in the Folio of 1623; these show many small changes that are typical of the fine tuning that a dramatist will attempt when intent on achieving exceptional effects in the performance of his script. They should encourage us, as well as actors, to study the text with every possible care.

Audience Response

The various ways in which Shakespeare encouraged audiences and actors to interact can both charge performance with energy and accentuate the seeming reality and immediate relevance of a play.

While present-day modes of staging seldom allow actors to take advantage of this, some non-theatrical events of our own times offer better parallels to playgoing at the original Globe: for example, political meetings when the issue is of immediate concern to the crowd, mass religious observances that are not strictly prescribed in order or form of words, popular music concerts, especially those in the open air, and many spectator sports. Some audiences are now so huge that other factors intrude but the way in which crucial games between a few skilled opponents are watched, the audience sharing in the excitement and relating personally to individual participants, provides a revealing contrast to the self-absorption of theatre audiences seated comfortably in a darkened auditorium and watching a self-contained, well-rehearsed performance of a play.

When players are close at hand and known to us as individuals, we can be caught up 'in the play' as audiences might have been at the Globe or the more intimate Blackfriars theatre. Verbal accounts of a final of the Men's Singles Championship at Wimbledon some years ago, before television influenced other forms of commentary, suggest the close attention of the crowd, its expectations and critical attitudes, and the gradual buildup of excitement that might have been experienced at early performances of Shakespeare. In the London *Times* of 8 July 1991, David Miller reported on a match between Boris Becker, an established favourite with the crowd, and Michael Stich, the latest in a series of German players whose serves and volleys had proved devastatingly effective:

> As the second set began to go the way of the first, Becker's nerves, extraordinarily, disintegrated. As he cursed, shouted and shook his fists at the heavens, the front row of Royal ladies smiled tolerantly like school parents watching someone misbehave on junior sports day. Becker was warned for time abuse; it was his reputation that was more threatened...
>
> Now came, for [Becker], the agony of the third set ... The executioner at the other end was unrelenting; and served to love for 5–4. As they changed ends, you could sense that Becker's intolerance of his decline had forfeited the crowd's sympathy. In that harsh way of the sporting public, they were ready for symbolic death.

The match finished with Stich's 'remorseless forehand return', and then:

> As the two young men embraced, you could sense the crowd's sudden forgiveness for the fallen champion's frenzy. He looked about 30. This modern game strips you bare. How long can Stich last in the goldfish bowl?

When we want to know the nature of the event in which Shakespeare imagined his plays being performed, a tennis audience offers a useful point of reference. The swift and complete changes of mood, exemplified in this *Times* report, warn against assuming that a drama awakens a single or constant response. The spectators' instinct to move ahead of the play, to identify with one player at a time, to mix emotional and moral judgements, to be harsh and pitiless, and, at certain moments, to become united in reaction, all indicate how a knowledgeable audience, in close contact with the actors, might be transformed when keyed up with expectation. And the players' responses suggest the competitive energy and intensified playing that might arise among members of the King's Men during each unprecedented and, largely unrehearsed performance. While actors and some of their audience will know ahead of time who will die and who survive or which two persons will go off stage together and at peace, neither party will know exactly how the end will be achieved, what passions, what access of power, or what revaluations will be involved in the conclusion.

When we try to assess what the plays do in performance, rather than what is said on-stage, we should give attention to expectation and anticipation, to delay and speed of fulfilment, to repetition of incidents as well as the clarification and understanding that derive directly from words. Forms of combat and chase should be carefully noted as basic structural devices that quicken attention and concentrate issues. On-stage transformations, either inward or outward, moments of bonding, efforts to contain irreconcilable differences, and the settling of accounts are all actions that give spectators special satisfaction. Although momentary actions and the presence of an actor are more immediately memorable and the means by which an audience is drawn into a play, the entire action of the play as its story unfolds is what transmits the greatest charge and holds an audience, even though few of them will realize that this is so. This part of a theatrical event is the hardest to evaluate.

★ ★ ★

Shakespeare could not have envisaged what the plays offer to audiences today, both playgoing and participation having changed so much. The elaborate scenery, complicated lighting, and carefully rehearsed performances to which we have become accustomed were unthinkable in earlier times. Yet present-day productions have originated, at least in part, from a study of the printed plays and can reveal new aspects of Shakespeare's artistry. Audiences are led to give concentrated attention to particularly significant words by finely tuned speech. Alterations of location or mood that are indicated in the text are reinforced by swiftly changing and impressive stage effects. A director's distinctive production that reveals a new 'reading' of the text is made possible by the same qualities in the writing that fostered the open and improvised performances of earlier times: a huge hinterland of meanings and sensations lies behind Shakespeare's texts and contains many paths to explore with many different intentions.

The most successful Shakespeare productions in our theatres are renowned for clarity of meaning and argument, efficient and elaborate showmanship, and finesse in performance, virtues which are now prized more than those of early performances. But they have limitations too. Most obviously, they no longer draw audiences from a wide spectrum of society or occupy a dominant place in popular culture. Secondly, the companies presenting Shakespeare are no longer part of a profession that is confident of its own future and financially self-supporting. Thirdly, performances cannot respond readily to the changing concerns of the public, being set in one form by means of long rehearsals and careful direction. Whether any of these shortcomings could be eradicated is a question that sharpens awareness of what the texts demand of actors, directors, and readers.

14

Asian Theatres and European Shakespeares*

Travel opened my eyes and mind to theatrical experiences I had not known before and, on returning home, I found that they had altered how I responded to Shakespeare, on stage and in print. First in articles and then in the book, New Sites for Shakespeare: Theatre, the Audience and Asia *(1999), I tried to understand the change and reconsider earlier responses.*

Critics, scholars, editors, directors and actors, all specialists who have a thorough knowledge of Shakespeare's plays, should seek out performances in totally different cultural contexts and in theatres with traditions alien to those of Europe. Such experiences can have more permanent and far-reaching value than theatre-going at home. It hardly matters what play is seen or who wrote it because our minds will not register new readings of a text: instead, we experience theatrical events of a different order than any we have encountered before. The most self-consciously traditional theatres are likely to surprise us most because they tend to be the least influenced by Europe. At performances of Kathakali or Kutiyattam in India, of Beijing or Sichuan Opera in China, or of Noh, Kabuki, or Bunraku in Japan, we become aware that the audience is giving a different kind of attention to the play, as if what is happening on stage has a different relationship to the offstage world. While many details of the performance will seem inexplicable or unnecessary, we will have extended our knowledge of the range of effects that theatre can create and seen colours in the theatrical spectrum that have been lost to sight nearer

* First published in *Shakespeare Jahrbuch*, 138 (2002), 11–22.

home. We should be able to roll back time and be better able to judge the effects that Shakespeare's plays were intended to have in performance.

When studying the verbal text of a play we do not hesitate to try to take account of the changes that time has brought to both language and culture. We want to know the original values of words and structures, especially those that do not disclose themselves to us at first. We read authors contemporary with Shakespeare who have now grown out of fashion, study depositions of witnesses living in England in his time, and look for evidence of Elizabethan social behaviour and personal presentation in paintings, sculptures, drawings, and embroideries. So we hope to rediscover the plays and increase our understanding of the meanings they may continue to have for us today. In very much the same way, we should try to learn the theatrical language and conventions that were in operation when the plays were first staged. No dictionaries exist to help in this but visits to unfamiliar theatres can, at least, give us a wider theatrical vocabulary and make us aware that audiences can be affected in ways that our established theatres seldom or never attempt. As we try to respond to texts as Shakespeare's contemporaries might have done, we should take any opportunity to see performances as close as possible to those in the theatres for which he wrote.

In recent years, replicas of the Globe Theatre with more or less respect for archaeological and historical scholarship have provided one way of learning more about the original performances of Shakespeare's plays. Yet the more earnest these attempts, the more apparent have become their limitations. We know now, more certainly than before, that how the Globe was used will not be revealed by imitating its architecture: a building will prompt questions about stage practice but no answers are enshrined in its fabric or the shape of its stage and auditorium. To learn the language of Shakespeare's theatre we have to envisage plays in productions, without variable stagelights or scenery, that could move from the Globe to the Blackfriars, and to the different performance-spaces of halls in royal palaces, great houses, town corporations and guilds, colleges and schools, together with inn yards and, sometimes, open spaces. More difficult still, we have to imagine performances by a permanent company of actors with a large repertoire of plays that, every season, included a stream of entirely new playscripts. And all the plays performed, including Shakespeare's, used words taken from the current usage of their audiences in private, social, political, and intellectual life. Few of these conditions are replicated by European theatre companies today, even when they do perform in a physical imitation of the Globe. Only in theatres of other cultures can we experience at first hand the effect of stage practices now lost to us at home. In Asia, as in Shakespeare's England, some highly sophisticated theatre performances, as well as very simple ones, are given with almost no technological support; companies of actors are often self-governing and their membership almost permanent; in some theatres, audiences are truly popular and drawn from many sections of society. While lacking public subsidy, some companies enjoy continuous financial success. As we witness performances that are very strange to us but have these features in common with those we read about in Shakespeare's day, we will wonder whether we have not been over-confident in trying to deduce what Shakespeare might have expected his plays to achieve in performance. Have we imagined only variations of what we have already witnessed on stage, because we have experienced nothing else? Have we received and judged the texts from a point of view and ways of seeing and responding that are inappropriate for Shakespeare's theatre? Have we been blind to signs in the texts that, in their own time, informed acting and stage business? Have we miscalculated the theatrical forces at work in the plays and therefore failed to recognise the kind of affect they had, and might still have, on an audience? Are the moral, psychological, philosophical, and political issues that we see in the words of the texts the same ones that would have arisen out of the performances as they were originally given and that Shakespeare would have foreseen as he wrote? Scholars, critics, and theatre people have been asking these questions for a long time but only recently have they had recourse to the wealth of living evidence that is available around the world.

I have not travelled far beyond Asia and so I shall restrict myself to examples of what can be learnt from some of the theatres I have visited there. At performances of the Jatra, the touring theatres of Bengal and Orissa, I have sat among large audiences, sometimes of two thousand or more, who have taken time off from ordinary life to go to the theatre. They see new plays that either represent contemporary life or reconstruct a mythical or historical past. Old plays are brought up to date by a free-moving, improvising fool and by textual insertions that emphasise contemporary relevance. To both old plays and new, an audience responds directly and openly, not only laughing, clapping, weeping, or talking among themselves but also calling out to encourage the actors, give warnings, or castigate. Its members share in a game, anticipating events and responding sharply to surprises: they are taking it all in as it comes, with immediate sensation and pleasure. The evening can be said to belong to the audience. Most of its members have come after work, just before eleven o'clock, and will attend to the play, in the company of family and friends, until 6.30 in the morning when, with the dawn, they go back to work. It is like a sport in which they are so directly and actively engaged that, in politically charged times, even a play on a historical subject has been banned because it incited disorder and anti-government demonstrations. (See, for example, Balwant Gargi, *Folk Theatre of India* (Calcutta: 1991), p. 33.) This audience, almost encircling the stage, is free to do as it wishes. Some members call out to the actors during a performance and gather around them at the close of the play. Others talk amongst themselves with little restraint and move around to see better or meet with other friends – activities prevented in our theatres by pre-sold, numbered tickets, watchful ushers, and sensible safety regulations. It is a head-strong audience that can become impatient and restless, more like the hydra-headed monster who would clap and hiss an Elizabethan player, "according as he pleased and displeased them" (*Julius Caesar*, 1.2.258–9). It can also be very quiet, its attention held as strongly by argumentative self-justification or confessional soliloquies as by thrilling fights and physical activity.

Sitting in such an audience, we may better understand why a Shakespearean Prologue would ask the 'gentles' among them to be patient and attentive. The Jatra plays and performances seem designed for both contact and combat between actors and spectators. Many speeches are spoken directly to them in order to address misunderstandings, explain what is about to happen, reflect on what has passed, or arouse active responses. Performance becomes a two-way engagement. Might Shakespeare have intended his actors to perform in this way, facing out front for much of the time and interacting with an audience that stood and sat closely around them? Were some of the speeches intended to restrain over-enthusiastic response, others to be purposefully provocative or unsettling? If we positively look in Shakespeare's texts for what can be said to an audience, we will find every play full of such possibilities, as they are in theatres that pay less attention than ours to the imitation of ordinary behaviour and do not subdue spectators by sitting them in the dark.

Jatra companies provide a particularly illuminating experience because, like the Chamberlain's and King's Men, they perform in repertory. A different play is given each night of the week a company is in town, unless one is repeated after a day or two to satisfy popular demand. The constant element in these performances is the company's actors, so that its leading members are both well known and well paid, appreciated for their individuality as well as their varying roles. Actors are the centre of attention and almost the sole means of communication. The small stage, like a boxing ring, gives little scope for crowd-scenes and has no scenery beyond a small rostrum or a single chair, even though the play's action may involve journeys to many different places and occupy the course of many years. There is, however, an orchestra, dancing, and singing, and the actors have the experience and discipline to sustain six or seven hours of performance.

Theatres in Asia are as different as the many languages spoken in a single country, the variety of theatrical events seeming endless. The widespread practice of cross-gender casting has often been noticed as an analogue to Elizabethan practice, but the most frequently cited examples are the Japanese Noh and Kabuki and the Indian Kathakali which all employ mature men as their heroines, not the 'boys' or young men of Elizabethan times. Better analogues are to be found in numerous regional theatres, including the Jatra, which are so local in their attractions and so financially self-sufficient that they do not take part in foreign tours or provide simultaneous translations and handbooks for tourists. Their style is, for the most part, rougher, bolder and more constantly active, less ritualistic or ceremonial, closer to ordinary behaviour, than the so-called 'classical' theatres of either Japan or India. These theatres freely adapt the convention of cross-gender casting, employing both young boys and mature men in female roles, and sometimes including actresses alongside them in the same cast: no barriers seem to exist between these very different performers. And how do their audiences respond? Again that varies, but unselfconscious sympathy and outright enjoyment are very evident and studies of Elizabethan boy-actors should probably take that into account.

While many Asian theatres should interest European Shakespeareans because they are irresistibly popular, engagingly contemporary, and financially profitable, as many more are worth attention for the subtlety and refinement of their performances and the hold they have over very small and dedicated audiences. Japanese Noh and Indian Kathakali are notable examples, although the achievements and audiences of both are at present being modified, not in response to contemporary tastes or artistic imperatives, but because of a financial need to go on tours to other countries and provide educational services alongside theatre performances. Kutiyattam is an ancient theatre that, while changing with the centuries, still requires and receives the imaginative involvement of very small audiences. Its complicated language of gesture and movement, its interplay of speech, singing, music, and silence, the compact theatre in which it is staged, and the rarity and length of its performances all make special demands on an audience, insisting on close and absorbed attention. The spectator, faced by a drama that is closer to a hieroglyph than a statement, tends to forget his or her own self; performance is a challenge to understanding and imagination, not an immediately gratifying experience. Because nothing is seen or heard that replicates ordinary existence and little stands out to irresistibly grab attention, the imaginations of creative actors and responsive audiences are free to react to the action in their own ways and draw on all the manifold sense-memories that each individual life has provided. This inner and private activity gives vivid life to the drama's fiction, not on the stage, but within the spacious and private consciousness of each member of both parties.

How do we know that this is so? Because no other explanation seems able to account for the quite exceptional dedication of the actors' entire lives or the entranced silences in which an audience can he held speechless and unmoving. While the strange and complicated physical representations of the drama are hard to understand or appreciate – outlandish, impractical costumes, grotesquely inhuman make-up, improbable physical movements – what is experienced in the imagination can be simple, compelling, and, sometimes, overwhelming. (See John Russell Brown, *New Sites for Shakespeare: Theatre, the Audience and Asia* (1999), pp. 71–82.)

If we have ever wondered whether an exegesis of a Shakespeare play were too subtle or our response to a moment of drama too intensely personal, Kutiyattam performances will extend our tolerance of both. And in Asia, it is not only ancient forms of theatre that sustain close attention; the productions of Suzuki Tadashi, that are often eye-catchingly visual in their use of large casts, will sometimes centre the drama on one almost motionless figure whose imagination and silent, inner tensions are the heart of the experience. In each of these examples – Noh, Kutiyattam, and Suzuki's theatre – what is seen and heard can lead an audience towards imaginary experiences that far outreach those of ordinary life. We should hesitate before insisting that Shakespeare's plays must always be accessible; they, too, may yield moments which utilise the same compelling power of imagination, even if only a few in an audience are able and willing to follow and "amend" what is on show (*A Midsummer Night's Dream*, 5.1.211).

Many of the older and regional forms of Asian theatre, being neither heavily influenced by Europe nor dependent on complicated set-design and technical support, are also of interest to Shakespeareans because they rely so continuously on improvisation. The actors are free to respond to an audience, speaking the words of a text as they wish and interpolating stage-business of their own. An audience experiences the drama as it takes life before their eyes, each moment in fresh creation, without pre-programming. The actors respond to the actual progress of the play's action on each and every occasion it is performed however accident and impulse may have affected them or whatever up-to-the-minute and local happening has caught their interest and that of their audience. As always and everywhere, improvisation can be careless, a waste of time and an intrusion into the progress of a drama, but Asian actors, who rely on well-practised routines as well as inspiration, are well able to maintain and heighten interest by improvised shaping of each episode and developing close and quick rapport with an audience as well as with other persons in the play.

The sophistication of improvisation in Asia is often as remarkable as its prevalence. In Kutiyattam, an actor's unrealistic postures and movements require very precise balance throughout the body while hands and eyes are exceptionally and continually active in making specific signals; dialogue is in Sanskrit, a language spoken only by scholars. The difficulties of this style of acting do not discourage improvisation but seem, rather, to encourage precision and invention in the use of it. In contrast, when faced today with the finesse and multiple demands of Shakespeare's dialogue, the usual resort of English-speaking actors is to avoid improvisation and take endless trouble to choose how each sentence and line will be delivered. In both private and company rehearsals, the text is gradually mastered and decisions made about how particular words will be stressed, lengthened, coloured, or passed over rapidly, how a sentence will be phrased and meanings pointed, and how metre will shape and time utterance. The technical and psychological demands of the text are assumed to be so great that only careful preparation can mark necessary shades of meaning and give an actor's performance coherence, authority, and power. The example of very sophisticated Asian theatres suggests on the contrary, that with adequate training and experience, Shakespeare's subtle versification and language could provide the stimulus for improvised performances that would respect the structure of the play's action and respond to the conditions of each performance on stage and in the auditorium. If such an instantaneous handling of the dialogue were practicable, an audience would experience, with the actors, a sense of adventure and exploration. This is how the plays must have been performed in Shakespeare's theatre with its daily change of a large repertoire and the absence of any strict managerial and technical control of production. If it were to be attempted today, a director would be of little use except, perhaps, in training, casting, and choice of visual presentation.

Besides a fuller understanding of the theatre language used in the texts, a change in critical attitudes is likely to develop after an experience of Asian theatre. The very act of sitting among audiences whose ways of life and ideas about life and art are very different from one's own will immediately draw attention to the difficulties of full comprehension. Yet, while ignorance of the verbal language is a colossal drawback, it is also an advantage because it heightens other perceptions. A visitor becomes watchful of what happens in the audience as well as on the stage and soon realises that communication is by many physical and habitual means to which he or she has no access. The explanation of why this costume or that gesture is used, why this tone of voice is adopted, why these particular persons are brought onto the stage, will often involve such long-engrained matters as the history of race, conditions and conventions of social life, the politics and ecology of the place of performance, the theatre's contact with other arts, the life-histories and family relationships of the performers. Nothing in theatre exists by itself alone or is created only in one moment; each unrepeatable detail is shaped by the context of performance and received in that context. Sitting in an alien theatre, one realises that no theatrical event can be adequately represented by quoting a text, describing on-stage action, or by showing videos of a performance: it grows out of an entire social context at a precise moment in time. Actors remodel the life-experiences they have ingested and only an audience from the same time and place can adequately appreciate what has been achieved. Performances that exist outside our own life experiences serve both as tokens of a common humanity and as reminders of theatre's inevitable involvement with the context of each performance.

When we are open to the experience provided, rather than fastening on whatever is understandable in our usual terminology, we quickly realise that we cannot respond as others around us and may come to think that this will always be so, even in a familiar theatre and with a familiar text, because we will not bring the same contribution as any one else to the shared event. Our responses will be conditioned by our own lived experience and social culture, as well as by whatever personal ability, scholarship, and familiarity with the plays we may possess. In considering what happens with any play in a theatrical event – that is, considering a text in the environment for which it was written – scholarship and criticism are bound to be both experiential and personally biased.

Another consequence of visiting Asian theatres is that we become aware that behind many of the surface differences lies a basic difference of purpose. We are used to thinking, with Hamlet and the critics and scholars of Shakespeare's time, that theatre is meant to be an imitation of life, its purpose "to hold, as 'twere, the mirror up to nature". We also believe that it has the moral function of showing "virtue her own feature, scorn her own image, and the very age and body of the time his form and pressure" (*Hamlet*, 3.2.23–24 and 25–28). In Asia these beliefs are also current, but a very different purpose for the theatre is proposed in the *Natyasastra*, the ancient theatre manual supposed to be handed down at the request of Indra, the greatest of gods. While inspiration will be derived from lived experience, theatre performance should not imitate life; it should recreate it.

On stage, everything is to be transformed in order that the production can create *rasa*, that is sensation, feeling, taste, or pleasure. While the word *rasa* is not easy to translate, either in its original or present usages, what a theatre performance is *not* is clear enough: it does not define meanings or encourage argument, and response to it is instinctive and not dependent on intellectual understanding. Anyone can appreciate *rasa*, irrespective of race, culture, or age; and, in performance, production, or playwriting, the achievement of *rasa* is more necessary than representing on stage an individual person with an individual history, physical characteristics, or psychology, more important than presenting theme or argument.

Does this critical position have any relevance for Shakespeare's plays? In spite of Hamlet's views, I think it does. The Chorus to *Henry the Fifth* offers a quite different idea, wanting nothing like ordinary life on stage:

> O for a Muse of fire, that would ascend
> The brightest heaven of invention:
> A kingdom for a stage, princes to act,
> And monarchs to behold the swelling scene!
> (*Henry V*, Prologue, 1–4)

Prince Hal is not said to behave like an everyday mortal, but to have risen

> [...] from the ground like feathered Mercury,
> And vaulted with such ease into his seat
> As if an angel dropp'd down from the clouds
> To turn and wind a fiery Pegasus,
> And witch the world with noble horsemanship.
> (*Henry IV, Part I*, 4.1.105–110)

Cleopatra claims that

> Eternity was in our lips and eyes,
> Bliss in our brows' bent, none our parts so poor
> But was a race of heaven.
> (*Antony and Cleopatra*, 1.3.35–37)

Puck tells the audience of *A Midsummer Night's Dream* to consider the play as a dream, not an imitation of life in waking reality, and Peter Quince's Prologue to "Pyramus and Thisbe" insists that everything is intended for its audience's "delight", a word that could be taken as an Elizabethan stand-in for *rasa* (5.1.41 and 5.1.114). If we only look for an imitation of life and a judgement on virtue and vice, we will miss an essential element of Shakespeare's plays that is, like *rasa*, sensational and immediately pleasurable. All the texts contain some elements that are not taken from 'nature' or the stuff of everyday life: gods, ghosts, spirits, fairies, prophets, and a host of unlikely events that philosophy or common sense would never sanction or explain. The Gravedigger in *Hamlet* may seem ordinary enough at first, even if overtly theatrical, but he started digging graves the very day Hamlet was born and is there to greet him when he returns to die in Denmark; he says that the skull he has picked up is Yorrick's in order to show Hamlet the present "favour" of the fool he had once loved. Rather than imitating life, these plays, on some crucial occasions, may be said to transform life as we know it and not be very much concerned, if at all, with the form and pressure of ordinary living.

Present-day critics who seek in the plays a reflection of social behaviour or an argument concerning personal and political morality will tend to pay little attention to their gods and those unlikely events that have little to do with the ongoing and formative processes of living. But these elements *are* in the plays and Shakespeare's brave and inventive use of language might serve as a warning that his entire work is likely to have been hospitable to pleasure, sensation, and fantasy, as well as to more sober, material, and socially significant matters.

Yet another reflection on our critical attitudes derives from the enjoyment of theatrical events when we do not understand a word that is spoken on stage. Not only do we follow the action and empathise with the persons in the play, but physical images from Asian performances will often stay locked within our minds long after we have returned to Europe. While our attention was being held and heightened by physical closeness to the performers, these theatres can only have spoken to us by colour, form, gesture, presence, and the effects of music and dance. We may reflect afterwards that this is not so very different from all good theatre, although our ability to retain words from a reading of the text will normally obscure the manner in which we have been engaged in the enacted drama. How does Hamlet die? How impatient is Cleopatra at the moment of death or how serene? Words of the text do not raise or give direct answers to these questions and yet on them the effect of a tragedy on its audience very largely depends.

By paying careful attention to what we do not fully understand, as we do when watching plays in alien theatres, we can school ourselves to appreciate the crucial moments in Shakespeare's plays when it seems that he had decided to stop writing dialogue and change to almost simplistic speech that can bear very little literary analysis. When Macbeth leaves the stage at the end of the tragedy he is fighting without uttering a word. He has previously told the audience what he thought or what he wanted his opponent to hear: "Lay on, Macduff / And damn'd be him that first cries 'Hold, enough!'" (*Macbeth*, 5.8.33–34). But he then faces what he believes to be inevitable and puts his intentions to the test of action. In those following moments of fighting – and actors tend to prolong them – something else will be communicated that must, in part, be instinctive and not willed. How does criticism assess that wordless response and the *rasa* that arises? Is the effect entirely dependent on the actor and the accidents of performance or can we learn to recognise clues in the theatrical language that the dramatist has used here or has developed in the play before this moment?

Having paid attention to plays without the benefit of words, we will be able to ask more questions about a play's meanings. At the end of a comedy how buoyant is the last dance, how uncertain the last joke, how resolved the differences of mind and sentiment? In criticism, we should take note of these ambiguities which, in performance, are quite as powerful as those of words and may influence the resolution of a drama more thoroughly than any verbal statement. By learning more about the unspoken processes of theatre and opening our minds to the whole range of what theatre can offer – a wider range than we can witness in the theatres of our own time and place – we may begin to answer these questions with more confidence.

Conclusion: Anyone's Shakespeare

In this book all the studies of Shakespeare in performance lead towards a realisation that, in this form of criticism and scholarship, as in a disaster at sea, the call must be 'each for himself!' or for herself. Not only is the subject of study and its context always changing, so also are the readers. Anyone studying the plays in performance brings to the task a random bundle of likes and dislikes, prejudices and blind spots, and these are liable to change with time. This study is like a sport, worth watching for spectators, enjoyable and sometimes difficult or surprising for participants. I hope the book will draw readers to watch the sport more closely and encourage new players onto the field.

Index